KRISHNA MENON

T. J. S. GEORGE

Krishna Menon

A BIOGRAPHY

TAPLINGER PUBLISHING CO., INC.
NEW YORK

First published in the United States, 1965

TAPLINGER PUBLISHING CO., INC.
119 W. 57th Street
New York, New York 10019

Copyright © 1964 by T. J. S. George

Library of Congress Catalogue Card Number:
65-17329

Frontispiece photograph by
LISA LARSEN

Printed in Great Britain

Contents

Contents

for

AMMU

Preface

THIS IS NOT a definitive biography of Mr Krishna Menon. For one thing, a full study of his fantastically varied life would have to be several volumes long. For another, Mr Menon simply won't help.

I am very grateful for the willing co-operation I have received from his numerous associates. They showed me letters and other documents, spent hours talking and answering questions, and led me on to other contacts. Had it not been for this generous assistance, this book would not have become as authentic and comprehensive as I think it is. The number of those who have helped me is so great that I do not venture to thank them here individually. I must, however, record my grateful appreciation of the help given by the India League, London.

The fact that Mr Menon is in active politics has also served as a damper on details in some sections. The full story of the political coup d'état that sent him out of the Government in 1962, his lone fight against taking Chinese friendship for granted and the 'palace intrigues' of some of his Cabinet colleagues against him are not only absorbing reading but also of vast political importance in India; but these must await a more propitious time before they can be told. A biography such as this will not be complete without a companion volume of Mr Menon's more important speeches. I believe that some day this gap will be filled, for the realization of the historical significance of Krishna Menon will grow as the years pass.

Among those who read the manuscript and made valuable suggestions are Mr Graham C. Greene, Mr Stephen Hugh-Jones and Dr A. T. Markose. I am deeply indebted to them.

Bombay, 1963   T. J. S. GEORGE

PART I

Madras

Ideas are, in truth, forces. Infinite, too, is the power of personality. A union of the two always makes history.

HENRY JAMES

The Man

THE world was not aware of V. K. Krishna Menon till well after 1947. And then he burst into the limelight with dramatic suddenness. What the world saw was a man in his fifties, full of eccentricities, volatile, fantastic and whimsical, a man who could be hated or adored but never ignored, a man who, in spite of obvious temperamental handicaps, was rising higher and rising fast in power and eminence.

Where had he been and what had he been doing for fifty years? What pushed him into the centre of the stage soon after freedom dawned on India? Why was he walking the earth as though it belonged to him? Not enough was known about his past to explain the phenomenon that stood before the world. Inevitably legends grew.

Krishna Menon is acknowledged to be a phenomenon that inspires a few, infuriates many and embarrasses all. This impression is not wholly unjustified.

But there is no place for legends in the life of Krishna Menon. His personality, with all its built-in handicaps, is the end-product of a logical evolution.

He was born into a society which was orthodox in the extreme and rigid in its religion. But in his own household his father stood out as an exception, being progressive, empirical and almost iconoclastic. Looking first at society and then at his father, Menon saw dramatized before him the contrast between stagnation and progress. The youthful desire to change the old order was strengthened by the realization that it was possible to do so.

The personal qualities inherited from his parents were no less decisive. His father, a prosperous lawyer and landlord, was famous for his blunt matter-of-factness and his sense of right, so much so that if he refused to accept a brief no other lawyer in

Malabar would take it on. He was domineering and uncompromising on the one hand, loyal and tender on the other.

The mother, an accomplished musician and scholar, was a temperamental person with a legendary obstinacy in matters she thought right. Whatever offended her common sense offended her – and whoever offended her was sure to feel the consequences. His mother was as independent as his father was dynamic. Those in Malabar who knew Menon's parents are not surprised when they are told today of his so-called arrogance, his imperiousness and obstinacy.

His was also a family accustomed to wealth. Menon's father belonged to a line of Rajahs who enjoyed royal privileges in North Malabar. Considerable luxury surrounded his years of childhood. Pomp was a familiar circumstance. Though, in the wake of idealism, Menon cut himself off from riches and their attendant pleasures, he is essentially an aristocrat in his attitudes and conduct. Careless about money, he can be reckless in spending. When the occasion demands it, he can impress the most sophisticated society with his expensive tastes.

It must have been a painful sacrifice for a man of wealth to go into voluntary starvation – as Menon did in London. For twenty-odd years he lived the life of an exile, denying himself even basic necessities, concentrating on the cause he thought important. Those who sacrifice everything for a cause develop certain assumptions when their labours have borne fruit. Menon was no exception.

Menon came early under the influence of two great individuals. The first was Mrs Annie Besant, the fiery Irish individualist who made India her home. Her two most outstanding characteristics, apart from her sympathy for the oppressed, were a deep faith in law and constitutionalism, and a conviction that work among young people was of paramount importance. Both beliefs have become articles of faith with Krishna Menon.

No sooner was he free of the spell of Mrs Besant than he found himself under that of Harold Laski at the London School of Economics. The Professor's socialism, couched as it was in faultless phrases and rooted in scientific reasoning, found fertile soil in Menon's mind.

Both Annie Besant and Harold Laski were highly controversial personalities in their time. Knowing them and admiring them,

Menon realized that a man of character could hardly avoid becoming controversial.

Long experience with the discipline of British politics gave the finishing touches to his personality. It was to qualify himself as a teacher that Menon first went to London. No sooner was he there than he became embroiled in political agitation. His primary activity was on behalf of Indian independence. But to him freedom was a universal right; the oppressed in India, the down-trodden in South Africa, the slum-dwellers in London – it was all part of the same unrelenting crusade. He became therefore not a mere observer of politics in Britain but very much a participant, both at the party level and in local government. This gave him a first-hand knowledge of and lasting faith in the machinery of democracy.

But this experience was bought at a price. He was adrift from his moorings too early in life and his isolation lasted too long. The result has been a rootlessness that persecutes him. He just does not belong. While on one side the total absence of a family prevented his emotions from finding natural outlets, on the other, the tensions of a one-man crusade in hostile territory for over two decades cut deep into his sensibility.

A colour complex grew in him. He was practically the leader of the left-wing socialists in the South-west St Pancras Labour Party. But the leadership of the Party – which was right-wing and opposed to aggressive socialism – snubbed him at every turn. Menon received the impression that somehow this was due to his dark skin. That impression never wholly left him. It made him, as criticism and rejection always does, strive for higher achievements. But it also gave him a bitterness which affected his behaviour and deprived him of the popularity that could otherwise have been his. Worst of all, it added to his sense of loneliness.

As he hardened through experience, so his appearance began to reflect the development within him. Menon's face is bony and rough-hewn, relieved only by the vast expanse of his forehead. His hawk eyes have such a piercing intensity that one's first inclination is to avoid them. His eyebrows are raised and arched in perpetual exclamation. His nose is an extended curve accentuating the thinness of his long face. His thick lips protrude during his moods of stubbornness. Providing a dramatic backdrop to his general appearance is an explosion of grey hair, restless and

3

permanently dishevelled. Rugged masculinity is the sum of these attributes.

Vying with his eyes and nose in expressiveness are his fingers. Wiry, coarse and unyielding, they can stress a point with more finality than a dozen well-turned phrases. He stands an inch short of six feet, the frailty of his frame making him appear much taller. He drags his feet as he walks, the result of prolonged under-nourishment in the 'thirties.

In 1947 freedom put an end to his years of struggle. But its coming also sharpened his prejudices and predilections. Suddenly liberated, Menon seemed anxious to rub in the fact that he was now the representative of a sovereign nation. Especially at international gatherings he seemed to delight in offending those who had till then looked down upon him with imperialistic disdain. Indeed, to many, Menon was insufferable in victory. He became the 'undiplomatic diplomat', the 'ugly Indian', the 'unspeakable Mr Krishna Menon', the 'most hated diplomat of the year'.

The world thought that Menon was glorying in this hated eminence. But the criticism in fact made him unhappy and bitter. He felt that he was being made into a propaganda symbol by vested interests. He could never brook anyone's questioning his bona fides, and the propagandists were doing just that.

Since 1957 Menon has mellowed. In that year he was elected to Parliament by popular vote and became Minister of Defence. The problem of fitting into the Indian environment after a quarter-century of self-imposed exile was a formidable one, but it had to be solved. He took to his native South-Indian costume and began to feel his way. The first steps were faltering. But by the time the next general election came round in 1962, he had arrived.

In the 1962 campaign he began to make an impact on the masses for the first time, despite his inability to express himself clearly in any of India's many languages. When the campaign ended and the results were announced, his victory was so shattering that even traditionally Menon-baiting foreign publications acknowledged that he had become India's second most important public figure.

But seeds of destruction kept growing in and around him. His propensity to alienate friends and antagonize people helped to build up a mammoth opposition lobby in his own country, with powerful support from abroad. He also manifested an uncanny

4

ability to influence fundamental policies of the Government of India, and the lobby was duly alarmed. He became the focal point of the all-embracing struggle for survival between the Right and the Left in India – a struggle which may well be chronicled as the most significant political fact of the era of Nehru.

Menon appeared to be always on the offensive. This attitude inspired the enthusiasm of the masses who flocked around him. But in the process he betrayed a fatal flaw in his make-up – an inability to appreciate the importance of party politics and of party machinery. He loftily cast aside all the time-honoured devices open to a political leader to strengthen his own position in the party. He went to the other extreme and continued to alienate the strong men of his party who, enraged by his 'arrogance', turned their considerable resources and abilities to the one purpose of crushing him.

Essentially an agitator, Menon needs a crusade to sustain him. In the old days the crusade was for Indian independence; later it was for socialism in India and peace abroad. The crusader's indefatigability made him crash through obstacles with a doggedness that was not always good for him as a politician.

But he did many things that were not good for him as a politician. He wore his emotions on his face. If he disliked a person, he made his distaste so glaringly obvious that he destroyed all hopes of a future entente. In the corridors of the Indian parliament, he would walk past important Cabinet colleague without so much as a nod of recognition, just because he disapproved of their ideas.

His contempt for the social graces is well known. A friend who has known him for a long time said, 'He is no diplomat. He is not even a politician. He is simply an unusually brilliant man.' Menon will not lift a little finger to make himself popular. The art of public relations, so important today, is abhorrent to him. When friends suggest that he should try to create a more acceptable public image of himself, he brushes them aside with the remark, 'So you want to sell me!' As one who has made great personal sacrifices for Indian freedom, he is contemptuous of those who demand a share of freedom's fruits merely on the basis of a term in jail or an arrest during the days of the Raj. As a man of exceptional abilities, he is intolerant of those whose only asset is the flair for insinuating themselves into positions of responsibility.

5

He is as impatient of mediocrity as he is over-generous to talent. Mediocrity being the commonest element in the world, he has gained the reputation of being a difficult man.

He is indeed difficult, but his arrogance is only a small part of the whole. Personal contact with him reveals that the rudeness and the unpleasant mannerisms are but a deceptive cloak beneath which hides a kind heart and an eternally hopeful disposition. A peculiar thing about Krishna Menon is that it is easy to hate him from a distance when you have only the man's public image to go by, yet it is impossible not to admire him when you have met him and come to know him in person.

But knowing him can be a trial. Menon is difficult to converse with. His mind moves so quickly, his intellect is so sharp, that it is almost impossible to keep pace with his thought-processes. Menon does most of the talking – and the conversation lapses the moment he thinks of something or someone else. Unfortunately this happens with embarrassing frequency.

He has the disconcerting habit of allowing his mind to stray in the middle of a conversation. The other party may be saying something vital, but suddenly Menon's eyes wander, a dead-pan expression clouds his face – and he is far away. This habit has created misunderstandings in the minds of many who, not knowing him well, see in his spurts of inattention a personal affront. In fact, this mental straying and the bouts of sleep at public functions are his ways of relaxing.

The superiority of his mind and his addiction to work have made him a hard task-master. He is a perfectionist and, like all perfectionists, is impatient of the imperfections he sees around him. This has produced in him a tendency to do himself what less exacting men would have left to subordinates.

Yet, in spite of all this, those who work for him are not only enthusiastic but also devoted and loyal. This must be due to Menon's habit of never sparing himself and to his ability to infect others with his own zeal for a cause. His missionary spirit is infectious. And his personal efficiency compels the admiration and co-operation of his staff.

Those who have been with him long say that only the superficial could take offence at his bluntness, for this bluntness comes from a loyal and affectionate heart. His outward rudeness is so identified with his innate frankness that close associates are uneasy when he is not rude. Miss Bridget Tunnard, who has worked as his secretary for many years, sometimes had occasion to protest, 'Damn it, boss, you are polite to me today! What have I done wrong?'

There is seldom an occasion when Menon shouts at a man and does not feel remorse later. A watchman at the gate of the Ministry of Defence in New Delhi, who knew no English, once irritated the Minister who knew no Hindi. The Minister flared up at him and went into his office. Minutes later he sent for the watchman. When the watchman, trembling with fear, entered the Minister's office, Menon told his secretary, 'I shouted at this man while I was coming in. Tell him I am sorry.' The watchman went out with tears in his eyes.

Arthur Lall, till recently Indian Ambassador to Austria and for many years a close associate of Krishna Menon at the United Nations, said to the writer, 'In the Indian Civil Service I have worked with some of Britain's best brains. But after 1947 I knew that we had a man who was far more intelligent than any of them.'

His intelligence is apparent not only in his ideas and the formulae he devises, but also in his speeches. A qualified barrister and holder of an honours degree in logic, Menon has a highly cultivated capacity for reasoning which makes him a powerful debater and advocate. He also has a gift for turning a phrase. He develops an almost fanatical attachment to a phrase he has coined. At one stage a favourite slogan was 'Independence, democracy, socialism'. He gave to India's contemporary vocabulary the remarkably apt phrase 'jute Press', denoting the fact that Indian newspapers, owned mostly by big industrial houses, are run by the barons in the same spirit in which they run their other interests, such as jute factories. He always castigates the Press for misrepresenting him, and once put it to reporters in these words, 'If I tell you I have eaten a banana, you will report that the banana has eaten me.' Speaking of non-alignment at an election meeting, he said, 'If we become aligned, we will be the target of those whom we are not with and the arsenal of those whom we are with.'

It is a deliberate policy with Menon to pick up words from familiar documents and underline them repeatedly until people stop taking them for granted and realize that they have a meaning. 'Social justice' was no more than a term in the Indian Constitution until Menon gave it flesh and blood. This technique has helped to a significant extent in the influence he has had on national moods and popular thinking.

Such phrases and epigrams combine with his penchant for introducing out-of-the-way information to make Menon's speeches a delight to listen to. He is a stickler for original research and asks his staff to find out all kinds of unusual data. They have a difficult time satisfying him and often desperation and frayed tempers follow, but Menon never rests until he has laid hands on precisely what he wants. When ultimately he makes use of the data in a speech, the staff as well as the listeners are left wondering at the range of his mind and the perspective he gives to his arguments.

When the Congo issue was news, he often began his speeches with the sentence, 'Some time when the Himalayas emerged, the African land mass broke off.' He would then describe how the colonial phase in Africa began when a British captain went there in a ship called the *Jesus* and returned to England with two hundred and fifty slaves. The Queen of England, he would continue, admonished the captain of the *Jesus* in true Christian spirit for taking slaves – and then knighted him. From this story of the Queen the speech would progress methodically to the King of the Belgians and finally to Moise Tshombe. The audience invariably felt that a man with so much detailed knowledge could only be believed.

Menon's speeches are so well constructed and so word-perfect that one would suppose that they were the result of considerable preparation and rehearsal. In fact he never prepares a speech. He has clear-cut ideas on every subject, studies an issue in all its aspects and has a great felicity of expression, so that when he stands before a microphone, the speech flows. Practice has perfected his technique. Today Menon's oratory may lack Nehru's intimacy and informality, but he has the quotableness of a Churchill, the arresting satire of a Disraeli, the purposefulness of a Cromwell. When Menon speaks in the United Nations, the delegates crowd in and the visitors' galleries fill.

Menon apparently loves speaking. At ceremonial dinners he can be seen sitting morosely, without even looking at the food, as though he were in a bad mood. But when it is time for speech-making he is a new man, full of animation, good humour and brilliance.

The Man

His humour has a peculiar wry quality about it. In October 1961, recuperating from a brain operation in New York, Menon was apparently in a glowing mood, looking at the flowers President Kennedy had sent and listening to doctors remarking on his tremendous will-power. When a group of Indian pressmen, seeing him shave for the first time in a week, said, 'You'll feel better after a shave,' Menon snapped, 'I will feel the same, but those who come to see me will feel better.'

Once, after he had been introduced at the National Press Club of Washington as a drinker of a hundred to a hundred and fifty cups of tea per day, 'sometimes taking the tea with ice cubes', Menon said, 'The figures are greatly exaggerated. I would never commit the sacrilege of putting ice cubes in tea. That would be like putting buttermilk in Scotch, though as a teetotaller and vegetarian, I wouldn't know just how whisky tasted. But I'm sure it would not be improved by buttermilk.'

His speeches, like his actions, show his optimism. This trait in him is something of a surprise since Menon's experience is of a kind that would have made most men cynical and frustrated.

Somehow he manages to keep afloat. In the worst of circumstances, he does not lose faith. Many were the occasions in the United Nations when, with pressures and cold-war interests pulling the nations in various directions, Menon faced certain failure in his peace-making efforts. But he never gave up. The successes that punctuate his career would not have materialized but for his conviction that, if only he were persistent enough, he could win.

As surprising as his optimism is his awareness of the meaninglessness of self. A favourite saying of his is that individuals die, institutions do not.

When the Press campaign against him during the 1962 election reached an unprecedented pitch and Menon's image appeared dangerously blackened, he did nothing to save himself. On the contrary, the ideological immorality of the newspapers made him launch a one-man campaign of his own against the Press. This was a grave risk to take at election time, but no advice could make Menon relax the tempo of his fight. He told the writer: 'What does it matter if I have to sacrifice my career? Somebody has to expose the true character of the Press, and if I am liquidated, I will still have done some good to the country.'

He never keeps personal papers. Documents that would have set the record straight have been thrown away. Results are all that matter to him, not the collection of evidence to establish his claim for the credit.

He derides biographies and biographers. 'Autobiographies,' he told the author once, 'are written by those who believe that the world is centred on them – and the world is not centred on any individual – and biographies are written by those who have nothing else to do.' A close friend of his collected a vast amount of material on his life and work and told him that she intended to publish them in book form. Menon threatened to sue her if she did anything of the kind. He believes that facts about his personal life should not interest anybody. 'Why should anybody care,' he often asked the author, 'where I was born and what kind of food I ate? All that matters is what I have done. You can analyse this work impersonally and that's all that need be done.' The author failed, despite perseverance, to induce Menon to speak about himself. He would only talk about his work, and that, too, reluctantly. Where the word 'I' should have figured, he invariably used words such as 'the Government', 'Congress', 'India'.

The so-called anti-Westernism of Menon would not have become the talking point it is today if the West had not, under the influence of the late John Foster Dulles, made a symbol of him and attacked him with malicious persistence. Menon was not initiating the theory of non-alignment or building up an Afro-Asian conspiracy against the West; he merely represented certain new forces that were coming into play in the post-war world. If the significance of these forces had been grasped by the United States and if the State Department had been sympathetic towards the aspirations of the new nations, the United States would have had less occasion to say that non-alignment was only a cover for communism. Towards the end of his career, Dulles himself came to look upon non-alignment and the Afro-Asian point of view with less suspicion. But by then the damage had already been done.

The intemperate character of the criticism made Menon more obstinate in the pursuit of his policies. His obstinacy in turn touched off more criticism. The vicious circle thus produced has done neither party any good. The propaganda has been so effective that today the average Westerner is unable to visualize a Menon who may be just as human as himself.

The Man

Menon is, in fact, just as beset with hopes, fears and aspirations as the ordinary man. He has, like anybody else, his weaknesses and his strength. Politically he is no more diabolically motivated than his Prime Minister. He feels as deeply as Nehru, but expresses himself more bluntly. The worst that can be said about him is that he is a professional Afro-Asian.

It is noteworthy that despite all the daemonic qualities attributed to him, Menon has always succeeded in attracting devoted friends. Those who have been close to him stay with him because they see in him, apart from his obvious talent, a fierce integrity. He has never stooped to dishonest political tricks, and he never expects others to do what he would not do himself. Deep in him there is a craving for companionship which makes him, in the right company, a very charming person.

One must see him in the company of children in order to understand this other Krishna Menon. His way with them is peculiar. For some unknown reason, they take a fancy to him even though his jokes have an adult tone. His smile, which has a winning warmth about it, is never more delightful than when he is with children.

His friends are unanimous in regretting that Menon has never married, for marriage would have rounded off many of his corners and given him the companionship he craves. To some extent freedom from office knocked off some of the edges. Soon after resigning from Government he visited Bombay, and people were surprised to see him unusually jovial, brimming with life and laughter. He talked leisurely, cracked jokes, played with children, teased grown-ups. He was really relaxed. One could see that it was the burden of office that had made him act strangely before, and that, tensions gone, he was a very pleasant man.

Menon is a man of Spartan habits. He is a faithful adherent to the Gandhian tenets of austere living. He is a vegetarian, a teetotaller and non-smoker. He never takes a solid meal, tea and biscuits constituting his staple diet. In times of heavy work he can do with as little as two hours' sleep and feel none the worse for it. He has not been known to take a holiday since the early 'twenties. He is used to hard living and his needs have remained frugal even after living conditions have eased. As Minister of Defence, he had at his disposal a spacious bungalow across the road from the

Prime Minister's house, but he confined himself to a small room at one end of it. This room, completely reflecting the occupant's personality, was a beautifully equipped den displaying numerous gadgets. Some, like an 'electric memory machine', were there primarily for their curiosity value, while others, like various types of telephones, were being used.

The room also contained several model tanks, pieces of artillery and patrol jeeps. Menon is fascinated by mechanical toys and plays with them often in his hours of solitude, manoeuvring tanks, flying aeroplanes, watching various animals perform feats on the floor at the touch of a button.

But essentially the room was a library, the books and magazines revealing the wide range of his interests – science and mystery predominating. Menon concentrates so fiercely while reading detective stories that he is known to finish a whole book during the forty-minute drive from Bombay city to the airport – and at the end he will remember even detailed points in the story.

Every time Menon goes out to a city or an airport, he buys books in scores. 'We don't know how, but he manages to read them all,' say his secretaries who cart these volumes to head-quarters. Not only does he read them but he is able to discuss the most involved technical problems in such fields as electronics and aerodynamics with experts. Menon's reading speed is remarkable. Even during his London days, he used to borrow sizeable volumes from friends in the evening and return them the next morning.

He has little interest in music and art. He has developed an intellectual objection to admiring ancient monuments and objets d'art generally. In the course of a speech at Agra in 1961 he said that he had seen the Taj Mahal only once and had no desire to see it again.

His whole life is attuned to a fast tempo. He does not waste time on trivialities such as food, and is not only able to assimilate books and reports with incredible speed, but also contrives to be physically on the move most of the time. While in office, he was the most mobile cabinet minister in India. There was a time when Bob Hope's gag about John Foster Dulles – 'He pays periodic visits to the United States' – could be applied to Menon vis-à-vis India. He thought nothing of going to the United Nations for a week-end. In India he travelled mostly at night so that he might have the whole working day at his disposal.

The Man

When he is abroad Menon gives full rein to his passion for shopping. After an exhausting day in the Palais des Nations in Geneva or in the United Nations in New York, he would spend hours window-shopping. When the fancy took him, he would go into the shops and buy in style – mostly books, toys and suits. He bought not only for himself but for whoever might be with him at the time. The only condition was that the beneficiary must leave the choice of his clothes to Menon.

For his own wardrobe Menon has accumulated a huge number of suits. It is the one indulgence he permits himself. The suits are impeccably tailored and have won Menon the reputation abroad of a well-dressed person. He cannot, however, wear good shoes.

His love of shopping is only one of his many feminine characteristics. Others are shifting moods, strong likes and dislikes, a proneness to choose the wrong men for friends. But through all this, there is a great persistence in fundamental matters. He keeps hammering away at his theme, repeating the same ideas and often the same phrases, until he has created the impression he wants.

It is possible to say that Menon's career has been a tragedy; and yet it is a triumph. He is a failure, and yet a success. In fact, fifteen years of office have produced a conglomeration of paradoxes. While he is obsessed with world unity and brotherhood among nations, he has divided humanity into two opposing camps – the pro-Menon and the anti-Menon camps. While his supreme passion is to submerge the self and emphasize work, the world has been so dazzled by his personality that it has failed to notice the work he has done. It was this grand paradox that overtook Krishna Menon in late 1962.

Imperious Parents

V. K. KRISHNA MENON was born on May 3rd, 1896, at Panniankara in Calicut at 9.48 p.m. The birth was registered by the municipal authorities of Calicut. Some time later confusion crept into the records and today almost all available biographical references on him mention 1897 as his year of birth. Material put out by the Government of India itself has helped to establish the mistake.

Menon's family records give precise details of the event. The *karanavar*[1] of his father's household, Komathu Govinda Kurup, was a meticulous man who maintained a voluminous diary, notebook after notebook of family details written in Malayalam, his mother tongue, in a neat and steady hand on carefully lined pages. The information given covered a very wide field – from the places he visited for the purchase of elephants to the number of bananas eaten by birds on a particular plantain tree on a particular day.

In the notebook for 1896, in the entry under 25 Medam 1071 (Malayalam era), he wrote: 'Tonight at 7 o'clock a servant came from Vengalil house with information that nephew Kunji-Krishnan's wife Lakshmi Kutty gave birth to a male offspring on Sunday the 22nd of this month after sunset at 48 minutes past 9 o'clock under the sign of Uthratam. I gave the servant three rupees.'

'Nephew Kunji-Krishnan' was Krishna Kurup, Krishna Menon's father, and 22 Medam 1071 corresponds to May 3rd, 1896.

The son of Komathu Krishna Kurup would not take the family name of Komathu or the caste name of Kurup. In the matriarchal system of society which obtains among the Nayars[2] inheritance is

---

[1] The eldest male member of a Hindu joint family in Malabar who, by tradition, enjoys unquestioned authority in the family group.

[2] Nayar, also spelt Nair, is a prominent Hindu caste in Kerala. They are martial by tradition and constitute an intermediary caste between the Brahmins and the 'untouchables'. 'Menon' is a suffix that denotes one of the many subdivisions of the Nayar caste. These subdivisions were largely based on occupations and Menons were supervisors or accountants.

in the female line, and a child's family name and last name would be those of the mother. So he was given his mother's family name of Vengalil and her caste suffix of Menon. Father Krishna Kurup, however, had a choice over the middle name, and here he decided to be strictly non-matriarchal. He gave his son two middle names, both his own. He (the father) was known in the family as Kunji-Krishnan and officially as Krishnan. Thus his son's name was entered in the records as Vengalil Krishnan Kunji-Krishna Menon. The incorporation of the father's name into the son's, the common practice in a patriarchal society, was quite unusual in the Malabar of that day. But Krishna Kurup was an unusual man.

The prefix *Kunji* and other prefixes like *Unni* and *Kutty* (all meaning 'the little one') were popular Malayali devices by which a regular name was converted into a childhood endearment. Some men carried these names even into adulthood. In school and even when he took his first degree, Menon was officially V. K. Kunji-Krishna Menon. As he grew older he dropped the prefix – much to the relief of those who had to use his name frequently.

At the time of Krishna Kurup and his uncle Govinda Kurup, Komathu *tharavad*, or joint family, lived in feudal glory in a rural area called Ayincheri, some fifteen miles east of Badagara which is thirty miles north of Calicut. Vengalil *tharavad* is at Panniankara, in one of the select residential areas of what is now Calicut city. While Vengalil enjoyed the amenities of town life, Komathu was far removed from urban conveniences. Even today there are no proper roads leading to Komathu; the house is in a spot accessible only by foot. From Badagara one can take a bus (a recent innovation) to Purameri and then walk the remaining eight miles. Or one can take a private taxi to Thodannur and then walk six miles. Local wits say, light-heartedly of course, that the house was deliberately built in an inaccessible corner by old man Govinda Kurup because, being rich, he wanted to discourage fund-collectors!

In this part of Malabar rock-studded hills disappear into low-lying marshland. Birds and crickets are disturbed only by the occasional cries of shepherds and farmers. Amid clusters of coconut trees and vast expanses of paddy fields, life moves leisurely on. Next-door neighbours may be five water-logged miles apart. Till early in the century buses were unknown and the commonest mode of transportation was walking. People still walk ten, twenty or thirty miles without flinching. The more well-to-do had their own canoes and palanquins in which they would be carried for miles by sturdy bearers. *Karanavar* Govinda Kurup did most of his travelling by boat and palanquin.

On the cover of his diary Govinda Kurup wrote simply: 'Diary book maintained from first of Kanni 1071 corresponding to Monday the 16th of September 1895 in memory of the Komathu Kurup called Govindan. Death matters have been written in red ink in order to be seen quickly.'

These death matters pertained not only to members of the Komathu *tharavad* but to any resident of the neighbourhood known to the *karanavar*. He was something of a local baron, giving advice on marriages, keeping an eye on trouble-makers, settling local disputes. Not only Nayar families in the area but also Muslims went to him with their problems. Even today this position of prestige is enjoyed by the *tharavad*, and a visitor can see an occasional villager standing in the courtyard with folded arms making his supplication to the present *karanavar*.

An entry in Govinda Kurup's diary mentions the expenditure of three rupees and seven annas (about five shillings) for salt, chillies, buttermilk, etc. which were supplied to the public in one of the family 'charity depots'. It was the custom among prominent families during the sweltering summer months to install a pavilion in a place accessible to passers-by and give them buttermilk, among other things. Govinda Kurup maintained a dozen such places as a humanitarian gesture.

On June 24th, 1896, Govinda Kurup was in an ebullient mood. It was his birthday, and he wrote,

> I have held a feast today, because it is my birthday, with 25 *edangazhi* rice in the Brahmins' outhouse and 200 *edangazhi* rice in my own house. Fed 35 Brahmins, made 12 people offer prayers and they were duly rewarded and the labourers were given three rupees each. Things for all curries and coconuts were supplied by *kutiyans* [tenants traditionally living on the property of a *tharavad*]. Excluding this, total expenditure is 54–3–9 [in rupees, annas and pies]. Nothing very much.

To those who have some idea of what a princely sum 54 rupees (roughly £4) represented in the India of the late nineteenth century, Govinda Kurup's last remark may symbolize the ultimate complacency of the feudal landlord. But to wealthy Kurup himself it was really nothing very much.

Govinda Kurup loved elephants, and loved to own them. All over Kerala till very recently owning an elephant was regarded as a mark of social status. Govinda Kurup's Komathu family had several of the animals, as befitted their high social status. His own favourites were Sanku, Sankaran and Gopalan. An elephant could cost anything from 1,500 to 3,000 rupees (£100 to £220 sterling). It was not a bad investment, for Sanku was rented out for a monthly payment of 140 rupees, while Sankaran used to fetch 120 rupees. Pages and pages of one year's diary are taken up by Govinda Kurup's travels all over the West Coast in search of a new elephant, the men he visited, the bargains he negotiated, the private impressions he formed of the men and their animals. This love of elephants was not extended to his horses, which he kept merely for purposes of travel.

Govinda Kurup's diary and account books are an informative commentary on the life and customs of the day. Now and again he records alms given to itinerant holy men. 'To a Brahmin on his way to Banares 0–4–0.' And sometimes: 'Towards Onam present to Rozario, the new police inspector in Badagara 20–0–0.' This was no bribe, of course, for Onam is the festival of gifts in Kerala and one had to do things according to one's position.

Govinda Kurup's finest achievement was the edifice that now houses Komathu *tharavad* in Ayincheri. The rare visitor who survives the six-mile walk in the blazing sun will be pleasantly surprised once he reaches the house. It is a palatial old-world mansion that stands high on a hill. Its walls are massive and its high roof is lined with layers of wood which somehow act as an air-conditioner. The wooden pillars have intricate carvings on their tops. There are outhouses and courtyards, and the main door into the house bears the proud inscription that it was built by the 'Kurup known as Govindan'.

It was Govinda Kurup's responsibility, as *karanavar*, to look after the upbringing of his nephews. English education was not common in those days. It was even held that contact with the English spoilt children. But Govinda Kurup had other ideas, and he sent his nephew Krishna Kurup to the Municipal School in Palghat to begin his revolutionary English education.

17

In course of time Krishna Kurup entered the Kerala Vidyasala in Calicut for his college education. This institution was later renamed Zamorin's College and still later the Guruvayurappan College. Young Kurup's two-year stay in Calicut was a turning point in his life.

There was in Calicut at the time a family that had settled there only three generations earlier. It was established by a powerful man called Raman Menon, who was a Dewan Peishkar under the Maharaja of Travancore. A Dewan Peishkar was the highest administrative post the 'natives' could attain in those days, and Raman Menon was right at the top of the social scale.

One day, on his way from Travancore to Calicut, Raman Menon stayed at the house of an old uncle. There he met an attractive girl by the name of Narayani Amma. Under matriarchy it was customary for one to marry one's uncle's daughter. Soon Narayani Amma found herself setting up a new *tharavad* in Calicut. It was called Vengalil.

Narayani Amma had four sons and four daughters. One of the daughters, Valyammalu Amma, was a gifted student of music and literature. She married a prominent Nayar from the aristocratic landlord family of Koothali. They had an only daughter called Lakshmi Kutty who was blossoming into youth when the rolls of the Kerala Vidyasala recorded the arrival of a northerner called Krishna Kurup.

Being a northerner in Calicut had its disadvantages. This was because an invisible barrier stood defiantly between North Malabar and South Malabar. The southerners and the northerners used to look down upon each other with some kind of disdain. The river Kora Puzha was supposed to be the boundary between the north and the south, and no woman from one area would be given in marriage to a man from the other.

There is a legend that illustrates the point. This is about the Goddess Mookambika who belongs to Mookambi, the northernmost point of Malabar. Her most ardent devotee was the Zamorin, the ruler of Calicut, which place unfortunately was in the south. Undaunted, the Zamorin wooed Mookambika and at last persuaded the Goddess to travel to Calicut with him. When they reached Kora Puzha, the northerner Mookambika could not possibly proceed further. There ensued a brief struggle, during which the Zamorin pulled the Goddess by her hands. The

Goddess escaped into her northern purity, but one of her bangles slipped off into the hands of the Zamorin. The indefatigable devotee brought the bangle to Calicut and installed it in a temple. This temple still exists in Calicut and it is called 'Thiruvalayanadu', which literally means 'the land of the sacred bangle'.

Occasionally, though, an enlightened family would come forward to break the barrier and establish a link between the north and the south. The Vengalil family had already set an example in this matter: the Koothali Nayar whom Valyammalu Amma married was from North Malabar. Krishna Kurup, being also from North Malabar, was a natural visitor to the home of Koothali Nayar in Calicut. He met Lakshmi Kutty there. Young, ambitious and idealistic as he was, Kurup asked for the hand of Lakshmi Kutty; he had no heart for the north-south feud. The Vengalil family welcomed the idea. But some of Kurup's own people back in Komathu were far from happy. His *karanavar* was among those who disapproved of the proposal. But Krishna Kurup was too idealistic and upright to recognize Kora Puzha as an impassable barrier. No objection could dissuade him from his decision. In 1889 Lakshmi Kutty became his wife.

There was only a terse reference to this event in uncle Govinda Kurup's diary. In September 1889 he wrote: 'I have learned from hearsay that nephew Kunji-Krishnan has gone to Telli-cherry with Vengalil Lakshmi Kutty whom he has married.'

Tellicherry, a northern coastal town, was the scene of the imperious Krishna Kurup's activities for the next four decades. By now he had obtained his Bachelor of Arts degree from the Presidency College in Madras, and had also become a lawyer. He had set up practice in Tellicherry in June 1889.

As towns go in North Malabar, Tellicherry was an important one. It was one of the centres of trade at the time of the East India Company. It was important enough to have a court with a bench of three judges. The fact that this court was right in the midst of an aristocracy which did not frown on litigation was an attraction to the brighter lawyers of the time.

It did not take long for Krishna Kurup to conquer Tellicherry. His sharpness and his grasp of law made him one of the two leading civil lawyers in the town, the other being his cousin T. C. Narayana Kurup. To their professional ability the Kurups brought, of course, the pomp and prestige of their *tharavad*. It is said that Narayana Kurup used to proceed to court every morning in a ceremonial procession, seated in a gilded monogrammed coach drawn by horses and with liveried attendants standing on either side wielding peacock-feather fans. Krishna Kurup maintained not only horses and coaches but also elephants in Tellicherry.

Krishna Kurup possessed something besides wealth and wit to qualify him for the pre-eminent position he obtained in Tellicherry. This was his integrity. He had the reputation of delivering an unofficial judgment of his own when a case was brought to him. If he thought it was a false plaint, he would throw out the brief and the man who brought it, and the man would never be able to approach another lawyer. But once he took up a brief, he fought for it with single-minded devotion. Kurup had the arrogance of righteousness.

Some old people in Malabar recollect the time when Krishna Kurup was proceeded against by a creditor. Kurup told the creditor that he wanted a little longer time to repay his debt. The creditor went to court. The plea was eventually dismissed because the transaction had by then become time-barred. Kurup waited until the time limit he had himself set was up and then he went to the creditor and said: 'The law was the law. Now, here is your money and give me a receipt.'

Kurup's fidelity to his word was so well known that he sometimes had to pay for it. This happened on one occasion when he was accosted on the road by a local acquaintance, poor but shrewd. The wily villager asked him, apparently as a joke, whether he could have one of Kurup's elephants. Catching the spirit of the joke, Kurup said: 'Sure, why not?' The villager then asked whether he could have it for five hundred rupees (about £39). This left no doubt that the man was joking, for the price of an elephant never fell below a four-figure sum. Kurup therefore kept up the joke, saying: 'Sure, why not?' No sooner had he mumbled his unsuspecting consent than the villager produced from out of his hollow walking-stick five hundred rupees. Kurup, though stunned, quietly took the money and let the man walk away with his elephant.

Krishna Kurup had eight children – Chinnammalu Amma, Janaki Amma, Krishna Menon, Raman Menon, Kochu Narayani, Kunju Lakshmi, Ammu Kutty and Padmavati. Krishna Menon's family nickname was Appa, while Raman Menon, the only other son, was called Appukuttan. Within the family Krishna Menon is still known as Appa.

Of the eight children only three are alive today – Krishna Menon, Ammu Kutty and Padmavati.

The children lost their mother when the eldest of them was hardly out of her teens. Lakshmi Kutty was a fragile woman of poor health, but the robustness of her mind and intellect more than made up for the frailty of her body. Following the fashion of the day, she was given no English education as a child, but she acquired considerable erudition in Sanskrit and music. After marriage, she engaged an English tutor and learned something of the language. Though short-tempered and irritable, she was also noted for her affection and charitable disposition. Anybody who went to her with a tale of distress was sure to return relieved. It was her obstinate nature that left a mark on everyone who came in contact with her. Krishna Kurup himself learned of this early in their married life. One day he locked the family safe with a combination lock which could be opened only with a five-letter formula. Lakshmi Kutty asked her husband for the formula, but Kurup refused to part with it. Lakshmi Kutty's pride was hurt. She threatened to open the safe by herself if the formula were not given to her. Knowing that that was impossible, Krishna Kurup laughed and went off to court. When he returned in the evening, however, the safe was open. Lakshmi Kutty had spent the whole day by the side of the safe, tried every permutation and combination patiently and systematically until she had struck upon the right arrangement. Kurup's amazement was the greater when he realized that his wife had done it without the use of paper and pencil.

Kurup grew to adore his wife. He used to tell his daughters that none of them would ever surpass their mother in brilliance and intellect. Soon after the eighth child was born, however, Lakshmi Kutty fell a victim to tuberculosis. Her death in 1911 was a blow from which the family never recovered.

With his wife's early death, Krishna Kurup was drawn closer to his children. Custom permitted him to take a second wife, but he never entertained the idea because he believed it would not be in the best interests of his children. Kurup's devotion to his family went beyond the limits of matriarchy. Indeed, he looked down upon the tradition of one's sister's children inheriting one's wealth, and insisted on giving his property to his own children. This, not surprisingly, led to some unpleasantness between Komathu and Vengalil.

Kurup's diary contains several instances of sheer joy at the arrival of some good news about one of his children. On July 20th, 1927, he noted with pride that he had received a cable from Appa saying that he had passed the B.Sc. examination with first-class honours. (This was the B.Sc. of the London School of Economics where Krishna Menon was studying at the time.) In May 1929 he noted, 'Private information to hand that Padmavati has passed the S.S.L.C. examination. Very glad.' But Appa was obviously the bright star of the family, and Krishna Kurup records how he once spent nineteen rupees to have a photograph of Appa enlarged and another rupee to have it framed.

Kurup could also be a strict father, but it was in the realm of ideas that he made the greatest impact on his children. He was a progressive. Without making a public show of it, he rejected many orthodox ideas of his religion and his society and set an example that inspired his children. It was, for instance, an almost universal custom among the Nayars of Malabar to have the ears of boys pierced for studs before they were five years old. Kurup saw no sense in this tradition and refused to touch his sons' ears.

Krishna Kurup's only religion was truth. For the rest, he did not care much which God was where. He was even immune to considerations of caste and used to create consternation in society by inviting the lower-caste Thiyas to sit in the same line as the Nayars whenever there was a marriage feast in the family. In food habits, too, he gave common sense precedence over custom; while Nayars were considered vegetarians, Kurup took meat and fish until he was medically advised to avoid them.

With his progressive disposition, it was natural that Kurup should have been politically active. He was responsible for starting a municipality in Tellicherry, and was its chairman for a decade. As a politically conscious citizen he was acutely conscious of the enthralment of his country. Those were the days when lawyers were in the front line of the battle for freedom. Big families unquestioningly identified patriotism with loyalty to the King Emperor. Komathu *tharavad*, though far away from the prying eyes of officialdom, used to have a large print of the British royal family in full regalia in the most prominent place on the wall. Almost a full page in *karanavar* Govinda Kurup's diary is devoted to describing, as though it were a personal domestic tragedy, the death of Queen Victoria.

But Krishna Kurup had a feeling that this was all wrong. He did not personally throw himself into the struggle, but he never left any doubts about where he stood. In his later years he was a habitual wearer of *khaddar*, the hand-made cloth prescribed by Gandhi as 'freedom's liverie'. In the 1932 Civil Disobedience movement, his nephew, also called Govinda Kurup, was arrested and put in jail. Krishna Kurup was outraged and ordered the removal from his wall of the picture of the King and Queen. Krishna Kurup declared at that time that he would go to jail himself. But he was old by then and in indifferent health and he never got to the 'front'.

Under the date-line January 5th, 1932, his diary carries a one-sentence entry in English: 'Mahatma Gandhi is arrested and confined in jail by a vindictive and stupid foreign government.' Kurup was undoubtedly a sensitive nationalist. It is little wonder that his son was fired with patriotic fervour very early in life.

From 1889 to 1933 had been a long innings, and Krishna Kurup decided that the time had come for him to rest. On April 11th he wrote in his book, 'From tomorrow I have decided to stop being an Advocate in Tellicherry. Today it is 43 years, 11 months and 15 days since I began as a High Court Vakil.'

He wound up his establishment and went for his retirement, not to his own *tharavad* of Komathu, but to Vengalil in Calicut where his children were living. The prolonged illness of his wife in Tellicherry had prompted him to build what is today one of the largest houses in the whole of Calicut. It is said that Kurup built it in such a way that it would be free from termites and pests and have few quick-wearing parts. It was the last word in constructional opulence: brass fittings for doors and windows instead of the usual iron! It was a two-storeyed palace rambling over a garden, cool with the shade of huge trees. It was to this house, which was under the care of his daughter Janaki, that Krishna Kurup turned in his retirement.

On June 15th, 1935, Krishna Kurup went out for his usual walk. He chatted with acquaintances and exchanged greetings with friends sitting out in their porches, when suddenly there was

23

a stab of pain in his left chest and the next moment he collapsed on the road. In a few moments, Krishna Kurup was dead.

Most of the personal characteristics that distinguish Krishna Menon and his surviving sisters today are obvious gifts from their father. Krishna Menon was proud of his father's reputation for integrity and his public eminence. Later, during Menon's theosophical escapades, father and son used to have serious differences of opinion accompanied by long and loud arguments. But Menon's admiration for his father never waned.

3

School

KRISHNA MENON'S childhood was spent in places scattered over Malabar. His early years were passed in Tellicherry where his father was practising. For high school and early college education, he moved to Calicut. He visited Komathu during vacations.

Krishna Menon was a frail child. This must have been the legacy of his mother, for his father was a sturdy out-door man. A good horseman and hunter, Kurup had celebrated the birth of his first son with a hunting party lasting many days, during which his guests were lavishly entertained. He wanted his son to cultivate the same interests as he had and presented the boy, when he was fifteen, with a pony. But the boy had his own ideas. He could not bear to see such a nice little pony being forced to carry a man on his back. So young Appa gave his pet a share of the luxuries that were his own in the house, including porridge for breakfast, and looked after the animal with diligent affection, never once riding it. Kurup appreciated his son's reasoning and let him do what he liked with the pony.

Menon's love of animals, which remains with him to this day, came to the fore again one day when one of his father's elephants was sentenced to death. The unruly animal had killed three attendants in quick succession and, seeing in him a source of further danger, Kurup agreed to have him shot. But Appa objected. He created such an uproar against the decision that Kurup had to reduce the death sentence to one of banishment.

Kurup was glad that his son was developing a mind of his own. But in so far as it concerned food, Kurup was unhappy about his son's ideas. Appa's anaemic appearance gave Kurup much anxiety and he used to put great pressure upon him to eat fish, if not meat. Menon always got out of it by saying that the bones

25

would stick in his throat. Of course everyone knew that the real reason for the young fellow's refusal was his sense of revulsion at non-vegetarian food. He even used to protest against the fashion of removing the tusks of elephants and keeping them as ivory showpieces in the house.

The indulgence with which the father accommodated the son's childhood ideas cemented their mutual affection. Menon's attitude to his father was almost adoring. He tried to dress like his father, old-fashioned cap and all, and even to talk like his father. His first textbooks carried signatures modelled after that of his father.

For his part, Kurup had high hopes for his eldest son. He wanted him to become not only a rider like himself but also a lawyer to whom, in good time, he could turn over his practice. He therefore encouraged every symptom of individuality on Appa's part. Sometimes he did so despite the frowns of society. Once a coachman employed by the family was involved in a criminal case and, in the absence of a witness to testify in his favour, there was a great risk that the court might find him guilty. Fourteen-year-old Krishna Menon, full of compassion for the poor man, volunteered to be a witness. The coachman was at first awestruck and the rest of the household felt scandalized. It was unthinkable in those days that members of aristocratic families should figure in criminal cases, even as witnesses. But this young aristocrat was insistent and, with the knowledge of his father, gave evidence on behalf of the coachman which ultimately led to an acquittal. The numerous relations of the family were outraged when they heard of the young fellow's recklessness. They protested to Kurup. But Kurup complimented his son for his compassion and his spirit of independence.

The privileged life that Menon enjoyed in his father's household was not without price. It gave him a sense of particularity and a reserved disposition. He kept aloof from the rough and tumble of school life. At the same time, among intimates, he was boisterous and domineering.

Menon's education began at Tellicherry. He studied at the Municipal School and also for a year at the high school of the Brennen College, a Christian missionary institution. Soon his mother's illness forced the family to move to Calicut where Menon was enrolled in the Native High School. The name of this school was changed in 1921 to Ganapat High School, partly to avoid the ugly word 'native' and partly to perpetuate the memory of the founder and first headmaster of the school, Ganapat Rao.

Years later, in 1955, Krishna Menon had occasion to recall his days in the Native High School and the training he had had there. In a message sent to the school magazine from the India League in London, Menon wrote: 'I have often recalled how much I have learned from my old headmaster. It sometimes surprises me how some of those things still help me in later life.'

This old headmaster, Ganapat Rao, was noted for his puritanical fervour and his almost fanatical religious outlook. After giving up the management of his school to his son, he spent the last years of his life as an ordained sadhu.

One year he put his foot down when he learned that the boys were going to stage a drama in which there was a woman's role. Krishna Menon was the boy selected to play this role, that of Gubba in *Alfred and the Cakes*. But Ganapat Rao would not allow a boy to masquerade in woman's clothes in public. In his view girls constituted a danger from which all boys had to be shielded. The boys in his own school were being meticulously protected from all contamination, and he would not permit an anniversary celebration to wreck the work of years.

The boys were nonplussed. Without Gubba, of course, there could be no *Alfred and the Cakes*, and without the headmaster's permission there could be no Gubba. They ruefully resigned themselves to forgetting all about their little drama. But Krishna Menon, the would-be heroine, was not to be dissuaded so easily. Exhibiting the first known manifestation of a knack that was to become famous in later years, he devised a formula to end the impasse to the satisfaction of all. He argued that the headmaster's objection was not to the presence of a woman in the play but to the masquerading of a man as a woman. Therefore he would play the role of Gubba without any masquerade. He would go on stage wearing trousers and jacket and recite Gubba's lines.

It was a childish solution. But the problem itself was childish. And of course the headmaster was agreeable to this compromise. Thus a dumbfounded audience had the privilege of seeing the lean and effervescent Krishna Menon, dressed in jacket and trousers, playing the role of an assertive woman. His appearance on the stage in such circumstances was a signal for the younger section of the audience to break out into jeers, catcalls and other expressions of excitement. But they had no effect on Krishna Menon's performance.

Krishna Menon did not have a bright record in school. The curriculum included Malayalam prose and poetry, English, elementary mathematics, some history and geography and physics. The textbooks were written by approved Englishmen and they extolled the virtues of the English servants of the East India Company while putting horns on the Indian rulers who opposed them. The history books almost invariably ended with a chapter on 'The Blessings of British Rule'. Menon bothered little about these studies. The sharp intellect which was later to win him honours was either dormant or still unformed.

School might have been uninspiring academically, but it kept young Krishna Menon busy. He was a restless pupil who showed some outstanding qualities outside the class-room. The urge to do things was strong. He was active in organizing reading-rooms and debating societies. He was known as a resourceful debater who could speak on any subject at short notice. Audiences seemed to inspire him. And he used to speak as often as he could in English, which was unusual for a high-school boy in Kerala.

The only sport that attracted Krishna Menon's attention in school was badminton, and he played a fairly good game. Generally, though, he was no sports enthusiast. Except that he was tall, he was physically unimpressive. And he seemed not to care.

His physical frailty, however, was never a hindrance to Krishna Menon's assertive tendencies. The hereditary characteristics of obduracy and determination were evident from his earliest days, and unhappy was the boy who ever fell into an argument with Krishna Menon. Once he took a stand, he would cling to it, right or wrong, and he would spend any length of time to convince others of his view-point. Among friends he was talkative, and the manner and matter of his talk marked him out from the common run of students.

When Menon held forth un-schoolboyishly about social problems and the like, there was nothing his fellows could do except to listen and take the first opportunity to run away. But Krishna Menon had another favourite subject on which the other boys could get their own back. This was the new house Krishna Kurup had just built for his children in Calicut. Proud of his family and prouder still of his father, Krishna Menon would go to school in the morning in a victoria and boast of his father and his wealth.

When Menon at last reached the school-leaving class, it was discovered that he was under age; a boy had to be fifteen before he could appear for the examination. As a matter of fact, he must have been exactly fifteen years old then, but the discrepancy in age had already crept into the records. There was nothing that could be done except detain the boy for a year. When he was officially fifteen, Krishna Menon passed out of school.

From school he went straight to his father's old college, then called the Zamorin's College. It was a second-grade college offering only the intermediate course, and Krishna Menon therefore spent but two years in this institution, studying ancient history, modern history and logic. The pattern of life in school was continued in college, though with more debates, more arguments and more extra-curricular activities. In 1915 he passed the intermediate examination and left for Madras and the Presidency College, again following his father's footsteps.

During his final year in school Menon lost his mother. After that he and the other children were under the care and supervision of Janaki Amma. She came to be a mother to them, and between her and Krishna Menon there developed a relationship of extreme tenderness and deep affection. She reputedly became the one person in the world who could exercise a great influence on Menon, but she never interfered in his official work.

Janaki Amma died very recently, on June 25th, 1963. She had been in hospital in Bombay for seven months and Menon was beside her bed at least once a week, whatever his preoccupations. Her death, though long expected, left the man utterly desolate. He was the 'kid brother' all over again, as he wept without making any effort to hide his tears before a swelling crowd of people. He carried his sister's body down four flights of winding staircase. The custom among Hindus is to carry dead bodies to the crematorium, the nearest relatives taking quick turns. Krishna Menon had one end of the bier on his shoulder, and he walked a mile and a half with the corpse of his beloved sister, refusing the customary relief. The procession was along one of Bombay's main thoroughfares, and passers-by were amazed to see Krishna Menon walking along the road carrying a dead body. When the crematorium hove in sight, he lost all control of his emotions and began weeping loudly and bitterly. So pathetic was his state that every one in the vast gathering at the crematorium wept too.

Janaki Amma had been managing the family estates left to Krishna Menon by his father at Kuttiadi and other places in Malabar. Some of them are huge estates growing coconut and black pepper. Both these commodities are like gold and, had the Menons been interested in making money, Kuttiadi alone would have made them millionaires.

4

A Taste of Revolution

A CERTAIN uniqueness has always been attached to Madras, the metropolis of southern India. It is delightfully orthodox, apparently impervious to outside cultures and has a long-standing reputation for high thinking and plain living. If one can conceive of a city where a library will beat a nightclub in popularity, Madras is it.

The lean young man who alighted in Madras Central Station on a hot June morning in 1915 was not exactly overawed by the grandeur of Madras; he was already an individualist capable of taking such wonders as the tramcar in his stride. Yet, as he walked out of the milling railway station with a coolie trailing behind with his box and bedding, Krishna Menon had a sense of elation. He was in a city of famous leaders and famous movements and there was much to look forward to.

Madras was and still is India's finest university town. It has a cluster of colleges each with its own tradition and reputation. The Presidency College is known as the home of aristocrats and sons of officials; the Christian College is thought to be the resort of the refined; the Loyola is the strict custodian of Catholic values; the Pachayyappa's is the receptacle of all and sundry. The student world in Madras had their own picturesque way of referring to these traditions; they talked of the Princes of Presidency, the Gentlemen of Christian, the Slaves of Loyola and the Rowdies of Pachayyappa's. It was among the princes that Krishna Menon's father had studied. It was to join the princes that Krishna Menon went in 1915.

The Presidency rolls at the time contained a few names that were to become famous in later years. Dr S. Radhakrishnan was a tutor in the Philosophy Department; Govinda Menon, later a judge in the Supreme Court of India, was in the same class as

Krishna Menon; K. M. Cariappa, later to be India's first commander-in-chief, joined and immediately left for the defence academy; Pattom Thanu Pillai, now Governor of the Punjab, was also there.

A straggling complex of red-brick buildings, the Presidency College overlooks one of the world's largest beaches, the Marina. Next door to the College and separated from it by the Buckingham Canal is the college hostel named after Queen Victoria. Round and about lies a satellite string of private lodges such as every college in Madras maintains. In these lodges students live together free from the rules and regulations of hostel life. The hostel is the approved residence of serious students; the lodges usually take in the tougher ones.

Freshman Menon never went to live in the Victoria Hostel. Like most students from Malabar he clubbed with other boys to form a lodge of their own. For some time this group was at Buckingham Lodge across the canal. That was its official name; it was more popularly called Buckingham Palace. Students maintained their own cooks there and shared the monthly expenditure, which would seldom exceed twenty rupees per head. It was cheap even by 1915 standards.

Menon was a B.A. student with history and economics as his special subjects. His professor was a young scholar named M. A. Candeth. Candeth had just returned from Cambridge where he had been a friend of Jawaharlal Nehru.

Candeth developed an immense liking for Krishna Menon. He could see that Menon's indifference towards his studies was only the result of deeper inner cravings, that the boy's keenness of mind bore no relation to his academic performance. In conversation he was very sharp and his sense of values elicited Candeth's respect. The professor used to say privately that this boy was on the verge of some unpredictable but potentially important development.

In fact Menon was reflecting a characteristic of his time when he neglected the class-room and took more interest in extra-curricular activities. Many sensitive Indians were doing just the same. They had a vague sense of national humiliation. They wanted to put an end to it and feel free and proud. But in those pre-Gandhi days the movement for freedom lacked precise ideas. There was no national commander-in-chief to give a sense of direction and purpose to the campaign. Therefore, the patriotically inclined had difficulty in finding outlets for their emotions. A general restlessness crept into them.

Menon's routine in Madras showed how restless he was. As a degree student in history, he continued his lackadaisical meanderings through the curriculum. History then meant European history, which in turn revolved round British history. Menon read prodigiously, but seldom his textbooks. His attitude during lectures (such as he attended) was one of cynical indifference.

At four in the afternoon lectures would be over and students would find themselves with a long evening on their hands. A good majority of them went to the playing fields. Menon, indifferent to sports as well as to his studies, would seldom be seen among them. Sometimes he would roam about the Marina talking animatedly to close friends. Sometimes he would visit cinemas. But he could not have been any great lover of the cinema for, when the lights came on at the end of the show, his friends almost invariably found him asleep.

Most of his time was spent in activities on behalf of the various social and cultural organizations in which he took an interest. He was a permanent fixture in all functions promoted by the College Union and by the various debating societies. He was elected secretary of the Malayali Club which included practically all the students from Kerala.

Fellow-students considered him an aggressive speaker. Teachers more often than not looked upon him as an embarrassment, for he spoke most of the time about the legitimacy of the freedom struggle and about the way in which indigenous aspirations were being stifled by the foreign government.

This kind of talk was considered all but treasonable, and Indians familiar with that phase of their national history will realize what courage it must have taken for Menon to speak as he did, and what reactions he must have caused among the students and the staff. The British Principal of the Presidency College was particularly offended by Menon's ideas. But Menon only made things worse by frequently referring in his speeches to the sycophancy of some of the Indian staff members.

Menon was not only a speaker but also a listener. Lectures by eminent men were fashionable in Madras. Wherever there was a public lecture by a well-known speaker on politics or social problems, he was sure to be present.

A by-product of these interests and activities was Menon's addiction to cycling. Either to attend lectures, or to round up speakers for some function he was organizing, or merely to visit people, he had to cover vast distances in the city. Soon Menon became inseparable from his bicycle. He would ride up and down and across the city, neither the insufferable heat nor the distances daunting him. He became so identified with his vehicle that cronies started saying that if a letter was addressed to Mr Cycle, Madras, the Post Office would deliver it to him.

Menon was doing everything an ideal student was not supposed to do – apparently frittering away his energies, and wasting much of his time.

One fine morning the defiant red-and-green flag of Mrs Annie Besant's Home Rule League was seen fluttering above the Presidency College. It was the time when Mrs Besant was soaring to dizzy heights of popularity and her Home Rule League had become the symbol of Indian Nationalism. The banner of revolution dancing above the Presidency College was a clear challenge. Awe-struck students collected in excited knots on the college campus and talked about the sacrilege in hushed tones. Indignant professors met and discussed the shame of their college. Citizens gathered on the promenade outside and, pointing to the flag, talked wildly. The news spread even to Government offices and police stations; and everyone was outraged.

Of course, the flag had but a brief moment of glory. It was promptly pulled down and the authorities turned to the task of punishing the culprit. Inquiries soon showed that the flag was planted on the college roof by Krishna Menon, and the Principal prepared to announce his expulsion. It is said that Professor Candeth intervened, arguing that it was the first indiscretion on the part of Menon and that he would personally see that it was not repeated. The Principal allowed himself to be persuaded.

The flag incident must be considered a landmark in the evolution of Menon's personality. It may be difficult, even for Indians growing up in the post-independence era, to realize the gravity of what the young student had done. It was an offence for which he could be put in jail. Menon had acted with the spirit and daring of a revolutionary, but without being associated with any revolutionary group or party. It was a spontaneous, instinctive defiance of authority. It showed the intensity of the passions that were stirring deep within him. It showed his total fearlessness, his contempt for personal safety. It showed that his taste for revolution was not an acquired taste but one that was born with him.

Menon may have been grateful for the chance he was given to stay on and complete his course, but he certainly was in no mood to turn over a new leaf. In fact, his love for politics and his disdain for studies continued to grow. It was no wonder therefore that he failed to get his degree at the first attempt. In the 1917 examination, he was successful only in Part I, that is, English. He had to wait until April 1918 before he passed Part II as well and became a Bachelor of Arts with a second class.

By now he was too preoccupied with extra-curricular activities to be worried about academic failures. The development predicted by Professor Candeth was coming.

But there was to be a further delay. Krishna Kurup, though upset by the performance of his son in college, still hoped that the boy would make good. He insisted on Menon's going straight on to the Madras Law College when he graduated from the Presidency.

Menon was not at all enthusiastic, but he was still not sure what he should do with his life. Idealism was spurring him in a particular direction, but he had formed no definite ideas yet. Krishna Kurup had his way and Menon took up law.

Soon after enrolling himself as a Bachelor of Law student, Krishna Menon proved that he was still the audacious revolutionary who had shocked the Presidency College by planting the flag of defiance on its dome. The Principal of the Law College, a Mr Davis who was famous for his Shakespearean recitations, was fastidious about propriety in dress, and he had decreed that India's future lawyers should never appear in college except in conventional college clothes. Menon made a point of going to the sedate Law College dressed in a typical South Indian *kurta* and *dhoti*. The Principal was all a-flutter. But it did not have the slightest effect on Krishna Menon who was quietly packing his bags on his own.

35

5

A Leader found

A POLITICAL tidal wave swept Krishna Menon out of the Madras Law College a few months after he joined it. It was a painful break, for it meant defying his father, who had a house in Tellicherry with gardens and outhouses, and after two more years Menon would have been able to join the prosperous legal practice in Malabar. To give it up and plunge into the kind of public activity that attracted him at the time was to invite insecurity and personal suffering. But the youthful Menon did not pause to think of the virtues of security. The call had come from Mrs Annie Besant.

It was around this time that the Indian National Congress began to develop into a national movement for freedom. From its birth in 1885 until the first decade of the twentieth century the Congress had been no more than an annual reiteration of India's loyalty to the British Crown. The founding fathers of the Congress were impressively abject in their reverence for the monarch. Faith in the sense of justice of the British people was total. The President of the Congress in 1896, Mohammed Rahimtulla Sayani, said in his presidential oration that 'a more honest or sturdy nation does not exist under the sun than this English nation.'

This was still the temper of the times when Krishna Menon arrived in Madras. He had a strong feeling that somewhere something was missing. The riots that followed the Bengal partition in October 1905 had shown that there was enormous power in the country awaiting leadership.

It was Mrs Annie Besant who took up the challenge. She had come to India in 1893 to spread the Theosophical movement. But the apparent inanity of the national movement had drawn her into the political arena.

The war was in full swing. The Germans were crashing through

Europe. England was in peril. Without so much as consulting Indian leaders, the Viceroy had dispatched huge contingents of crack Indian troops to Europe. These soldiers soon became a legend in Flanders and their qualities of endurance and courage were recognized as major contributions to the victory of the Allies.

When the Indian Army won such unstinted praise, the Congress took over with a resolution saying that 'in view of the profound and avowed loyalty the people of India have manifested in the present crisis, this Congress appeals to the Government to deepen and perpetuate it and make it an enduring and valuable asset of the Empire by removing all invidious distinctions here and abroad between His Majesty's Indian and other subjects ...'

Choosing to jump from theosophy to politics at this moment, Mrs Besant electrified the nation with the very first idea she put forward. She objected to the Congress resolution on the basis that it presented the Indian problem as a matter of reward. Things such as autonomy and self-government, she said, were not to be India's as a reward for loyalty; they were India's as a matter of right. She boldly demanded the prohibition of imports from countries from which Indians were excluded, and introduced for the first time the idea of reciprocity in Indo-British relations.

After this the Congress never looked back. By 1917 Mrs Besant was President of the Congress.

And yet the Congress was but a small part of Mrs Besant's field of activity. A woman with tremendous capacity for work, she founded a series of organizations to press the programmes she believed in. Politics was only one of her interests and it was only a means to an end. The ends she had in view concerned the soul. She set up groups for social service, for religious study, for educational work, for the organization of youth. She bought a printing press and started from Madras a daily newspaper called *New India* and a weekly under the name of *Commonweal*.

Mrs Besant's special target was youth. She was always interested in schools and student organizations. At the height of her almost legendary popularity, she turned her special attention to galvanizing young people into action. She disaffiliated her educational institutions from the University of Madras and started a National High School at Adyar. Students everywhere became a powerful pillar of Mrs Besant's programmes, so much so that the authorities were constrained to promulgate a special order prohibiting students from participating in politics. The order led to increased political activity among students and added to Mrs Besant's popularity.

The white-haired old lady was all action. Her drive and dynamism lent an aura of magic to her personality. She was full of fire and full of vibrant ideas. She was a natural leader and, at a time when Gandhi had only just arrived from South Africa and was still watching and studying the situation in India, she provided the inspiration the nation sorely needed.

This was precisely the kind of leadership the young idealist from Malabar was waiting for. Even while he was in the Presidency College, Krishna Menon was inspired by the ideas of Mrs Besant. As he devoured every column of every issue of *New India* and *Commonweal*, Krishna Menon saw in Mrs Besant everything he valued and longed for – action, fearlessness, a flair for youth programmes and social work and above all a sense of discipline and a belief in legality. Mrs Besant was a passionate believer in correct constitutional behaviour, a principle which was soon to lead to her unpopularity and political eclipse. Krishna Menon, the inheritor of a profound sense of righteousness from his parents, saw this ultra constitutionality of Mrs Besant as a glorious characteristic; he himself was to become a convinced advocate of constitutional proprieties in his mature years.

At first he was content to watch and admire from a distance. Then he began actively propagating, in his own limited circle, the ideals of the Home Rule Movement. Soon after he joined the Law College he realized that he had to throw himself completely into the movement.

The emotional appeal of Mrs Besant's movement was heightened for Krishna Menon by the imposition of the Government's notorious Security Act and what followed. The Act demanded exorbitant financial deposits from publications critical of the Government. Protest meetings began to be held every day in every corner of the country and *New India* came thundering out against the new evil. Almost every issue of the paper carried editorials signed by Annie Besant tearing apart the Press laws in her strident, closely argued language. When *New India* itself was asked to put up a security deposit, the public spontaneously started contributing money until, within a few days, the entire amount was in the hands of an overwhelmed Mrs Besant.

A Leader found

Then there was the internment of 1917. Scared by the effectiveness of Mrs Besant's systematic campaign, the Government restricted her to the resort town of Ooty. The internment was a foolish measure because it produced results exactly the opposite of what the Government had intended. Montagu, then Secretary of State for India, noted in his diary: 'I particularly like that Shiva who cut his wife into 52 pieces, only to find that he had 52 wives. This is what happened to the Government of India when it interned Mrs Besant.'

When she was released after three months, she travelled in a triumphant cavalcade to Madras. From the Central Station all the way to the Theosophical Society's headquarters at Adyar in the suburbs of Madras she was wildly cheered. In that crowd was Krishna Menon.

When he entered the Law College Mrs Besant was already President of the Congress. The flow of inspiration from Adyar was steady. Here was a place where one could do useful work. Here were ideas one could serve. The pedantic atmosphere of the Law College made Adyar seem even more attractive.

Menon made up his mind. One evening he went to Adyar with his bed-roll – and never returned. It was the development everything had been leading up to – the count-down was past and the Menon the world was to know was airborne.

It may be of interest today to recall that another prize Mrs Besant had bagged some years earlier was way up north in Allahabad. This was the then thirteen-year-old Jawaharlal Nehru. Years later Nehru was to write in his autobiography: 'I was deeply moved by her oratory and returned from her speeches dazed and as in a dream. I decided to join the Theosophical Society ... and Mrs Besant herself performed the ceremony of initiation.'

Along similar lines two lives were moving which were destined to meet and discover in each other an amazing identity of outlook.

Adyar was then a nerve centre of India. Ever since Mrs Besant had made it the international headquarters of the Theosophical Society, it had become the meeting ground of the outstanding brains of the day.

Ideas flowed from Adyar. Even the first rumblings of trade

unionism in India were heard from there, for it was such leading lights of the Theosophical Society as B. P. Wadia and later B. Shiva Rao who organized the workers of Perambur, an industrial suburb of Madras. At one stage Mrs Besant organized what she called the Madras Parliament, a unique institution which sought to give Indians practical experience in the machinery of democracy; when the House met, the Chief Justice of Madras and such great figures as V. S. Srinivasa Sastri, S. Satyamurti and C. P. Ramaswamy Aiyer were on the front benches. Adyar, though a small suburban village, was an intellectual metropolis with the daily *New India* spreading its influence.

Krishna Menon entered this metropolis with enthusiasm. He shared a bachelors' apartment on the banks of the Adyar river. His life there was austere in the extreme. He slept on a wooden cot, bathed in an earthen pot in an outhouse, ate meagrely. He dressed carelessly in a Madras *dhoti* and coarse *kurta*. He could often be seen barefoot. He was somewhat diffident and shy as he entered this new and unaccustomed life. He seldom mixed with people for the sake of the company. Except when he was out and about on duty, he preferred to be by himself. Work had suddenly become a passion. Nothing else mattered.

The spiritual side of the Theosophical Movement seemed to have attracted Menon little. He welcomed the discipline and the austerity in so far as they helped him concentrate on his real interests. Of these the two main ones were politics as crystallized in the Home Rule League, and the concept of national education spearheaded by Mrs Besant.

The nucleus of Mrs Besant's educational network was the National University. Dr George S. Arundale, a British educationalist of great eminence, was in charge of this institution whose chancellor was Rabindranath Tagore. It attracted to its faculty some of the most brilliant minds of the day. Menon enrolled himself as a student in this university and later became a lecturer.

From the beginning he seemed to have won the esteem of Dr Arundale. He identified himself with everything Arundale undertook, impressing the Professor with his consuming devotion and eventually becoming his secretary.

By 1918 scouting had become a rage in Madras. Only the previous year had the Indian Boy Scouts' Association been officially launched by the National Congress under the initiative of Mrs Besant, who was its President.

Mrs Besant turned her attention to scouting initially as a protest against the oath prescribed by the founder of the movement. This oath asked for loyalty to 'God and King' with no mention of country. Mrs Besant argued that this was a very wrong thing to ask of an Indian boy. The argument ultimately led to her organizing India's own scout movement. Later Baden-Powell was to visit India, understand and appreciate the validity of Mrs Besant's stand and bring about a merger of the Indian Scout Movement with the world organization.

From the time it was started the movement had fired the imagination of young and old alike in India. It became a national duty. Mrs Besant gave it brilliant organizational leadership. She appointed as her Chief of Staff Mr F. G. Pearce, who was fresh from the University of London and who had had training in scouting. As assistant to Pearce Mrs Besant picked Krishna Menon.

Menon threw himself heart and soul into scouting. He trained himself rigorously and became a qualified Scout Commissioner. He kept copious notes on the duties of a scoutmaster, on camp hygiene, scout signs, first-aid, etc. These notes, neat and exhaustive and still preserved at the India League in London, show how seriously he went about the task of equipping himself.

The first scout troop in Madras was organized by him at a place called Komaleeswaranpet and it was called the Mohammed Troop. It soon became the model troop in the city and carried off all the badges and trophies. Again, of all the Rover Troops in Madras, his own, called the Ashoka, became the most famous. He also organized cycle squads and sea scouts. He made it a habit to visit his scouts every morning before they left for their schools. He was a strict disciplinarian and insisted on punctuality. Early morning rallies would find him at the appointed place well ahead of time and his scouts knew that it would be unpleasant for them if they came even so much as a minute late.

The organization of scouts was the first big responsibility with which Menon was entrusted. He carried it out with great efficiency. Old-timers still remember what a striking, if somewhat incongruous figure was cut by Krishna Menon, lean and lanky in his khaki uniform, hardly able to achieve visual smartness but making up for it with the fire in his eyes.

The success that attended his work in the Boy Scout movement also gave him a new confidence in himself. He felt that he was, after all, on the right track. Menon was happy. In happiness he grew more dedicated. He began developing habits and characteristics that were unusual. He seemed hardly aware of the diversions other youngsters of his age went in for. Once he took up an assignment his application was total to the extent of neglecting food and sleep. The concept of leisure began slowly to fade from his scheme of things.

His dedication grew so profound that he joined a special organization Mrs Besant had founded called the Brothers of Service. This was an exclusive order admitting only those whose entire life was placed at the disposal of Mrs Besant for national work. It was something like the Servants of India Society, except that the Brothers of Service were expected to be more self-effacing, more hard-working and more rigorously disciplined. The order had its own uniform as well – a long white tunic with a blue cord tied round the waist.

Menon was a habitual wearer of this uniform when it was decided that he should go to Malabar to organize the scout movement and other public activities in that part of the south.

6

The Prophet

M ENON returned to Malabar in 1920.
Adyar had suddenly lost its political significance, Mrs
Besant having opposed Gandhi's idea of civil disobedience and
consequently become a back number in the Congress. Disobedience, civil or otherwise, was anathema to Mrs Besant, who
believed in sticking strictly to the law of the land. Gandhi's
recourse to fasts revolted her. In most ways she and Gandhi were
incompatible. Her appeal was to the head, his to the heart.
She was very British in her loyalty to the Crown. She wanted
India to have complete freedom, of course, but only as a member
of 'the Indo-British Commonwealth'. Gandhi popularized the
slogan 'within the Empire if possible, outside if necessary', and
was working for the latter by 1929. The eventual evolution of
India as a republic within the Commonwealth was a fusion of
Mrs Besant's ideas with those of Gandhi and one of the catalytic
agents that brought about this fusion was Krishna Menon. But
in 1920 the possibility of such a fusion was never even imagined;
only the irreconcilability was noticeable. As Gandhi took over
leadership of the Indian movement, Adyar withered.

Politically rejected, Adyar stepped up its non-political activities.
Mrs Besant's apostles began to go out in all directions preaching
the gospel of theosophy, social work, national education and
above all the scout movement.

Young Krishna Menon was a natural choice for Malabar. His
devotion to the cause was great and he had proved his organizational acumen. He was therefore appointed Scout Commissioner
for the Malabar-Cochin territory.

To Menon, return to Malabar had a personal aspect. In the
eyes of his people and society, he was returning home with an
unfulfilled mission. He had failed to get a law degree, had achieved

43

nothing else worth while. His family and old friends were confused when they saw him arriving in the odd tunic of the Christ, complete with long hair combed back. Twenty-four years old and this was all he had to show!

His father, Krishna Kurup, was crestfallen. He had tried his best to keep his son in the Law College and had felt let down when his entreaties were ignored. And now here was the young man proclaiming by his very costume that he was beyond redemption. It was a cruel shattering of fond hopes. Appa was the brightest of his children and he had always dreamed of taking him into partnership.

Much of the disapproval Menon encountered in Malabar might have been due to a sense of fear among his well-wishers. The young fellow had jumped into the unknown. His elders could not predict what his activities would lead to in terms of his own future. At the same time they knew what official repression meant; the way their boy was going about was an open invitation to the minions of law. Fear, disappointment, confusion and anger were the emotions the Christ-looking Menon inspired among his people. Kurup was upset by what he regarded as his son's quixotic take-off. For several painful years he continued to feel distressed.

The strain caused by society's disapproval of his ways weighed heavily on Krishna Menon. But he was not apologetic. Like a prophet, he was convinced that he was doing the right thing and that others were in the dark. It was ignorance, he told himself, that was at the bottom of their disapproval. This in turn gave strength to his beliefs for, in essence, all his activities were directed towards the removal of ignorance and the creation of a socio-political awareness in every individual.

When one remembers the general mood of the time, the yearning and the groping and the searching that was going on in India, one realizes that by now Menon must have been a fanatical idealist. There was a passionate nationalistic fervour in the air, though the ultimate objectives were undefined. In young hearts there could be no place for anything other than a sense of service.

It was not a time when criticism could go very far. The sensitive young men participating in nationalist work were proud of their 'one-track minds'. They were messiahs who could not be dissuaded by the criticism of those they thought had failed to see

44

the light. They were determined and dedicated and they never stopped to think of consequences.

The criticism he faced made no impression on Menon. If his family could not understand the importance of his work, he would prefer to forget his family. It was an attitude typical of the time. He paused briefly to explain his convictions and ideas – but only briefly. Soon after arrival in Calicut, leaving critics to criticize, he threw himself into a mad round of activities which took at least a section of Calicut by storm.

At the top of the list of priorities was scouting. The movement caught on. Menon travelled all over Malabar and Cochin, organizing troops and setting up units in every town. Wherever two boys assembled in khaki he was personally present to tell them about the importance of the movement and to guide them.

The significance of the scout movement in relation to the development of Menon's personality is that it brought out the revolutionary's instinctive reverence for discipline and collective work. The struggle for freedom had not yet assumed an organized character. All that existed was a popular craving to become politically independent. Those who felt deeply about it regarded the discipline and organization of the foreign power as the cause of its success. It was by virtue of superior military discipline, by strength derived from the industrial revolution, that the British had succeeded in subjugating India. Indians lacked unity, discipline and strength. If they were to stand on their own feet, it was necessary for them to develop a sense of organization and team-work. Scouting was the patriotic opportunity to organize the nation's youth into one disciplined unit, with a precise sense of mission and service. Menon saw the scout movement as a basis of nation-building.

His non-scouting activities were also in the direction of organization and preparation. He founded in Calicut the Nineteen-Twenty Club, a sort of intellectual coffee-shop where angry young men could gather and talk their heads off.

Menon set up a second platform in Calicut. This was called the Social Service League. While the Nineteen-Twenty Club served the purpose of a study group, the League afforded an opportunity to young men of the locality to be of practical service to the community.

The long-robed, long-haired cyclist became a familiar figure in

Calicut as Menon went about meeting people, holding discussions, arranging meetings. One day while returning from an evening discussion group Menon was stopped by an acquaintance, who took a long look at him and said,

'The way you dress and go about, you look like a crack.'

'I'm glad,' said Menon. 'Let the light enter through the crack.'

This man was too determined. Witticisms and innuendos could not deflect him. Slowly people began taking note of him and realizing that his activities were planned and purposeful. His local conspicuity was also due to the fact that he was invariably trailed by C.I.D. men. This was a compliment accorded by Authority in those days to anyone who had to do with patriotic work. Menon accepted the presence of the detectives with ironic good humour.

It was during these years in Calicut, while working on his own and for the ideas that inspired him, that Menon developed the first characteristics of the crusader he was to become. Life became all work and no play. The righteous obstinacy inherited from both his parents was at work. He added a note of relentlessness to every activity he launched. His zeal knew no bounds as he pressed ahead through project after project. He was fast becoming an irresistible force. Classmates who had looked upon him as a very average boy now realized that this was no ordinary man.

For almost three years Menon went on with his crusade in Calicut. Then it was time to make a move.

Dr Arundale was planning a trip to England. As an education-alist engaged in pioneering activities in India, his name was well known in Britain and he had been invited to preside over a conference at Letchworth. The conference was organized by Mrs Ensor, founder-director of a co-educational school which was enjoying a great reputation in England.

Arundale was a successful talent-scout. He used to help Mrs Besant pick young men of ability and give them opportunities for development. When the idea of going to Letchworth for the educational conference was finally accepted, he also decided to take a couple of promising youngsters with him. It did not take Mrs Besant and Arundale long to make their choice. Krishna Menon was one of those selected. The idea was to secure educational facilities for them in England and give them the best of training in the fields of their choice, so that they could return to

India and become leaders of the national resurgence movement that had grown from Adyar.

When Krishna Menon was informed of the plan he was immediately enthusiastic. Arundale was already a man he admired and he thought it a great opportunity to be able to go with him to England. He had been told that a six-month stay in England would make him a qualified teacher and he could return to the National University in Adyar and settle down there as a professor.

Through a friend Menon informed his father of the plan. At first Krishna Kurup was not enthusiastic. Of course, he liked the idea of his son going to England. But teaching? That was not what he had planned for his son. He could not possibly hand over his practice and his property in Tellicherry to a teacher. Couldn't Appa use the opportunity to study law? Couldn't he return as a great barrister from London and electrify Tellicherry with his brilliance and scholarship? Appa could. Kurup was told that Menon would take advantage of his trip to London to acquire a degree in law. Kurup's joy was unbounded. At long last his dream was going to materialize – and in a manner he himself had not foreseen, for Appa was going to be not just a Bachelor of Law from Madras but a barrister from London. He volunteered to finance his son's trip.

On a humid June day in 1924 Menon boarded an Italian ship in Bombay. He felt strange in the new Western-style suit he was wearing. But Dr Arundale took him under his protective wing. The party sailed for Venice. From there they went overland to London. Victoria Station was foggy and rain-soaked as the wide-eyed Indian youth alighted there one dismal morning. Everything was strange. Everything was also cold, insufferably cold after all those years of cycling in the scorching Madras sun.

But it was London. It was opportunity. At the age of twenty-eight, life was beginning.

PART II

London

He never glanced in the mirror
of History, never even thought
what posterity would think of
him, but simply did his work.

LUNACHARSKY on Lenin

7

India League

As he looked around on his arrival at Letchworth in 1924, young Krishna Menon saw that the world was grim indeed. Fascism was gaining ground in Europe, but the democracies were complacent. Far away in India Gandhi was all but dying in a British jail. It was a year of bloody communalism in northern India. The British public was not even conscious of the national movement that was going on in India. As a sensitive idealist Krishna Menon felt the urge to jump to the fore and do something.

Letchworth was saturated with education and theosophy. Neither his mental make-up nor the challenges of the times were calculated to make him remain in such placid waters. With his background of political activity and social service in Madras, it was only natural that Menon should look beyond Letchworth into the stormy seas of politics.

But he was no longer the impetuous youth of Madras. He knew that for the success of whatever voyage he might be undertaking, he would have to equip himself academically and intellectually. The environment of conflicting interests and contradictory loyalties in which he found himself demanded of those who wanted to contribute their mite a seriousness of application and steadfastness of approach. No more for him the days of undergraduate adventure.

Menon started his career in Britain by enrolling himself for a teacher's diploma course. He taught history for a year at St Christopher's School in Hertfordshire, and obtained his London diploma in 1925.

Teaching could not contain Krishna Menon. His mind turned in other directions, but he had no intention of returning to India in a hurry. The revolutionary in him was now fully aroused and he saw a prolonged struggle lying ahead of him. He did not see the struggle as merely an occasion for adventure. He was so conscious of its importance that he wanted to prepare himself thoroughly by studying economics, political science, history, law, philosophy and psychology.

In London's India League, the only real home Krishna Menon has ever had in his life, huge crates of papers are stored in an attic. The patient researcher can unearth scores of notebooks written in a steady slanting hand. They are lecture notes taken down by Krishna Menon and they bear witness to a very serious student, well-read, impeccably neat and with an eye for essentials. The subjects range over a wide field. There are notes on British industry, industrial organization, international trade, statistics, principles of currency, public administration, commerce and colonization, political and social theory, history of political ideas, philosophy, principles of education. A few pages of one notebook show that he even tried to pick up some shorthand, but apparently this plan was soon abandoned. These notebooks represent the solid foundations of an intellect that was to become the envy of friends and the despair of adversaries.

The London School of Economics was then enjoying a unique reputation and prestige under Harold Laski. Menon studied political science there for two years. In 1927 he obtained his B.Sc. degree with first-class honours. He was then thirty-one years old.

By this time it was becoming clear that the prospect of an uninterrupted period of study was out of the question for Krishna Menon. The course of events had put him in an environment of political activity and he realized that as an Indian nationalist he had work to do in England.

It was a time when indifference on the part of the public was combining with determined propaganda by the Government to produce a hopelessly distorted picture of India in Britain. The national movement in India was hardly known among the common people of the United Kingdom. All they knew was that His Majesty's Government was saving India from anarchy and chaos and that this noble work was being obstructed by 'incompetent' Indian leaders who were 'a collection of inferior Kerenskys'. Such were the phrases used and the information given by the British newspapers of the time. The anti-Indian campaign was vigorous and systematic and it was being carried on, to use

Krishna Menon's own words, 'by men who draw their incomes from India and spend the evenings of their lives in maligning her and her people'.[1]

The situation incensed Menon. Here was a challenge that called for the immediate attention of India's national leaders. The war for liberation might be essentially a home-based one, but it was desperately in need of a second front in Britain. Englishmen were enjoying a democratic system of government and this made the work of the publicist a very important one.

The outline of a solution to the problem soon presented itself. In 1912 Mrs Besant had established in London the Home Rule for India British Auxiliary. This organization sought to win support for Indian freedom mainly in the House of Commons. In 1923 it had been re-named the Commonwealth of India League. The resolution suggesting the change of name was moved by Mr Jinarajadasa, who later became President of the International Theosophical Society, and was seconded by Mr H. S. L. Polak, who had already become known as a disciple of Gandhi and a great pacifist. In fact, both the Commonwealth of India League and the British Auxiliary were manned by friends and followers of Mrs Besant. Quite naturally Krishna Menon with his Adyar background had gravitated to the Commonwealth League when he arrived in London.

Menon found the League, as it was functioning then, too soft and too quiet to be of much real use. The vilification campaign against the Indian freedom movement was so furious that only an equally furious campaign in support of India could produce any result. Here was an active and thriving organization that could do the job. Menon began flooding the League with new ideas, new programmes, new horizons. The leaders of the League could recognize a good worker when they saw one; in 1928 Menon was elected the joint secretary. That clinched the issue. Here, Menon told himself, was his duty. His return to India could wait. The immediate job was to put life into the League and build it up as an advance post of India's national movement. Without realizing it, Menon was settling down to a crusade that would last two decades.

But Menon's concept of what the League should be and how it should work differed substantially from that of the older members.

---

[1] Letter to the Editor of *New India*, Madras, dated January 17th, 1937.

Menon had little time for their theosophy as such. This discrepancy was to lead to a parting of the ways and a remoulding of the organization along radical lines.

The Commonwealth of India League at that time had its headquarters at 203 The Strand. Peter Freeman, a Member of Parliament, was its chairman. The object of the League was officially stated as being '... to work for Dominion Status for India, thus making her a partner-member in the Commonwealth of Great Britain and the self-governing Dominions'. The short form of its objective, 'To Work For Dominion Status for India', was printed on the League's stationery.

With Krishna Menon around, the activities of the League began to acquire a new dimension. He pressed for an extension of the League's scope, more intensive field-work among the general public, the mobilization of student and worker opinion in favour of the cause. Most important of all, he wanted a redefinition of the League's aims, substituting the phrase 'freedom and self-determination' for 'Dominion Status'.

This was an echo from India. A war of controversy had flared up among the leaders of the Congress movement over the phrase 'Dominion Status'. The elders wanted the Congress to accept it, while younger men, led by Jawaharlal Nehru, opposed it and called for full independence instead. The difference of opinion was so great that Nehru set up the only faction within the Congress with which he was ever associated, the Independence of India League; it was a pressure group that functioned until the Congress accepted independence as its goal. In this struggle Menon found himself on the side of the radicals and he tried to swing the Commonwealth of India League round to his way of thinking.

In a detailed memorandum to fellow members he explained what was wrong with 'Dominion Status':

1. It lays stress on India being within the British Commonwealth and for a *British* organization to do that savours of compulsion.

2. For the above reason the term militates against the usefulness of the League as a bridge-builder between India and Britain, because it puts us falsely out of alignment with Indian claims, with which in reality we fully agree, and alienates us from the Indian co-operation we seek.

3. The term is not congenial to the rapidly growing body of radical opinion in Britain which appreciates the Indian objection to being a Dominion by compulsion, and acknowledges freely the justice of Gandhi's demand for the 'substance of independence' and is increasingly speaking of independence and self-determination rather than Dominion Status in deference to Indian feelings; although to them and to us, the term means the same thing. Thus our retention of it tends to alienate British support as well as detract from our prestige in India.

4. We anticipate the possibility of a technical Dominion Status, not embracing real Indian freedom, being proposed for India; this, if it were brought forward and even rejected, would put us in a false position. We do not think the spirit of Sir Malcolm Hailey is dead in the British attitude towards India and we do not want to be involved in hair-splitting mental gymnastics which would further affect detrimentally our prestige in India.

Menon knew that Dominion Status virtually meant independence. But he also knew that this point, taken for granted by Englishmen for Englishmen, could be overlooked or twisted in the case of India. The Statute of Westminster had not yet come into force. Menon's opposition to Dominion Status was therefore on legal-constitutional grounds. He wanted to forestall any dialectical complications over its interpretation. 'We think,' he said in another memorandum, 'that greater good both in world affairs and in the domestic concerns of both nations will result from free and equal partnership within the Commonwealth. But we acknowledge the right to separate and we seek to make that acknowledgment explicit.' Menon obviously meant what he said for, after independence, he was to become a great advocate of India's staying within the Commonwealth.

But in 1930 his stand was too radical for the conservative elements of the Commonwealth of India League, for Menon was clearly trying to align the League and its work with the Congress movement in India. This was not particularly appealing to the theosophists in the League, because Mrs Besant was no longer a member of the Congress. The stage was set for Menon's break with the theosophists.

He did not have much trouble choosing between theosophy and his political ideas. Two years under Harold Laski had already decided the issue. Much as he loved and respected Mrs Besant, Krishna Menon could see that the Indian National Congress symbolized the mass movement in India for freedom and that it was important for the Commonwealth of India League to work with the Congress.

This was yet another milestone in Menon's political evolution. While at Adyar he had not been a supporter of the Congress. As one who admired Mrs Besant and her values, he was even sceptical of the strange new ideas the Congress was developing under Gandhi. But it did not take him long to understand the significance of the new ideas. As Mrs Besant drifted away from the Congress in disgust and anger, Menon found himself watching it carefully and studying the implications of its new policy directions. It was all right for Mrs Besant to shrink away from Gandhi and the Congress; politics was only of secondary importance to her, and she had theosophy to which she could return. To Menon, politics in the sense of national liberation was the primary concern. He could not therefore bring himself to drop it and confine himself to theosophy.

He knew that the theosophist elders in the Commonwealth of India League were resenting his attitude to the Dominion Status issue and generally to the League's work. But, just as criticism in Calicut did not deflect him from his chosen path in 1920, the disapproval of the theosophists did not affect him in 1930. He had no doubt at all that the League should stop handling politics as an incidental business, that it should become insistent and aggressive, that it should work in co-operation with and parallel to the main movement at home.

He pressed his case against Dominion Status. Besides being logical, his arguments were also practical, as the memoranda made clear. Consequently the radical wing gained the upper hand in the League.

Gradually the elders began dropping out, among them Mrs Besant and H. S. L. Polak. It was the second painful break in Menon's life. But there could be no compromise between personal emotions and social ideals, between affections and duty. Much as he adored his father, he broke with him because he was convinced that work for Indian liberation was more important than becoming a rich lawyer. Much as he revered Mrs Besant, he accepted the fact of breaking with her because political work was a matter of life and death for the messiah in him.

Both experiences were of a nature that sharpened Menon's dedication and zeal. Separation from those he had tended to hero-worship made him devote himself even more fanatically to the cause. The break with Mrs Besant completed Menon's evolution into a fiercely single-minded political animal.

In the League itself the resignations of the elders created some confusion. In a 'personal and unofficial' circular, the Joint Secretary of the League explained: 'Although it is not practicable to embrace all who consider themselves friends of India in one organization (such an attempt would savour of Carlyle's facetious suggestion of a Society for the Amalgamation of Heaven and Hell), there is no sufficient reason for any division amongst us which would cause a weakening of the forces working for Indian freedom.'

There was no weakening. On the contrary there was a tremendous strengthening of the work for India because, by the end of 1930, the Commonwealth of India League had ceased to exist and a new organization under the name of India League had unfurled its flag in London. Its object was, 'To support the claim of India to Swaraj.'

8

Persuading the British People

THE CRISIS through which the Commonwealth of India League
passed in 1930 was only a pale reflection of the crisis that had
overtaken India. The Lahore Congress had authorized the All-
India Congress Committee to launch a programme of civil
disobedience and on March 12th Gandhi had started his epoch-
making Dandi march to defy the salt-tax regulations by taking
salt from the sea. On April 5th, when he actually broke the law,
the nation exploded into a frenzy of civil disobedience. Arrests
followed, but the movement grew. There were stray incidents
of terrorism here and there, but the revolt was mostly non-violent.
The British Government for the first time knew the power and
potentialities of the new weapon that Gandhi had forged.

Krishna Menon watched this explosion of mass emotions with
awe and pride. He was not initially a believer in civil disobedience,
preferring argument as his own political weapon. But the shattering impact of the Gandhian technique compelled attention;
whether or not one approved of it intellectually, one had to
grant its effectiveness in India at the time. Menon was convinced
more than ever that he was right in trying to relate political work
in Britain to the Congress movement in India. Though the India
League he fathered was a non-party organization, he himself
became a Congressman and a Gandhian.

As India declared 'war' following the Dandi march, Krishna
Menon began an intensive propaganda campaign to tell the
British people of the implications of what was going on. He spoke
from every available platform, including soap-boxes in Hyde
Park, and filled the pages of his *India News* with information about
the issues at stake. The tone of his writing was typical. There was
never any haranguing, but only a sustained emphasis on the
fundamentals of constitutional liberty and the meaning of

58

governmental policy decisions in India. Propaganda was not twisting facts, but making facts available. With this end in view, he prepared a standing list of prominent Indians whom he could call upon for articles on the various aspects of life and government in India.

On the political level it was the post-Simon-Commission[1] period of bitterness in India. At the India League they were thinking in terms of a campaign 'attacking the Government if need be in case the policy of the Government after the publication of the Simon Report is unsatisfactory to us'.[2]

It was also the time of the first Round Table Conference, and preparations for it had started early in the year. At least two Indian leaders going to London for the Conference, Sir C. P. Ramaswamy Aiyer and Sir Sachidananda Sinha, were known to Menon through Mrs Besant. He wrote to them giving details of the work that was being carried on in London and offering the machinery of the League for their use. The offer was made to them in their personal capacities so that ideas that could not be put forward officially at the Conference could be aired through *India News* and from the platform of the League.

Most of Menon's efforts immediately after the formation of the India League were directed towards establishing the League as an integral part of the Indian national struggle on the one hand and, on the other, towards making its presence felt in England. Departing from the line of the Commonwealth of India League, he charted his course in the belief that 'our work here should have the moral force of India behind it'.[3] He wrote to everyone he knew in India asking for correct information on political developments and for other assistance. 'I cannot help thinking,' he wrote to Sir Sachidananda Sinha, 'that if some of our leaders would give a certain part of their attention to sustained and well-directed action at this end, it would pay.' The Congress leaders

[1] The Simon Commission, led by Sir John Simon and with Clement Attlee as one of the members, was appointed by the British Government with a view to 'reporting whether and to what extent it is desirable to establish the principle of Responsible Government or to extend, modify or restrict the degree of Responsible Government then existing' in India. The vagueness of the terms of reference and the failure to include any Indian representative on the Commission made India rise in revolt against the Commission. Its two-month tour of the country, in February and March 1928, was marked by an unusually successful Indian boycott accompanied by police firings, lathi charges and other repressions.
[2] Menon in a letter to Sir Sachidananda Sinha, June 18th, 1930.
[3] Letter to Editor of *New India*, Madras, January 17th, 1930.

did become aware of the India League and of the fact that it meant business, but it was to be a few years yet before they officially recognized the League as their own London limb.

The need to become recognized in Britain was even more pressing. Until then, work for India had been carried on in London as a spare-time job. The Commonwealth of India League was known only to a small circle of theosophists, M.P.s and political leaders, and the authorities knew it as a harmless little group of people who were best ignored. There was no question of Krishna Menon's allowing himself to be ignored. He persuaded well-known Englishmen to become officers of the League, Bertrand Russell becoming Chairman. After the organizational preliminaries were over, the League began implementing a forceful programme.

To understand the evolution of the India League's personality after 1930, it is necessary to understand one of Krishna Menon's strongest characteristics. An aggressive revolutionary, he is an uncompromising believer in constitutionalism. Debate displaces direct action in his scheme of things. The seeds of this trait were sown during his early formative years by his father and were later nurtured by Mrs Besant. In England it grew into a major aspect of his personality, for in England he could see constitutionalism in practice. He saw that it was necessary to fit his programme into the framework of British tradition.

The activities of the India League fell into two broad divisions: field-work, and lobbying in Parliament. On both fronts Menon might well have been attempting the impossible.

One can appreciate what the India League was up against when one realizes that the political mood of the British in the 1930s virtually ruled out any intelligent popular interest in the questions raised by distant India. The summer of 1931 saw a financial crisis overtaking Britain. Ramsay MacDonald's Labour cabinet was irretrievably split. In desperation he made a deal with the Tories to form a National Government. All through these years unemployment remained dangerously high.

Thus, after 1931, the English were too preoccupied with their own problems to worry about those of others. The ordinary working man had far too much to do looking after his own job. The ordinary political leader found it trying enough to avoid being submerged under mass frustration. Marxism became fashionable among the politically educated. To them 'imperialism' really had a meaning. But again, the tremendous events in Europe totally overshadowed anything else.

It must also be remembered that throughout the colonial period India's publicity channels were exclusively in the hands of British authorities. The censorship was such that even foreign correspondents in India had difficulty in sending their stories home. Dr Pattabhi Sitaramayya refers in his *History of the Indian National Congress* to an American reporter who found it necessary to fly to China in order to file a story on the historic 'Quit India' resolution of the Congress in 1942. The censor and the British propagandist had together given to the ordinary Briton a picture of India which had no relation to the facts.

Menon had concluded that if independence were to be achieved by constitutional means, it was necessary first to demolish the wall of ignorance that stood between India and the people of Britain. This meant extended propaganda among the people. Menon knew it was a herculean task, but he was encouraged by his firm belief that a system should never be identified with the individuals in whose name it was being carried on. The imperialism of Britain, he felt, was something apart and distinct from the people of Britain. This attitude was to become a principal plank of the Menon creed; in later years, while bitterly criticizing the administration of the United States, he often confused many by giving expression to an admiration for the American people.

In this tendency to distinguish a people from their system, he was manifesting another point of contact with Jawaharlal Nehru. Explaining capitalism to his daughter, Nehru has written in his *Glimpses of World History*: 'Capitalism is like a stone: you can never get food out of it however long you may cook it. All you can do with it is to remove it altogether. There is no use getting angry with individuals.' This philosophy must have contributed a great deal to the persistence with which Nehru and Menon have tried in post-independence years to stay close to Britain and the Commonwealth.

Krishna Menon began his work among the people. The office of the India League became a centre of high-powered propaganda. Pamphlets, periodicals, speeches and appeals poured out. Lectures and public meetings were organized with impressive frequency. They all had one objective: to let the people know facts. With facts he would appeal to their sense of justice. Intellect and conscience became the League's twin targets.

Menon did most of the work personally. He wrote numerous pamphlets on the issues of the day and supplemented them with articles in the liberal newspapers and periodicals. The London *New Statesman and Nation* and the New York *Nation* often carried his signature, while Britain's daily papers were flooded with his letters. All Indian national occasions were marked by some function or other in Britain. Speakers at public meetings included such notables as Harold Laski, Stafford Cripps, Palme Dutt, Reginald Sorensen, Monica Whately, Ellen Wilkinson and J. B. S. Haldane. The very fact that big names were associated with the India League gave it a status and importance that could not be ignored.

Many of the League's functions were enlivened by skits, shadow-plays and film shows. Indian singers and dancers appeared frequently in London. There were readings from Tagore by Sybil Thorndike and from Nehru by Lewis Casson. At the time of the great Bengal famine in 1943 the League organized an India Relief Committee as well as a Businessmen's Appeal for India to collect donations. Demonstrations were held, as well as a flag day. Every time there was a function arranged by the League, London was plastered with stimulating posters. In 1943 it was 'Death For 15,000 in India. Food Now! Demand Government Action and Help Relief!' In 1945, against the background of intense political activity following the end of the war, this exhortation appeared on the walls of London as it did in the publications of the India League:

PEOPLE OF BRITAIN! URGE

A SETTLEMENT WITH INDIA NOW!

DEMAND

RELEASE OF THE PRISONERS!

END THE FAMINE!

OPEN NEGOTIATIONS!

A NATIONAL GOVERNMENT!

SEND

RESOLUTIONS, LETTERS AND TELEGRAMS

IN INDIA WEEK TO:

Persuading the British People

1. The Prime Minister, 10 Downing Street, S.W.1.
2. Mr L. S. Amery, India Office, S.W.1.
3. Your M.P. at The House of Commons, S.W.1.
4. Your trade union or political party H.Q.

Menon himself became an indefatigable speaker. Liberal groups scattered all over Britain suddenly became aware of an organization in London working for Indian independence and they kept writing to him to come and speak at their meetings. There was hardly a progressive political meeting in London at which Krishna Menon did not speak. At week-ends he visited other areas. Even the severity of the English winter could not slow Menon down. On wintry nights, acquaintances now recall, he could be seen huddled in his worn-out overcoat picking his lonely way back to the Strand after an engagement somewhere. He would travel two or three hundred miles even if, at the end of it, he addressed only a small gathering.

The dedication with which these engagements were carried out helped considerably in educating the British public. Menon was so utterly sincere that his cause attracted many individuals who later became pillars of the League and life-long friends of India.

Reginald Sorensen, M.P., well remembers the occasion when he first met Krishna Menon. When he was a minister at a small Unitarian church in Walthamstow he used to hold a mid-week discussion group with about twenty to thirty of his members. One occasional attender was an old lady who sometimes distributed leaflets about India. Through this Sorensen discovered an organization called the India League and its secretary Krishna Menon. His curiosity aroused, he contacted Menon and invited him to address the small group, which he did. Menon's characteristic intensity and fervour made the group almost feel that he was addressing the whole British people. Moreover, Menon's willingness to speak to a humble group in an obscure Walthamstow church hall also made an impression and awakened Sorensen to the moral significance of India's cause. From that evening Sorensen became a staunch supporter of the India League and its purpose and a constant voice for India in public life, within the Labour Party and in the House of Commons.

An eighteen-year-old girl, unaccustomed to politics, chanced to hear Menon at a meeting and was moved. She went home and wrote in her diary (July 1940):

I must write down my first account of a real political meeting. The speaker was an Indian named Krishna Menon. K. M. was tall, slim, with longish wavy hair, greying slightly, a hooked nose, fierce dark eyes, and looking in short very much the prophet.

He was introduced by the chairman of the [local] Socialist party. This man was the absolute antithesis of the Indian. The latter was really great and was putting all his energy into a call to all humanity. The former was a local, slow-talking, small-dealing, petty-minded organizer. I do not mean this unkindly -- very possibly one must have these organizers, but by comparison with the greatness of the Indian he sank into insignificant mediocrity.

In his speech introducing the speaker, the chairman declared with as much force as his false teeth would allow that it was disgusting and tragically unjust that the B.B.C. would not play the 'Internationale' before the news as with those of other allies. Point two, he had strong views about the unbearable injustice of the Government's banning the *Daily Worker*.

Then the speaker – he commenced by telling the chairman that he didn't care two pins whether they played the 'Internationale' or raised the ban on the *Daily Worker*. In his estimation the people should have been less apathetic before it was too late. Besides, how could he work up any enthusiasm over the banning of one paper when in India 700 a week were banned?

His foreign intonation, but obvious education, and his dry wit and not-too-well-hidden contempt of so much that is English helped to make his speech really enthralling from beginning to end.

Again the boring chairman ... again the subject of the 'Internationale' and the *Daily Worker*. What an anticlimax! Then the former was played and, because of the ferocious heckling of the man immediately behind us, we were all forced to stand as though it was the national anthem.

Besides addressing meetings himself and arranging public functions, Menon also set up a service to help other speakers. A regular desk in the India League sent to colleges, associations and others interested what was called *Notes for Speakers*, a little cyclostyled fact-sheet crammed with points that could be made use of by lecturers and writers. The League was also in touch with prominent Indians visiting London and would arrange lectures by them. There were also special committees for concentrated action in specific fields. There was a Labour Committee, a Women's Committee, a Students' Committee. Branch units of the League sprang up all over England. It was a relentless war on ignorance and apathy.

The war extended to fronts other than India. Even during his freshman days in Madras Menon had tended to see the question of Indian Independence in a global perspective. To him India was not an isolated case, but rather a typical example of international colonialism. Colonialism was an evil that stretched across the world and it had to be tackled as such. He had the perceptiveness to 'see a world in a grain of sand', to feel as intensely for the farthest colonial outpost as for his own India. In London this vision grew so that, while his activities centred on India, their scope extended to subject peoples all over the world.

Menon's campaign was so thorough that he also maintained a torrent of correspondence. Many were the citizens who either telephoned or wrote to the League for information on all kinds of matters. Some were genuinely interested in knowing about India, some wanted to ridicule Indian nationalism. To all of them Menon wrote personally. A typical letter, dated June 25th, 1931, was written to a Mr George Grainger who had sent Menon a newspaper-clipping about Gandhi's clothes and wanted his comments. Menon wrote:

> In reply to the news-cutting which I return to you, there is nothing savage about Mr Gandhi's clothes. A very large section of his countrymen, probably the majority, can afford only as much clothing as Mr Gandhi wears. (The average consumption of cotton cloth in India is between nine to thirteen yards per year per head.) Englishmen in India wear the clothes to which they are accustomed in their own country, irrespective of the climate. Surely it cannot be

wrong for an Indian leader to dress like his following. In any case, it is not Gandhi's clothes but his ideas and what he has done for his people that worries his critics. If they were worried about the unclad condition of millions of their fellow-subjects in India, Britain's rule of that country would have directed its main energies to the improvement of the economic standards of its masses.

The two-page single-space letter goes on to explain Britain's role in the Cawnpore communal riots. This kind of correspondence was a time-consuming business. But it was worth it. For one thing, it helped the League to establish personal contact with a large number of Britons. For another, no one could argue with Menon's facts, figures and logic – especially when they came in the form of a personal letter.

Primarily a one-man show, the India League might have been expected to make only a limited impact. But the cumulative effect of the League's field-work was out of all proportion to the organization's size or resources. There was in Britain practically no public opinion for India when the League started its work. Within a few years there was an unmistakable mobilization of progressive opinion in defence of India. For every heckler who put 'blimpish' questions to the lean and famished Indian speaker in Hyde Park, there were several who listened patiently and then kept in touch with the speaker and his League. Students, factory hands, mineworkers, liberal thinkers and progressive M.P.s were forced to realize that colonialism was not a wholly civilizing mission after all, and that the millions on the other side of the fence could have a point of view of their own. For the first time the national movement in India found a solid beach-head in the minds of the British people. The war for liberation had been carried right into the heart of enemy territory.

9

Lobbying M.P.s

LOBBYING was a legacy left to the India League by Mrs Besant. Krishna Menon was quick to realize that the job was of primary importance. For any public opinion to crystallize into positive action, efforts had to be concentrated at the policy-making level, which in England meant the Houses of Parliament. Menon started lobbying on a scale and with an intensity the like of which the British Parliament has rarely seen since. It was also to lead to Menon's association with the Labour Party.

As the India League went to work, it developed a pronounced Labour Party bias. So much were its activities confined to the Labour Party's area of influence that some even criticized the League for not appealing to the British people as a whole above limitations of party allegiances.

However, the League's affinity with the Labour Party was a natural development. The Conservatives were incapable of harbouring any liberal notions on colonial matters and, even if it had tried, the League could not have drawn very close to them. Labour, although as diehard in practice as the Tories on colonialism, was at least ideologically committed to anti-colonialism and equality among all peoples. Events indeed justified this; soon after a Conservative Prime Minister refused to preside over the liquidation of the British Empire, a Labour leader moved the Independence of India Bill in the British Parliament. Of course, Menon's own ideological inclinations contributed to the League's Labour bias. Although he welcomed assistance and support from wherever they came, he himself was a member of the Labour Party and an active worker.

It was the London School of Economics that supervised this maturing process. The neo-Marxism of that phase of Harold Laski's life had a positive influence on many men of Menon's generation. Its effect on Menon too was profound. Differing from the ideas of his father and Mrs Besant in that it was scientifically orientated and ideologically complete, it came, moreover, during his years of maturity. It has therefore remained the most abiding influence on Menon's ideas.

Krishna Menon and Laski grew to be great friends and mutual admirers. Their relationship was not entirely one of professor and pupil. When he started studying at the London School of Economics, Menon was already an active political worker. He was bright, inquiring and of a very serious disposition. These were qualities that Laski admired in his students. He thought the young man a bit of an eccentric, but he also knew that it was an eccentricity that flowed from a Messianic zeal.

Menon was stimulated by Laski's iconoclasm. His teaching technique was one of promoting a critical examination of everything that came up, rather than inducing acceptance of time-honoured notions. The predominant idea was that of the rightness of resistance to authority. Nothing could have fitted in better with Krishna Menon's intellectual mood.

Added to this was Laski's personal generosity, not so much with his money as with his time and influence. He was always ready to oblige his students with advice and introductions. No one who went to him ever returned empty-handed. This must have appealed especially to foreign students who were studying far away from their homes.

The greatest of Laski's qualities as far as Menon was concerned was his belief in Indian independence. Laski was quite outspoken about this, as he was about all colonial and imperialistic issues.

Menon became so devoted to his teacher that he said of him later: 'A very great man. It will take one hundred years to realize the profundity of his thoughts.' Encomiums of this kind have come but rarely from the lips of Krishna Menon.

Menon was to take full advantage of Laski's interest in India. As the work of the League gathered momentum, he drew upon Laski's prestige and influence to increase the League's own status and efficacy. Mrs Frieda Laski recalls:

He was always pestering my husband to do things. I have never known anyone so devoted to a cause as Krishna was to

India's. He was pestering everybody in order to propagate the cause. So we used to call him 'nuisance student' in an affectionate sort of way. The telephone in the house belonged to him. At nine every morning there would be a ring and I used to say 'That must be Krishna' and sure enough it was. My husband had genuine affection for Krishna. Krishna was unique over here.[1]

This intimacy with Harold Laski was sufficient to pull Menon and the India League into the vortex of the Labour Party, for Laski was already a powerful voice there. The Party's own system of functioning speeded up the process. The branches of the Labour Party, like socialist groups everywhere, have always maintained a machinery for continuous discussion of current issues. These study groups encouraged party members to examine various issues in depth. A question such as the independence of India was a natural topic for study at these gatherings. Such study invariably led to an appreciation by the Labour rank and file of the Indian point of view, in contrast to the traditional exclusiveness with which the Tories tended to look on all imperialistic matters. It was not surprising, therefore, that the League's message found greater receptivity in Labour ranks.

The specific object of Menon's lobbying was to get voices raised in Parliament in defence of the Indian people. To ensure this he persuaded friendly M.P.s to become active members of the League and to keep in regular touch with events in India. The League had a Parliamentary Committee attached to it and the committee had special representatives on the League executive. At one time there were as many as a hundred M.P.s on the League's membership register.

As it turned out, gaining support inside the Labour Party was more difficult than lobbying in Parliament. The leaders of the Party were simply not interested in India. The notion that the white man was doing a favour to the black or the brown by ruling him was common to both Tory and Labour leaders, the difference being only one of degree. Even Nehru had found, vide his *Autobiography*, that 'in matters of imperial policy there is little to choose between Tory and Labour in England. It is true that

---

[1] To the author in London, June 1961.

the Labour rank and file is far more advanced, but has little influence on its very conservative leadership.'[1]

For Krishna Menon the enlightenment of the rank and file of the Labour Party was sufficient inspiration to go on. The sympathy at the bottom, he argued, was bound to spread to the top eventually. Some of the leaders were already favourably disposed towards India – Harold Laski, Cripps and Aneurin Bevan. But the unsympathetic far outnumbered the sympathetic. Some of them were even personally hostile to Krishna Menon. Ernest Bevin topped this list. Also included in it was Clement Attlee, though after he became Prime Minister, his attitude changed to one of wholesome respect.

Understandably, Menon's initial efforts to get the support of the party for Indian independence proved extremely difficult. His method was to move suitable resolutions at party conferences and canvass support for them. But the party bosses invariably dodged a discussion with such procedural manœuvres as putting the resolution at the end of the agenda.

Occasionally when a resolution did come up for discussion, the official opposition to it was open and unrelenting. At the Southport conference in 1934, Menon submitted a resolution 'expressing the conviction that it is imperative that the principle of self-determination for the establishment of self-government for India should be implemented forthwith'. Typical of official Labour Party attitude to the subject then was the statement made by Arthur Henderson, who had been Foreign Secretary under Ramsay MacDonald. Urging the withdrawal of the resolution and refusing to give an undertaking on behalf of the executive to carry out the policy of self-determination for India, Henderson said: 'We have laid

---

[1] Why was the Labour Party, committed as it was to socialism and equality, unfavourably disposed to India's demand for equality? An answer to this puzzling problem came from Sir Stafford Cripps. In an article in the *Congress Socialist* in January 1936 (written at the request of Krishna Menon, incidentally), he wrote: 'Although the British workers have suffered with their lives as the tools of British imperialism, it is the undoubted fact that so long as the capitalist system survives in one country the standards of workers are indirectly improved by the imperialist exploitation of the other lands by the British ruling class. It is this fact coupled with generations of education in the false pride of "imperial patriotism" that makes it difficult for the British worker to see imperial problems through the eyes of his comrades in other parts of the Empire ... There are very few people in the Labour movement in Great Britain who have had the time or opportunity to gain a close acquaintance with the problems of India. The rest are easily confused by all the technicalities which can be so easily raised and over-emphasized in any discussion of the Indian problem.'

down very clearly that we are going to consult if possible all sections of the Indian people. That ought to satisfy anybody.' The resolution was of course thrown out.

But Krishna Menon was not to be so easily defeated. Nor was he discouraged. It is a measure of the doggedness with which his League worked on the leaders that, eleven years later, the same Labour Party accepted a resolution which declared that granting freedom to India was a necessary step in the struggle against Fascism. One year after that commitment the Labour Government decided to quit India. But those were eleven years of sweat and toil.

The eventual success the League scored both in the field and in Parliament was due in no small measure to Menon's self-effacing personal life. Britons saw that the campaign for Indian freedom was being carried on by an organization which was living precariously on a shoestring and by a man who was living more precariously on less. Indian independence was not seen even as a remote possibility at the time. There was no material reward to look forward to. At the same time the work demanded of a man everything that he had. In the circumstances Menon's total absorption in the work of the League and the obvious sacrifices he was making in terms of his own health and career compelled admiration and sympathy.

Voluntary enthusiasm was the only capital that came the League's way. Critics like Ernest Bevin used to say derisively, 'We know where you get your money from.' The fact was that there was precious little money coming from anywhere. A major source of income was the collections at meetings; Menon would send his hat round and gather a modest sum at the end of each political gathering. If he was lucky the collection would be sufficient to defray the expenses of the particular meeting. And he was not always lucky. The only other source of revenue was donations. But the friends of the League consisted mostly of workers, students and Labour Party members who were not known for their impressive bank accounts.

Menon's own approach to the problem may be gleaned from a letter he wrote acknowledging a donation.

Dear Lady Ginwalla, [he said] I have just been told that you have agreed to give us two half-crowns a week towards

71

the running of the League ... As you are no doubt aware, the League is in a bad way financially. At the present time we have to make every effort to keep up Indian propaganda and I hope that all of us working together will be able to achieve something.

Menon welcomed money if it came; if it did not, he went ahead with his work just the same.

The strength of feeling against India was strong enough to prevent the League from raising any funds from the public. Once the Chairman of the League, Peter Freeman, M.P., issued a public appeal for funds to carry on the work for India. No sooner had it appeared in print than Sir Montague Webb wrote to the *Daily Mail*: 'Who is Peter Freeman? ... No work need and should be done in Britain since India is not a country or a nation.'

So precarious was the League's financial position that on more than one occasion it had to close down some of its publications. These publications were of primary importance in the League's work, and Menon used to spend considerable time and energy over their preparation. It was with a heavy heart that he closed them down. As soon as the finances improved, even if it was only for another brief period, he used to start new periodicals to keep the fire burning.

If the financial strain did not drive the League out of existence, it was largely due to the fact that the League's establishment expenses were next to nothing. The pivot of the movement took no salary; on the contrary, whatever he was making for himself from other jobs went into the League. His total absorption in his work, however, attracted to the League a large number of voluntary workers – Quakers, labour leaders, communists, students, women. He was grateful for any help and felt that 'if we are doing anything useful it is because a team of people who have little of the goods of the world give of their best whole-heartedly'.[1]

Menon himself gave everything – including his health. He not merely was impecunious: he looked it. Lean, unathletic and thin by constitution, the hardships of his London life made him look underfed and emaciated. The strain of such endless and concentrated activities as he was engaged in would have made

[1] Letter to Sir C. P. Ramaswamy Aiyer, July 27th, 1930.

even a robust man wilt. Menon refused to recognize the strain, and this was to lead to a dangerous nervous and physical breakdown early in 1938. His father at home was opulent enough, but relations between the two had again become strained. Kurup learned that, instead of studying law, Menon had entered politics again. He was not prepared to encourage this. A solitary entry in Krishna Kurup's account book records the dispatch of 560 rupees to his son in London in 1929.

In the beginning scholarships saw Menon through. But as he became engulfed in political work and the period of the scholarships ran out, the situation changed. With his intellect and academic distinctions, he could have had a lucrative career in London. But there was no time even to think about making money; work was an obsession.

Forced by circumstances, he tried to earn some money from activities connected with his main mission. Thus he practised law for a while, and became a publisher. He was also the London correspondent of a number of Indian newspapers and periodicals. These increased his work-load a hundredfold, although the total income was hardly commensurate with the time consumed. Often he had to depend on friends for a half-crown for his personal needs.

Sometimes, during the early years, attractive offers of jobs would come from India. A friend at the University of Lucknow wrote in February 1931 'just a line to say that there is likely to be a vacancy of a lecturer in political science in our University from August 1st, 1931, in a grade of 250 rupees – 25 – 450 (plus 12% Provident Fund to be contributed by the University). If you wish to apply for the post, please send an application together with your testimonials ...' The prospects of a steady income would have appealed to any other man forced into such privations as Menon was facing in London. But he had no time to think of prospects.

It was inevitable in the circumstances that Menon should drift into starvation. He started living on tea, twopenny buns and potatoes. Ascetic by temperament, he perhaps found this less difficult than others in his position would have. But his body did not take kindly to it. Menon became ill and frequently bedridden. But the protests and warnings of the body failed to change the man's routine. In sickness, he would still work, with a vast collection of medicines scattered around him. Defeated, the body did the only thing it could: it adjusted itself. Menon today has no proper digestive system; he cannot stomach a decent meal. On the other hand, he flourishes on tea, consuming at least thirty cups every day. A few biscuits complete a diet which has confounded medical experts.

Even his intimate associates hardly knew where he lived. They had a vague idea that he had some sort of a garret in Camden Town in the borough of St Pancras, but beyond that there was no information. All they knew was that he could be seen in the office of the India League till about three or four in the morning every day, making his own tea and writing and writing.

The small hours of the morning were spent mostly in writing letters. He would type out the more important ones himself, and this must have been a greater strain on the recipients than on himself. A letter to Sir C. P. Ramaswamy Aiyer, for example, begins by saying, 'Since it is nearly daybreak and I may miss the mail, I must be brief.' He then goes on for five pages of single-space exhortations and concludes, 'I must apoligise for the quatnties of typing errors in this. I hope it leguble.'

Both in terms of work and in terms of the extraordinary personal sacrifices involved, Menon's career in the India League was awe-inspiring. It destroyed his health, but it built up India's cause. Those who came in contact with him were stunned into admiration. His own life provided a compelling human parallel to the formidable intellectual undertones of the India League's campaign.

IO

Mission to India

NINETEEN HUNDRED AND THIRTY-TWO was a tumultuous year in the history of India. The Gandhi-Irwin Pact which, only the year before, had ended a sorry period of bitterness in the country had suddenly collapsed, following the failure of the second Round Table Conference in London. Hopes which had risen to great heights had unexpectedly crumbled. Irwin was replaced by Willingdon, and India was pushed into an era of repression the severity of which was appalling. Stiff ordinances were issued one after another, defiant elements were treated without a trace of mercy, force was employed with the express purpose of frightening the nation into submission. Gandhi himself was arrested as soon as he returned from London. The jails overflowed and the cry of a country in anguish rose to heaven.

People living in Britain had no idea of what was going on in India. The official propaganda line was that the India Government was following a progressive 'dual policy' – that of maintaining law and order on the one hand and striving for constitutional advance on the other. All media of information available to the British told them that the Government's policy was an unqualified success and that more and more Indians were supporting the authorities. The Congress Party alone, it had been made out, was obstructing the Government, but then, the Congress Party represented only a 'microscopic minority' of the Indian mass.

The British public believed this, but the few who had direct contacts with India were increasingly disturbed. Private sources talked of unprecedented atrocities in India.

Suddenly the sensational story of a Scottish missionary broke in the House of Commons. This missionary, the Reverend Forrester Paton, was the victim of police terror in India. He had been beaten, wounded in the ribs, legs and arms and then drenched

75

with coloured water in a mad moment of rage by the minions of the Government of India. The Reverend Forrester Paton happened to be well connected in England, and his outraged friends raised the issue in the Commons. For the first time the eyes of many ordinary people in Britain were opened.

It was a challenge and an opportunity for Krishna Menon. The India League decided to confront the English people with the facts. But this time the usual method of holding public meetings and issuing pamphlets was not enough. The situation was so grave that it called for a new approach. The time had come, the India League resolved, to send a fact-finding mission to ndia.

From resolution it was a short step to realization, with Krishna Menon working overtime to raise the funds, plan the itinerary, set up the contacts and brief everyone concerned. With the help of Bertrand Russell and Harold Laski, he completed the job quickly. A team selected with an eye on the integrity and public acceptability of each member was announced. It consisted of Monica Whately, Ellen Wilkinson and Leonard Matters, all Labour M.P.s. Menon himself was named secretary of the delegation. The project was widely publicized in Britain as well as in India.

H. N. Brailsford was one of those who gave Menon a list of Indian contacts. In a hand-written letter beginning 'Dear Menon,' Brailsford emphasized the importance of the villages. 'A useful man,' wrote Brailsford, 'is Professor N. G. Ranga who is a Socialist and an economist.' (It is interesting to note that today the Professor is Chairman of the anti-Socialist Swatantra Party and a leading critic of Nehru and Krishna Menon.) Brailsford also wrote, 'Try to see Jawaharlal Nehru in jail. He's worth several hours talk. I was allowed to see him alone.' Others Brailsford recommended included 'M. C. Chagla, a Muslim lawyer in Bombay'. (Chagla was Indian High Commissioner in London until September 1963.)

The powerful publicity machinery of the British Government moved into action immediately to neutralize the India League delegation. It said that the delegates were hirelings of the Congress Party, going on a conducted tour. Conservative M.P.s and even the Viceroy came out with declarations that the delegation was out to present the Congress view of India and bring back a distorted picture. The delegation was prepared for this propaganda offensive and worse. But they were not prepared for what they saw in India.

It was Krishna Menon's first visit to his native land since his departure to England in 1924. He was now thirty-six. Eight of his most impressionable years had been spent in London. The orderly life of the British people, their general well-being and their strict conformity to democratic principles had made him realize the more poignantly the tragic plight of India. When he actually saw life in India after an interval of eight years, he could hardly believe his eyes. Here was a nation lying prostrate in blood at the feet of a cruel master. It was a crushing experience.

The delegation sailed from Venice on August 5th, 1932, reaching Bombay on the 17th. It left Bombay on the return voyage on November 7th, having spent eighty-three days in India. The four members often split up so that they could cover a larger area and obtain more individual contacts. They went from Bombay via Poona to Madras. After spending a fortnight in the four linguistic regions of South India, they travelled through Orissa to Bengal and Assam, and then to Bihar and the United Provinces, Punjab and the North-West Frontier Province. They came down to the plains via Delhi, covering Sind and Gujarat on the way. They travelled through the territory of some Indian princely states also, although most of the time was spent in what was known as British India.

The delegates met and talked to Indians of every class, creed and shade of opinion. They interviewed leaders of the national movement and many who were not directly engaged in politics. They called on officials, Indian and British, and on employers and trade unionists. They met village headmen, policemen, representatives of women's organizations and thousands of individual villagers. It was anything but a conducted tour. The delegates met opposition leaders, British residents in the country and non-political personalities as well as Congressmen. Nor were their hosts always Congressmen. Avoiding hotels as a matter of policy, the delegates were guests of individuals and organizations including the Servants of India Society and such non-party liberals as Tej Bahadur Sapru. The delegation was conscious that a mighty propaganda machinery was working against them. They avoided actions which might have been construed as partisan and did everything that could convince an objective observer of their integrity.

Almost from the day they landed in Bombay, the delegates began to witness scenes and hear stories that strained their credulity. From Punjab to Madras and from Assam to Kerala, it was one uninterrupted tale of brute force callously used. Coming as it did from Britain, this terror stunned a nation that had expected only justice and fair play from the English. A liberal of the stature of Pandit Madan Mohan Malaviya was constrained to declare in an interview with the delegation, 'This present period in India's history of torture and repression is one that I never believed, before I went through it, could possibly come under British rule. We know at last that we have to deal with the brute, and not with a human thing of heart and mind.'

The British members of the delegation were ashamed. Krishna Menon was outraged. But all they could do was to collect evidence of the atrocities and transmit it to the English people in the hope that British protests and action would effectively alter the course of policy in India.

The atrocities that Krishna Menon saw were humiliating. It was a time of processions in India. In the south they saw several groups of volunteers, numbering less than a hundred each, marching with a flag and singing national songs. The Government of Madras had ordered that there should be no clashes and no show of force in the presence of the delegation. The police plan therefore was to arrest the demonstrators quietly and not to beat them. In each case the procession was stopped after a while and the men were arrested. Menon saw the arrests. But in Calicut, his native town and the scene of his early social activities, he saw something more.

A procession was marching along with the usual songs and the ubiquitous flag of the national movement. As in other cases the procession was soon stopped by the police. Then, suddenly, a shower of lathis fell upon them. The men immediately squatted on the road, whereupon more blows fell upon their defenceless heads.

In a few moments, however, the police noticed that the crowd which had gathered in the buildings on either side of the road was looking the other way. The police chief followed the gaze of the crowd and suddenly discovered that the India League delegation was approaching the scene from the opposite direction.

There was an instantaneous change of mood among the policemen. There were no more beatings. One of the constables went into the police station right in front of which the beating had taken place and came back to arrest the men. The whole body of volunteers followed the police into the station without any resistance.

The spectacle was a revealing one for Krishna Menon; if this was what could happen in the proximity of the delegation, they could well imagine what was going on elsewhere. Later Menon visited the 'People's Hospital' in Calicut and saw the many citizens who were still suffering from the wounds inflicted by police lathis several weeks before. It was a strange home-coming.

Madras was perhaps the most notorious of all the Indian provinces for police cruelty, and the Malabar Special Police was a force known all over the land for its sub-human behaviour. The mere news that a contingent of the M.S.P. was on its way to a particular area was sufficient in those days to freeze the people's blood. As a native of Malabar, and after seeing some of the horrors of which the M.S.P. was capable, Menon experienced a sense of profound revulsion.

What he saw in Calicut, however, was little compared to the story of a man he met in the South Indian city of Madurai. An impecunious washerman had committed the offence of wearing hand-spun *khaddar* and picketing a shop. He was beaten severely and then taken to the police inspector's house. No one knew why the inspector was particularly against this poor man; all they knew was that, after some more beating, the inspector poured paraffin on the man's hair and set it alight. The inspector's wife was horrified and screamed aloud. In deference to her, a constable put out the fire. The inspector again belaboured the man with a ruler in one hand and a lathi in the other. The beating continued for a long time and then he was taken in a truck and dumped in a remote area.

Incidents of this kind were common occurrences. The delegation met little girls who had been cruelly disfigured with beating, old men whose bones had been broken, women who had been raped and then maimed. An extract from the notes of the delegation relates a strange 'offence' and the strange punishment it elicited,

Mohan Kaul is a young fellow of nineteen years of age, son of an ex-government official. He refused to salaam at the call

79

of Sarkar Salaam in Rajshai jail. He was put in standing handcuffs and given other punishments. Each time he was brought before the superintendent, he declined to make the required obeisance. Altogether he suffered five and a half months of solitary confinement. After the first three months, when he was still adamant about his refusal to salaam, he was put into a cage with his hands fettered behind his back. The cage was 7 by 5 feet. In this cage Mohan Kaul spent all hours of the day and night; he was obliged to take his food and answer the calls of nature in it. (Sarkar Salaam or Salute The Government was a 'disciplinary ritual' enforced on all prisoners. It was said to involve humiliating postures and the performance was ordered when visitors went to see the jail. It was the cause of much resentment among prisoners and much more vengeful punishment by the officials.)

Their own visits to the jails only confirmed the worst fears of the delegates. The regular jails were overflowing and the authorities had been forced to construct several hundreds of temporary jails all over the country. They were mostly barbed-wire encampments on unprepared fields which were often infested with scorpions, worms, vermin and sometimes snakes against whom the prisoners had no protection. The delegates saw the food, half-cooked and gritty. 'The eating and cooking utensils we saw in Peshawar made one sick. In Bengal the grain we saw contained worms. When we commented on it we were told it was cattle food. But prisoners and ex-prisoners said it was their own food.'

The delegates also noticed with dismay that the jails contained many children aged from ten to sixteen years. The hard labour given to them was inhuman. In oil mills, for instance, political prisoners were made to run like bulls, eating while they worked. Sometimes the hands of the prisoners were tied to the mill.

It might have been thought that all these inhumanities were the work of some isolated sadists in positions of power. But the pattern was too widespread to lend credence to such an assumption. Besides, the delegates also collected evidence of the haughty attitude adopted as policy by the British residents in India. The colonialists were callous about the human suffering that was going on around them and in fact asked for tighter repression, bullying those officials who showed signs of softness.

Mission to India

The Calcutta branch of the European Association said in its report for the month ending March 15th, 1932,

> Reference was made in the last month's report to the question of the behaviour of political prisoners in Dum Dum jail. In response to the Committee's representations, the Government promised that strict discipline should be maintained, but the Committee has since been informed that there has been no improvement in the state of affairs. The Committee have arranged to approach the Home Member in charge of jails personally, and if no satisfaction can be obtained in this way, the matter will be pressed on Government with the utmost urgency.

The Council of the European Association meeting in Delhi in February urged more repression than the ordinances imposed. The Bombay branch addressed a letter to the Home Department listing measures that should be taken to crush the Congress movement. It even proposed that 'persons in the employ of Government may be sent in the guise of ordinary citizens to picket shops, demand the goods of mills banned by the Congress, with the police in readiness to arrest picketers if any coercion or intimidation is used.'

Even some Englishmen were outraged by the revelation. Dr Hogg, the Principal of the Madras Christian College, volunteered a great deal of information to the Indian League delegation and said in a private document,

> Government desires and with all my heart I desire, that Indian youth shall not be seduced into sympathy with revolutionary methods and yet Government is taking the most direct route to this undesired result ... The combined effect of the horror I know people are feeling at brutalities witnessed, their indignation at the lathi charges on inoffensive bystanders, their resentment at the indignity of the coloured water-douche and at the inhumanity of prohibiting immediate succour to the injured, is rapidly alienating persons whose habitual disposition has been strongly loyal.

But before the delegation left, it had occasion to feel that the official assessment of conditions in the country was something completely unrelated to the actualities. This was brought home to the members of the delegation when, at the end of their tour, they interviewed the Viceroy on October 13th, 1932.

Willingdon was in an imperious mood. He condescended to exchange some pleasantries with the delegation; after all, they were straight from England, and the one seedy-looking native who was with them was of no consequence anyway. After saying that more English people should visit India and see conditions for themselves, the Viceroy asked the delegates what they had observed in particular. Having spent most of their time in the villages, the delegates talked about the actual conditions of starvation existing in the rural areas, of the starved peasantry in general.

'Starved! What do you mean?' exploded the Viceroy.

The delegates told him that in the United Provinces, round about Allahabad and elsewhere, a state of famine existed. In one village, they said, they had seen people living on berries.

'There is no famine anywhere in India,' declared the Viceroy. 'When famine exists it is reported to me. Strange that you should have come to India to find famine when my officers do not report its existence.'

The delegates thereupon changed the subject and talked about the great influence of Gandhi. They wondered whether he could not be released.

'The little man can be released tomorrow,' the Viceroy said, 'if he will only agree not to break the law. I have known Gandhi for twenty years or so. I do not regard him as a saint. He is a very shrewd politician. He has always refused to co-operate with me. The fellow said at the Round Table Conference that civil disobedience was an article of faith with him. What is to be done with a man like that? Let him come back here and break the law? When he did return and began that nonsense I simply had to arrest him, and I would do it again ... For the life of me I can't see what's wrong with my action.'

So much for the Viceroy's inspiring philosophy. As for his grasp of the situation in India, he told the delegates without batting an eyelid: 'Eighteen months ago things were in a mess. I will guarantee that conditions are today a hundred per cent better and I go further and guarantee that the people are a hundred per cent happier.'

Menon was stung.

In a 536-page book[1] the India League broke the story. There was no passion or sensationalism in the tone of the report; the mere facts were sensational. The report gave the documents in full, gave figures and details with clinical detachment. It presented a detailed analysis of the ordinances, the political and sectional parties, the Government's relations with the people and their parties, official methods of propaganda and repression, the excesses of the police, Press and labour conditions, the boycott movement. It detailed how the delegation itself was watched and how its inquiries were hampered in many ways. It described how the police penalized those who helped the delegates, how plain-clothes men were posted in their trains, buses and even private meetings, how the delegates were actually threatened on a few occasions and how police agents were sent to them as 'representatives' of groups of opinion. The delegation concluded,

> A good deal of time was spent by members in villages and they hold that there the communal feeling is non-existent, that there exist stark illiteracy, want and crushing taxation, that the police are considered to be a coercive force menacing the security and peace of the villager, that Gandhi's name is a household word, that the Congress is the most powerful party in the country. The delegation also noted lack of confidence in the Government on the part of the people and the failure of repression to crush the national movement.

Krishna Menon personally supplied 'the considerable research involved in the preparation of the historical part' of the report.

The book was subsequently proscribed by the India Government, but it shook Britain. It was the one comprehensive document that shocked the apathetic sections of British public opinion into a realization of their Government's colonial crimes in India. It exposed the myth of 'law and order' and the tragedy of the so-called dual policy. It exposed the lie of the Congress being a 'microscopic minority', of the vast majority of Indians being supporters of the Government. It also showed the British Government as a tyrant pursuing self-defeating policies. It established beyond doubt that there was no constitutional advance at all being made in India. It proved that the economy of the country

---

[1] *The Condition of India*, from which the foregoing quotations have been taken.

was being systematically destroyed. *The Condition of India* was perhaps the greatest single contribution made by the India League towards a proper appreciation of the Indian case by the British people. Typical of Indian feelings on this achievement was the editorial comment in the Madras *Hindu* of November 10th: 'The gratitude of India is due to the delegation for the unselfish spirit and courage evinced by them during their arduous tour.'

When he returned to London towards the close of 1932, Krishna Menon plunged straight into the propaganda battle necessitated by Conservative criticisms of the delegation and its work. Derisive comments were appearing in the Tory Press, while on the floor of the House serious allegations were made by Government leaders. Leaving it to friendly M.P.s to defend the delegation in Parliament, Menon sent a torrent of letters and notes to the daily Press. No critic was allowed to escape without a reply. When the Secretary of State stood up in the House and painted a diabolic picture of the League delegation, Menon wrote to the *Manchester Guardian*,

The answer given in the House of Commons by the Secretary of State for India to a question concerning the character and work of the India League Delegation is inaccurate in essentials and mischievous in its implications. Before the delegation left for India it obtained introductions to officials in India from responsible quarters in London. As Secretary of the League and of the Delegation, I endeavoured to obtain an interview with the Secretary of State which, however, was not granted. Sir Samuel Hoare's secretary at India Office, however, received me *on behalf* of his chief ...

Sir Samuel Hoare alleges that we 'were not disposed to credit accurate information when it was supplied' to us. Some of this 'accurate information' that the officials supplied to us proved to be contrary to our personal observation. Further, if our object was to obtain a picture of India as supplied in the official versions, we need not have gone to India. We, however, discussed local and general Indian problems with officials and in some cases to our advantage ...

Reference has been made to the source of the India League's and the Delegation's finances. The Delegation made an appeal both in India and in this country. There has never been any secret about any donation received by the League. It is impossible, even were it thought necessary, to keep anything secret from the Government since correspondence to and from India is tampered with. But the donor to whom Sir Samuel refers is a very poor man himself, and such donations as he makes to public causes are collected by him from friends ... Collecting or paying into Congress funds is a crime in India, punishable with imprisonment and confiscation; the powers of the Government in this respect are used to the full.

The Secretary of State also refers to the 'understanding that the Delegation intended to make a serious and impartial study of the situation and take no public part in politics'. This certainly has been our intention and our endeavour all through our stay in India, though we had given no pledges in this respect. The Delegation did not engage in Press or public propaganda; the restrictions they had imposed on themselves compelled them to remain passive observers of grave wrongs on occasion, and they obtained little satisfaction from officials to whom complaints were made. Such interference as there was with the Delegation's work in India did not come from the Congress or from other Indian parties but from the police and government officials.

Sir Samuel Hoare's attempt to discredit our investigation carries with it its own condemnation. He should allow his compatriots and the rest of the world to judge the results of our inquiry on its own merits. To abuse one's opponent is not the most convincing or the soundest mode of argument.

The letters and statements were being widely read, and the people were responding. 'I do want to congratulate you', Horace Alexander told Menon in a personal letter, 'on the success of your undertaking. It seems likely that what you are able to report up and down the country will affect public opinion more than anything yet ... I thought your letter in answer to Hoare was excellent. I think that Hoare was so anxious to blacken your characters. It showed that he knew he couldn't ignore you.'

But Menon was a bitter man by now. The complacency with which the Viceroy had denied their findings and the ease with which the Secretary of State had uttered patent falsehoods

provided a cruel contrast to the spectacle of national maltreat-
ment he had just witnessed in India. What he had seen was a
dreadful insult not only to his country but to all the ideals which
he valued. That it came from a nation whose parliamentary
traditions had elicited his respect aggravated the pain. Only his
intellectual trait of absolving a people from the crimes of a system
prevented him from becoming a life-long enemy of the British.
Thanks to this trait, he continued his faith in the ordinary people
but became a sworn enemy of the system.

In subsequent years Menon has been called pathologically
fanatical in his fight against colonialism. If this is true, the
reasons lie deep in the hell he saw in 1932. An overt sympathizer
of India has stated: 'Menon has a look of suffering in his face even
at the most peaceful moments ... There is a look of ancient and
remembered wrongs in his eyes. The tempest of his wrath rises
from oceanic depths.'[1] Menon has never been personally mal-
treated by a government or an official. He has never been im-
prisoned, nor has a lathi ever fallen on his shoulders. But he has
had more than his share of sacrifices and suffering. The garret
days of London were sufficient to break any man. The kind of
work he was doing and the way he did it amounted to self-
immolation. He saw his prolonged suffering as the product of the
system under which he was living. But personal misery was
nothing to him; when he saw the ordinance rule in India and the
humiliations it inflicted on his people, the dam burst. The sheer
viciousness of the terror made him react like a wounded tiger.

---

[1] Vincent Sheean, *Nehru: The Years of Power*, p. 249.

An Indian in St Pancras

EIGHTY-THREE days in blood-stained India gave Krishna Menon the strength and the equipment to plunge into his campaign in London with renewed fury. He felt he had an unassailable case and he belaboured the public and the politicians with it. He became more insistent at Labour Party forums, hurling facts at questioners. Frustrated by the obstructionist tactics of some Labour leaders, he decided to go into British politics so that he could have a say at the decision-making level. He became the official Labour parliamentary candidate for Dundee, but he was to break with the party before he fought the election.

There was, however, another elective post which he won, making local history. A year after his return from India preparations for borough elections were being made in St Pancras where he lived, and party colleagues suggested that he should stand for a seat. He fought and was declared elected for Ward 4 in 1934 for a three-year term. He became so prominent a borough councillor that he stayed on continuously for fourteen years, increasing his majority with each successive election. Others who were on the council with him at one time or another included Mrs Barbara Castle and Mrs J. B. S. Haldane.

Councillor Menon's record in St Pancras is still remembered as an example of the importance a relatively small position can develop under an imaginative man. He threw himself into the work with a devotion that equalled his devotion to India. This was a surprise to many. To Menon himself it was but the natural thing to do. Just before deciding to fight the election he had told a friend that the slum-dwellers living behind King's Cross Station in St Pancras were as cruelly exploited as the oppressed in India. If he were elected, he had said, he would fight for better conditions in St Pancras as part and parcel of his other struggle – India's independence.

The attitude was a reflection, all over again, of Menon's 'world-view idealism', of the breadth of vision which motivated him. The affairs of the Borough Council assumed a new importance under him. Colleagues of those days remember him as a dynamic councillor with a blistering tongue.

During his fourteen-year term Krishna Menon served on all the committees of the St Pancras Borough Council, but it was in the Library Committee that he made his mark. He became its chairman in 1945 when the Labour Party obtained control of the borough.

Some fellow-councillors have said that he was given the innocuous Library Committee because the diehards were afraid that, if he headed a more important one, his dynamism would turn the borough upside down. Library was thought to be a safe spot. But the diehards underestimated the Indian dynamo.

The old librarians of St Pancras still shudder at the memory of Menon and of all that he demanded of them. He was a severe task-master. Often he called meetings of the Committee rather late, but he made up for it by paying for tea and cakes out of his own pocket. The meetings would last for hours with all members except the chairman taking time off for snacks. The chairman never seemed bothered about food. Mrs Lena M. Jeger, who was a fellow-councillor then and who later became a Labour M.P., remembers Menon's 'great ability to switch his mind from, say, Indian independence and give one hundred per cent attention in St Pancras to, say, how many new books we should buy'.

Menon would look at the number of pubs in the borough and remark, 'We must have as many public libraries here as pubs.' To translate the ideal into practice the Committee was geared to action. Menon worked on the theory that libraries were books, not great buildings. He therefore never went in for ostentatious display, but concentrated on building up a large central store-house. He extended the library service in the borough by opening temporary branches in every corner of it. He organized conferences on the library service for teachers, voluntary organizations, cultural groups and the like. He also set up a travelling library, a gramophone records section, exhibitions, Sunday concerts.

Soon there was a local information centre at the Town Hall,

lectures to children on educational topics, a Book Week. The chairman's report for February 1946 said enthusiastically: 'The small children's library has accommodated as many as 47 boys and girls in the lending department and 22 in the reading room at one time, and 50 children were at the same time waiting in a queue to enter the library. The circulation figure for one week in February was 3,000 volumes.'

His greatest achievement in St Pancras was the Arts and Civic Council, a representative organization of the cultural, educational and voluntary groups in the borough. It was inaugurated in the Town Hall one Sunday evening by Dame Sybil Thorndike, with Krishna Menon in the chair. The function was further distinguished by a piano solo by Leonard Cassini. The Council was Menon's way of galvanizing the cultural forces in his borough and bringing them out for the benefit of the citizens as a whole. Under its auspices he began the annual St Pancras Arts Festival.

Menon's services to St Pancras were equally distinguished during the chaos of the war. Being the terminus of three important railway lines in London, St Pancras was a favourite target for enemy bombers. By the end of the war the borough had been turned into a shambles. With men returning from the front in their hundreds, it was one huge transit camp of misery. The Borough Council reduced itself to a three-member unit for the duration of the war and Menon was one of them. He served as an indefatigable civil-defence worker and air-raid warden.[1]

It is little wonder that in January 1955, St Pancras conferred the Freedom of the Borough on Krishna Menon 'in recognition and appreciation of his eminent services to local government while serving as a member of the council and in manifestation of the very high regard and esteem in which he is held by the citizens of the borough.' His was the second distinguished name in the St Pancras roll of Freemen. The first was George Bernard Shaw.

Menon's emotional attachment to St Pancras has continued since 1947 and so has St Pancras's regard for him. As the representative of free India he was able to obtain from the Borough Council a site for a monument to Mahatma Gandhi.

St Pancras must figure prominently in any study of Krishna Menon's political make-up. It was here that he had his first taste of administration and government. It was here that he first faced

[1] See chap. 14 for a fuller account.

89

an electorate. Fourteen years of experience in local government gave him a background that added considerably to his political worth. It was valuable training.

St Pancras is also significant in so far as it provides a clue to Menon's present-day attitude towards the West or, to use an unhappy term, the white man. In St Pancras he gave leadership to the white man – both in peacetime and in war. During the war years he saw life in the raw; he realized that, in the face of suffering, there was no distinction between the white and the rest, that the white was as much in need of help and sympathy as the others. To the extent that he personally extended help and leadership, it gave him a sense of confidence in himself and a feeling that a leader was a leader whatever the colour of his skin. His fourteen years of intimate association with British life gave him a certain understanding of Western civilization which, in turn, has been a source of great confidence in world politics.

While he was involved in the affairs of the St Pancras Borough Council and simultaneously keeping his India League campaign at full pitch, Krishna Menon was pursuing his academic studies. After obtaining his B.Sc. in Economics in 1927, he had switched to psychology at University College, London. One of the subjects he selected for research during this period was, strange as it might sound, the psychology of the actor. 'I want to study human nature in all its facets', he told a friend who was surprised by the choice of subject.

For his final thesis, however, he chose a more appropriate theme, 'An Experimental Study of the Mental Processes Involved in Reasoning.' This study enabled him not only to understand the processes of reasoning but also to develop a reasoning capacity which, before long, was to become famous. His experimental study of reasoning gained him a Master of Arts degree in 1930.

Thereafter Menon went back to the London School of Economics and continued to study as and when he could find time. By now his studies had become necessarily a spare-time job – and there was very little spare time available. Not many would have had the obstinacy or the intellectual stamina to stick to their studies under the circumstances. But Menon did, studying political science and law simultaneously. He was now a 'chronic' student. By 1934, two years after the shattering trip to India and ten years after his arrival in England, at the age of thirty-eight, he obtained the M.Sc. degree from the L.S.E. with a thesis on 'English Political Thought in the Seventeenth Century.' The same year V. K. Krishna Menon, B.A., B.SC., M.A., M.SC. was called to the bar at the Middle Temple. Later on he was to be made a barrister-at-law, *honoris causa*, of the King's Inn, Dublin.

Meanwhile, new developments were taking place in India. The gulf between the conservative and progressive wings of the Congress Party was widening and assuming dangerous proportions. The tempo of the national movement in general and the civil disobedience campaign in particular had generated new forces that demanded recognition. The peasants were awake, and so were the workers in the urban areas. There was an unmistakable leftist nip in the air.

The most concrete shape this mood assumed was a faction inside the Congress movement. Jayaprakash Narayan, an idol of young India, found himself in jail with half a dozen other stalwarts who happened to share his strong socialist views. They brought into being the Congress Socialist Party in 1934.

Jawaharlal Nehru was then the hero of all socialists, and the C.S.P. leaders looked to him for inspiration and guidance. But, characteristically, Nehru contented himself with giving them his moral support; he never joined the group or officially associated himself with it. With Nehru party unity was an obsession that brooked no interference and he would not think of joining any faction.

Characteristically again, Krishna Menon joined the C.S.P. with enthusiasm. Though faithfully following the broad policies of the Congress movement, Menon had always been emotionally attracted to the socialist wing of the Congress Party. He became the C.S.P.'s secretary in London.

Two years later, referring to the C.S.P. in an article in an India League publication, Menon said: 'Socialism has now become the main issue in Indian politics. The Congress Socialist Party has leavened nationalism and, while it has wisely refrained from splitting the Congress, has forced the economic issue to the front ... It has checkmated the tendencies that threatened to interpret Indian liberty in terms of power for the Indian possessing classes.' In a few lines Menon had summed up his faith in socialism and in the necessity to have a clear definition of Indian liberty. He had also given expression to his belief that the Congress had to be maintained as a united force for the sake of building up a socialist India. It is interesting that Menon was using practically the same words used by Harold Laski in the course of an article on India. 'It would be tragic indeed,' Laski had written in the *Congress Socialist* on April 11th, 1936, 'if the attainment of national self-government were to mean no more than the exchange of the control by British capitalism for that by Indian capitalism.'

But Menon's hopes about the C.S.P. proved to be short-lived. His voluminous correspondence of the period with the leading lights of the party – Jayaprakash Narayan, Asoka Mehta, M. R. Masani – shows that he was not in agreement with the near-blind copying by the C.S.P. of the phraseology and methods of Western socialism. There was hardly any attempt at adaptation. Menon was also offended by a streak of Trotskyist deviation he suspected in the movement. The party's journal, the *Congress Socialist*, he thought, gave the impression that the Trotskyist drift was too pronounced to be ignored. If this was the case, he felt, 'quite frankly, I am afraid I must reconsider my relations with the whole business ... I am not a communist but I am much less a liberal. Abstract justice is all right for parlour socialists. The campaign to isolate Russia ... is industrial fascism as Mr W. J. Brown, not a communist – anything but – calls it.'[1]

Besides, Menon was frustrated by the Indian socialist leaders' failure to keep him posted with party news and detailed policy directions. When Masani gave up the General Secretaryship of the party, Menon's only intimation of it came from Press reports and he had to write to Jayaprakash Narayan and Asoka Mehta asking for confirmation and the name of the next General Secretary. 'I fear,' he wrote to Asoka Mehta, 'that our liaison work has broken down a little and it has to be revived.' Apparently it was never revived. Menon, himself a thorough worker, got the impression that the C.S.P. was neither serious nor persistent enough to do much good for socialism in India. He drifted away from the party. Jayaprakash, Asoka Mehta and Masani are today among Krishna Menon's bitterest critics in India.

In retrospect, it seems that the decline and fall of the C.S.P. was a grievous loss for India. Had it flowered into a healthy

---

[1] Undated letter to M. R. Masani, probably 1937.

organization, the large number of gifted socialist leaders who are today sulking in hopeless frustration would have been active in constructive politics. It would have helped the growth of opposition forces in India and prevented parliamentary democracy from becoming a one-party democracy. It would have avoided the unenviable situation where the only meaningful alternative to the Congress Party in India is the Communist Party. It would have also made the post-1947 Congress a more homogeneous party instead of the amorphous mass it has become. In short, it would have saved India from the political cynicism that has taken hold of it today.

A year after the Congress Socialist Party was founded, Menon came in contact with a man who was to become the greatest single factor affecting his career – Jawaharlal Nehru.

12

The Great Friendship

WHILE Krishna Menon was recasting the India League in his own image, Jawaharlal Nehru, seven years his senior, was already a bright star in the Indian firmament. The first time Nehru seriously attracted Menon's attention was the 1930 session of the Congress at Madras. Just back from a visit to Europe, Nehru had stood up before that predominantly conservative Congress and asked for 'complete independence' – a radical idea when the Congress was talking about Dominion status as the ultimate goal. Naturally it led to a sharp clash between Nehru and the Old Guard of the Congress.

But with that speech Nehru struck a chord in Krishna Menon. The young agitator in London began to see in Nehru a reflection of his own cherished ideals. Nehru was for a radical approach, so was Krishna Menon. Nehru was taking keen interest in labour matters, and so was Krishna Menon. Nehru was paying a great deal of attention to the organization of youth, and so was Krishna Menon. When Nehru urged that independence and socialism should be the twin goals of the Congress, Menon had no more doubts left.

Menon first met Nehru in 1927 when Jawaharlal, along with his father Motilal, visited London en route for Moscow. They met again in 1932 when Menon went to India as secretary of the India League Delegation. These were cursory meetings. It was in 1935 that they really got to know each other personally. His wife's condition having grown critical in Germany, Jawaharlal had been abruptly released from jail and he had hurried to Europe by air. Kamala's health improved briefly and Nehru decided to pay a visit to London.

Informed of this decision, Menon got in touch with Nehru

early enough and began making preparations. He wrote in December to Nehru,

> Please let me know whether you would like me as an individual or as the India League to handle the arrangements, it being understood that all requests for interviews will be submitted to you. If I had the privilege of knowing you for a longer period I would have said that I must be trusted not to make a mess of it and if anything went wrong people would only blame me.[1]

Nehru went to London without any commitment to the India League. However, from the moment he landed in London, he realized that Menon was in command. The League did handle the arrangements. Subsequent events proved that the two made a great impression on each other. Menon's best expectations were confirmed and he was convinced that the progressive, idealistic and socialistic Nehru was India's brightest hope for the future. Nehru was struck by the broadness of Menon's vision, his obsession with work for India and his apparently inexhaustible energy. The seeds of a famous friendship were sown.

Nehru stayed in London for a fortnight. His programme was a crowded one, but essentially it was a fortnight with Krishna Menon. The friendship was at first more personal than political.

After his departure for Germany, Nehru wrote frequently to Menon, giving him, along with a lot of chit-chat, a day-to-day account of his wife's progress. On February 28th, Kamala's 'lovely face that used to smile and smile so well' smiled for the last time, and a crushing emptiness crept into Nehru's life. Significantly, Nehru increased the frequency of his letters to Menon, finding great consolation in this correspondence. 'My dear Menon' became 'My dear Krishna', and letters that went out of London began with 'My dear Nehru' instead of the earlier 'My dear Mr Nehru'. Throughout his journey back to India the correspondence continued, Nehru pouring into his letters every thought that crossed his mind, personal as well as political.

One interesting exchange during these days concerned Nehru's

[1] This letter reached Nehru in Europe at a time when he was said to have been in touch with M. R. Masani. The Congress Socialist Party had already put Menon in touch with Masani and Masani claims to have recommended Menon to Nehru. Masani, now General Secretary of the Swatantra Party, is rueful as he recalls the episode.

famous rebuff to Mussolini.¹ On February 25th, Nehru gave the
first intimation of what was coming.

> I am writing this to you to prepare you for a possible
> shock. My aeroplane from Marseilles stops in Rome and we
> are supposed to spend a night there. Information of this had
> been sent to an Indian student there whom I know. He
> writes to say that Mussolini wants to see me during my short
> stay there. This is very embarrassing. It is quite possible that
> the Italian Press might invent many things and then it will be
> difficult to set about correcting and contradicting …

Menon was outraged. The rape of Abyssinia was only four
months old and it was unthinkable that the symbol of Indian
freedom should flatter the Fascist leader with a personal call. He
shot off a strongly worded cable to Nehru asking him to avoid
Mussolini whatever happened.

From Cairo Nehru wrote again,

> I received your frantic telegram. To ease your mind and
> to prevent you having any further sleepless nights on my
> account, I am sending these few lines to you. The Rome
> visit is over. It was a most embarrassing and ticklish affair but
> I survived it with a display of extreme tact and extreme
> firmness …

As far as the India League was concerned, there are grounds to
believe that Nehru had quite a few criticisms to make during his

---

¹ Nehru was afraid that if he met Mussolini, the interview might be made use of
for Fascist propaganda. Indian students visiting Italy had been so used against their
wishes and sometimes without their knowledge. Italy had also published a bogus
interview with Gandhi in 1931. Mussolini was as anxious to meet Nehru as Nehru
was to avoid a meeting. The Duce tried to trick Nehru into an interview. The incident
is described by Nehru himself in *Discovery of India*. 'On arrival in Rome in the late
afternoon, I was met by a high official who handed me a letter from the Chef de
cabinet of Signor Mussolini. The Duce, it stated, would be glad to meet me and he
had fixed 6 o'clock that evening for the interview. I was surprised and reminded him
of my previous messages. But he insisted that it had now all been fixed up and the
arrangement could not be upset. Indeed, if the interview did not take place there was
every likelihood of his being dismissed from his office. I was assured that nothing
would appear in the Press and that I need only see the Duce for a few minutes. All
that he wanted to do was to shake hands with me and to convey personally his con-
dolences at my wife's death. So we argued for a full hour with all courtesy on both
sides but with increasing strain; it was a most exhausting hour for me and probably
more so for the other party. The time fixed for the interview was at last upon us and
I had my way. A telephone message was sent to the Duce's palace that I could not
come.'

first visit. These did not arise from any lack of appreciation of the need for such work in London; they came rather from an appreciation of Menon's personality. A rival organization of Indians in London called the Friends of India Society had also contacted Nehru offering to handle his arrangements for the visit. Nehru did not know what forces were pulling in what directions; all he knew was that the India League had already persuaded men like Harold Laski and Stafford Cripps to work out the arrangements in connection with his visit.

Once in London, Nehru could see signs of rivalry between the two Indian organizations. He realized that Menon, dedicated and aflame with patriotism, had antagonized other Indians and thereby perhaps weakened Indian work in Britain. The peacemaker in Nehru was upset: he suggested a closing of ranks.

Menon's reaction was contained in a letter he wrote to Nehru in July 1936, after the latter's departure. He said,

> You may remember that I did not succeed in getting down to discuss politics with you while you were here as someone or somebody butted in! I say this merely because I do not want to be thought of as being either out of action or, what was it, 'autocratic'. I am getting on with what I think is probably worth doing ... and I feel that in time you will also perhaps admit that we have our uses. In this atmosphere, work for India, whatever its uses, cannot be done by intermittent stunts and relying on people who have not given us any cause to think that they can be relied on ... I have no desire to be made use of by individuals, my countrymen or otherwise, who find in all this something to play with. In a mass movement like the Congress all sorts of people get in and even take up positions, but there will never be a mass movement on India in this country.

Nehru must have been aware, no doubt, of the tendency on the part of some overseas Indians to jump on the nationalist bandwagon for the glamour of it. And he could recognize a rare example of dedication when he saw one. As time passed, Nehru's earlier criticisms seemed to melt away. He came to rely on the League and attach considerable importance to its work.

Krishna Menon's firebrand socialism must have impressed Nehru. On his return from Europe after this visit, Nehru was

unusually forthright about his socialist convictions. Ever afflicted
by intellectual doubts, perhaps he had found encouragement in
Menon's forthrightness. His presidential address at the Lucknow
session of the Congress (April 1936) was of a tone that clearly
frightened the conservative sections of the Congress. Their
reaction was expressed by Dr Pattabhi Sitaramayya. Noting that
Nehru had confessed his socialism as far back as in 1929 at the
Lahore Congress, Pattabhi remarked in his *History of the Indian
National Congress*, 'When seven years later he presided over the
Lucknow session he reached the logical fulfilment of socialism –
namely communism.' This is the only statement from a Congress
source on record which goes to the extent of calling Nehru a
communist, and it shows how radical Nehru's views appeared to
the Old Guard of the Congress then.

Lucknow was only the beginning. Thereafter, well into the
war years, Nehru was to pass through a period of frustration and
emotional crisis. He felt ideologically different from the rest of
the Congress leadership, unable to reconcile his convictions with
the general direction the Congress was following and unable to
change his ideas or effectively change the direction of the Congress. This period of disappointment was to draw Nehru closer to
Krishna Menon. The more he felt isolated from the Congress, the
more he turned to Menon.

Following the Lucknow session Nehru wrote often to Menon
expressing his desire to resign the presidency of the party. He
found the presidential chair a bed of nettles. But, being Nehru,
he was unwilling to take a step that could directly or indirectly
affect the unity and prestige of the party. Menon's own approach
to the problem was that the Old Guard's opposition to progressive
ideas was an added reason for Nehru to remain at the helm and
try his best to push his programme. He could see the adverse
propaganda effect of the rift within the Congress and cautioned
the leaders in India about it.

The Press [he told them] has been making the most of the
difficulties encountered by Jawaharlal Nehru in his position
as President of the Congress. Every impression of disagreement with the socialist policy which the Congress Socialist
Party and Nehru are putting forward is received with great
rejoicing and the sentiment that this socialist trend is merely

a passing phase and will be stamped out by the more reason-
able sections of the Congress.[1]

Nehru's resignation never materialized. But the worst was yet
to be.

Britain had imposed a new constitution on India in 1935.
All sections of nationalist opinion were vehemently opposed to
this because Indian leaders were given no say at all in its framing.
Nehru took the initiative in setting up a Civil Liberties Union
with Rabindranath Tagore as President and Sarojini Naidu as
the executive chief. The idea was to expose the fact that the new
Government of India Act was, under the guise of constitutional
progress, in fact a device to curb liberties.

Menon saw the point and set his machinery in action in London
to tell the British people the real nature of the Act. He organized
a Conference on Civil Liberties in India and focused attention
on the iniquities of the new constitution and the restrictions it
imposed on citizens. Sufficient was done to prick the propaganda
balloon which had proclaimed the new constitution as the
harbinger of a bright new future for India.

Though fiercely opposed to the constitution, the Congress
decided to fight the elections it stipulated. The polling took place
in 1937 and it gave Congress a landslide victory; it won an
absolute majority in five provinces and emerged as the largest
single party in four others. But victory landed the Congress in
an unprecedented crisis.

Should the Congress accept office or should it not? If it accepted,
the British Governors, who were the constitutional heads of the
provinces, could use their special powers to frustrate the
ministries. If it refused power, it would in effect be abdicating
parliamentary responsibility and providing the Government
with an excellent excuse to carry on without the inconvenience
of elections and opposition parties. What followed was a battle
royal, plunging the country into one of the longest and bitterest
constitutional and legal debates in colonial history.

The bitterness was most marked between the conservatives
and the radicals inside the Congress movement. The latter saw
the crisis as a deliberately planned affair with the Old Guard
playing into the hands of the imperial power. Nehru was in

[1] 'London Letter' in the *Congress Socialist*, June 1936.

favour of putting an end to the whole business and launching a mass campaign for real freedom as distinct from the guided independence offered by the constitution.

The British love few things more dearly than a protracted debate on principles, and the Indian constitutional crisis became a subject of lengthy argument in Britain. It became Krishna Menon's job to present the Indian angle, expose misinterpretations and challenge the neat adaptations of principle put forward by Tory diehards. Meetings, pamphlets and letters to editors became a daily occurrence. When a newspaper persistently distorted the Indian viewpoint, Menon would personally go to its office and engage the editors in argument. Sometimes he was able to report a welcome change of tone as a result of these personal contacts. But for Menon's activities, the British Press and government officials would have found it easy to present to their people the picture as they wanted it to be seen.

The constitutional debate in India irritated Menon. He did his own probing in Whitehall and was convinced that the British Government was implementing a well-thought-out plot in which the constitution, the elections and the crisis that followed it were all carefully prepared stages.

Menon's analysis of the situation makes interesting reading. He wrote,[1]

> There is no damned crisis except that they choose to call it one. The Government is terribly anxious to make the Congress take office. If the Congress takes office even for a day it dispenses with the necessity of an election or the use of Section 93 in October as the assemblies would have met within six months as required by the Act. If Congress holds on to office or is encouraged to remain for a few months the budget will be through and then the Governor can carry on with a dummy ministry, sacking the Congressmen or forcing their resignation. It is a very clever manœuvre. For heaven's sake let us realize that the time has now come to call a halt and take the Congress out of legislative politics.

About the British knack of talking one out of one's rights,

> If the provinces function the federation will also take effect. There will be more formulae and more speeches and willy

[1] Letter to M. R. Masani, undated.

nilly the Governors may give some sort of an assurance that is not an assurance and is one at the same time. So this is the time to say that the Viceroy's speech says nothing new, it is supercilious in that he is trying to tell us what this constitution is, as though we are a lot of imbeciles ... Does anyone imagine that authorities in India or here will do anything to interpret the Act in such a way that there is the transference of power in reality? The answer is no.

About the Gandhian way,

I am terribly afraid that the Mahatma will come out with some long-drawn-out formula. I have no doubt that he sincerely thinks that office acceptance is good. I do not hold doctrinaire views on it and if Congress had not been so very 'up on the high horse about it' in the beginning, the best banner would have been to walk into office and to have said so at the elections.

This lengthy letter to his colleagues in the Congress Socialist Party emphasized two significant aspects of Menon's political attitude. Firstly, his deference towards Mahatma Gandhi, which he shared with Nehru. Like Nehru, he was unable to understand many of the Mahatma's actions or to agree with them. But, like Nehru again, he tended as far as possible to let the Mahatma have his way. He drew the particular attention of his socialist friends to the importance of 'not calling Gandhiji or his followers names. It loses more support than anything else.' Secondly, again presenting a parallel with Nehru, Menon had a line beyond which he was not willing to go in the pursuit of factional ends. His letter repeatedly said that the leaders of the C.S.P. should be with Nehru at Allahabad during the crisis in order to strengthen Nehru's hands. He was emphatic that it was no time for factional feelings or partisanship, but for a solid united front.

Menon wrote to Nehru also on the constitutional crisis though in less picturesque language than he used while writing to Masani. It helped Nehru in this period of isolation from the Congress. It gave him, as Menon's letters always did, moral support in his hour of depression and loneliness. Most important of all, it made Nehru feel that Menon had an exceptional grasp of constitutional matters. He was a reliable adviser to have around.

This impression was to play a crucial role in 1947 during the negotiations for the transfer of power.

Nothing, however, could change the Congress from its course. The crisis ended the way the conservatives wanted it to end. The Congress assumed office. The oddity of the situation was well brought out in the policy statement of the Congress Working Committee on the eve of acceptance of office. It asked the ministries to 'combat' the constitution and simultaneously avail themselves of their power to implement constructive programmes. In other words, the Congress governments were asked to take advantage of a constitution they were pledged to fight. No one was surprised when the ministries later resigned, the freedom struggle took on the character of mass struggle again and the Government, of course, stepped up repression. Menon's fears had come true and Nehru's cup of sorrow was full. Nehru was so desolate that he left India, seeking comfort for his tormented soul in the company of Menon. Within three years of their meeting the two had already come to look upon each other for strength, support and solace.

What lay behind the rapid flowering of this affinity? An important factor was the similarity of their political backgrounds. In their teens both were hypnotized by the Theosophical Movement. Nehru in Allahabad and Menon in Madras came under the personal spell of Mrs Annie Besant. Again both drifted away from theosophy after a few years to become involved in more active politics. The two men also had their English education in common. What Harrow and Cambridge did to Nehru, the London School of Economics and University College did to Menon: they made each of them, in Nehru's words, 'more an Englishman than an Indian'. Nehru and Menon are the two most 'complete Indians' in public life today in that they are totally unaffected by sentiments of language and region – sentiments that have become all-powerful in free India. The years in England also infused in them a kind of split outlook – undiluted hatred for British imperialism side by side with unreserved affection for the British people. Gandhi's attitude was identical, but he developed it as a principle, as an offshoot of his moral philosophy. In the case of Nehru and Menon, it grew naturally out of their personal contacts with the English, their prolonged observation of and participation in the English way of life in England.

The Great Friendship

These parallel experiences were sufficient to make Nehru and Menon take to each other. Added to these was the identity of their ideological outlook which had also grown independently before they met. Nehru's radicalism, latent from the time he wanted to join Gandhi's *satyagraha* society and was ordered out of the house by his irate father, had received a socialistic orientation – and a profound one at that – with his visit to Russia in 1927. The same year he had also attended the anti-imperialist conference at Brussels. Since then Nehru had been emotionally attached to the ideals of communism, though its dictatorial methods repelled him. Menon, a revolutionary from his student days in Madras, had been converted into a scientific socialist by Harold Laski and he had become an enthusiastic admirer of the Russian experiment. His attraction to communism was not emotional as Nehru's was, but rational; yet his objection to communism's totalitarian techniques was as strong as Nehru's, for they were contrary to the constitutional proprieties he had learned to respect.

Besides their socialism the two were also vehemently anti-Fascist – but this was not the kind of vague dislike of Fascism which most rational people developed in the 'thirties, but a positive and consuming hatred of it flowing from a deep understanding of Fascism's potentialities. In brief, both Nehru and Menon had passed through remarkably identical processes of intellectual evolution, and when they met in London it was as if each saw his own reflection in the other.

The political circumstances of the time provided the cement for the friendship. The momentum of the independence movement had swept Nehru into the company of leaders with whom he had little in common besides the over-riding passion of the day. There was his father, Motilal Nehru, whom he admired but whose world was different from his. There was the Mahatma whom he loved and obeyed, but whose ideas on economics differed widely from his. There was Sardar Patel who was, more than Gandhi, inclined towards capitalism and the business community, and whose attitude to events outside India bordered on cynical indifference. There was Maulana Azad whose scholarship and erudition provided a source of inspiration to Nehru, but who was unable to give him any political stimulation. Among the younger elements in the Congress there were many for whom Nehru had deep ideological sympathy – men like Jayaprakash Narayan and Acharya Narendra Deva – but he found their enthusiasm too doctrinaire for his taste. Subhas Bose, another progressive leader with whose ideas Nehru often found himself in agreement, was too much of an extremist to be accepted as a trusted political companion. Nehru was in the fullest sense of the term lonely. It was then that he came across Krishna Menon, a man who was deeply and profoundly committed to socialism but who was at the same time constructive enough to accept the discipline of the Congress movement. Nehru had at last found a comrade.

Krishna Menon, too, had been lonely. His was a one-man war in London and he was desperately anxious for help, particularly help from India. Passionate about the content of freedom, he was tremendously concerned about the strengthening of socialist forces in India so that freedom would not dawn on a politically unprepared people. But he was not in India to contribute to this directly. All he could do was to throw in his lot with sincere socialists working in India. He found in Nehru the perfect combination of idealism and practical sense, 'one of those rare personalities in public life who combine intense activity with vision and detachment'.[1] Most other leaders struck him as either too much to the right or too much to the left, while Nehru symbolized for him the best guarantee of the kind of freedom he visualized for India.

Apparently it was a friendship that grew in spite of themselves. Neither seems to have consciously cultivated the other. From the personal angle there were no deep-laid plots or ulterior motives. It was a time when friendship with Nehru could not be thought of as a form of political investment. Slow in taking to anyone, Menon was unreserved in giving his devotion to a hero once he met one. His loyalty to Nehru has remained undiluted and total through the years.

In the late 'thirties they had links other than ideology to hold them together. Nehru's 1935 visit to London coincided with the completion of his *Autobiography* and the efforts to have his *Glimpses of World History* published in London. Menon had by then already become a well-known figure in London's publishing world; it was one of the ways in which he tried to earn something. He naturally became Nehru's literary agent in London. He arranged

[1] From Menon's Foreword to *Glimpses of World History*, 1939.

for the publication of the *Autobiography* by the Bodley Head, for whom he himself acted as an editorial adviser. He suggested certain revisions and additions to *Glimpses of World History* and had the book illustrated by his friend and noted left-winger, J. F. Horrabin. In the second edition of the book Menon's name appears as editor.

Menon also edited several of Nehru's other books. *Unity of India* was brought out in 1941. *Parting of the Ways* and *The Cripps Mission* were published with forewords by Menon. His aim was to make Nehru's voice heard in Britain. In the process he himself became enraptured by the voice and developed great insight into Nehru's mind.

As his agent in London, Menon used to receive from Nehru all manner of instructions, advice and explanations. In March 1937 he received a letter of instructions which threw light on one of Nehru's least-known personal problems – his self-consciousness about his name. Nehru wrote,

> One small matter. I am getting rather fed up with my name. It is always being mis-spelt and mispronounced. The other day a B.B.C. announcer got hopelessly muddled over it and went on ha-ha-ha-ing. Unfortunately I cannot change my name but I propose to make a slight change in the way it is written. Jawaharlal consists really of two Hindustani words: Jawahar and Lal. In India one usually combines the two, but this long word has got a terrifying look about it and foreigners cannot get hold of it. So it would be better in future to separate the two. My name should be given as: Jawahar Lal Nehru.

This must have been one of those brainwaves that came and went. Menon does not seem to have had any occasion actually to split his friend's name in print.

A notable feature of Menon's friendship with Nehru was its strong personal quality apart from all the political, intellectual and ideological overtones. They liked each other as individuals. Cut off as he was from his own family, Menon might have found in the strong family instincts of Nehru a consolation. And the brotherless Nehru who had always been lonely in his home might have been inspired by Menon's affection and devotion to accept him as a brother. Even in the first months of their friendship,

Nehru's letters invariably contained a sentence or two about his wife or daughter. Long and ponderous letters from India would end with a sudden disarming sentence like 'Indira arrived yesterday. She looks well.'

Menon did not know the art of such personal touches. It is curious that in correspondence Menon never once addressed Nehru by the familiar term of 'Jawahar' or 'Jawaharlal'; it was always 'My dear Nehru' or 'My dear Jawaharlal Nehru'. But this was never an indication of his real relations with Nehru; it could have only been an offshoot of his South Indian unfamiliarity with the endearing variations of North Indian names. For a true barometer of their personal intimacy one must turn to some of the utterly charming letters Nehru wrote to him. They bear witness to Nehru's early disposition to share his innermost thoughts with Menon. When Nehru was upset or moody (a frequent occurrence), it became his habit to write to Menon to gain relief. One of these letters may be quoted here in full for the light it throws on their relationship. It is a moving letter written in long-hand on three sheets of notepaper.

May 17th, 1939   *Lucknow*

My dear Krishna,

I have been sending you letters from time to time dealing with various matters that arose. I shall continue to do so, for the mind goes on functioning through sheer habit. So also I shall carry on with my usual activities, though I realize more and more how I am losing in efficiency. But I want to tell you briefly my state of mind. It is bad. I have lost all pep and feel devitalized and my interest in life itself seems to be fading away. Don't be alarmed, I can still function fairly effectively and it may be that I shall recover some of my vitality. At the moment however, the outlook is not encouraging. Most of the things that I value and for which I have worked seem to be going to pieces, and it is not surprising that I should also disintegrate in the process. Nearly all the conceit I possessed in such ample measure has been knocked out of me. I suppose this is a gradual process and many things contribute to it. Events in India, events elsewhere. What has happened in Spain has affected me greatly as a deep personal sorrow. What has happened and is happening in India, being nearer to me, affects me continuously. The kind of human material that I see around me, the all-pervading pettiness and vulgarity, the mutual suspicion and back-biting and so many other things distress me beyond measure. Everywhere the wrong type of person is pushing himself to the front, everywhere disruptive forces are growing. Perhaps I exaggerate, perhaps all this is inevitable, and is not peculiar to India in the present phase of the world.

It is possible that I might not have been affected by all this quite so much if I had retained my own peace of mind. Having lost that in a huge measure, the shield that protected me has gone. The heat and my indifferent health make matters worse.

I wrote to you two and a half months ago that I was very ill mentally. I had received a sudden shock which upset me more than almost anything else had ever done. I was afraid of a breakdown but I avoided it and during those days of mental agony, I sat down and forced myself to write those articles – where are we? I adjusted myself gradually and became more normal. But I was too much shaken up and the after effects continue.

I am sorry to write to you all this and to distress you. I do so to enable you to realize somewhat how I am functioning at present. Partly also to relieve myself. There is hardly anyone here to whom I can speak with frankness about myself. But please do not worry. It is a phase which will pass perhaps.

Yours,

JAWAHARLAL

13

Partners in Foreign Policy

WHEN Nehru and Menon met in 1935 they discovered that they shared a common interest in international affairs. Under Nehru's impact the Indian National Congress had begun to take cognizance of the global context in which its own struggle was set. But Nehru's enthusiasm for foreign affairs was no more than a source of amusement to some senior leaders of the Congress.

It is said that a leader of the stature of Sardar Patel was cynical about foreign policy even after independence. According to one story, he was once asked whether India would take a firm stand on the Indonesian issue. The Sardar furrowed his forehead and said, 'Indonesia, Indonesia ... now, let me see, where's Indonesia? ... Well, you had better ask Jawaharlal about that.'[1]

In Krishna Menon Nehru met a person who felt as intensely as he himself did about the significance of international developments. Being in London Menon was perhaps more immediately conscious of the impact of world events on the Indian struggle and vice versa. As he saw the situation, it was necessary for Indian leaders to give and receive support from other peoples in a similar plight and with similar ideas. He was anxious that the Congress should become active on the international front, that it should get into the world picture. Nehru was happy to find a man who could team up with him.

The teaming-up assumed an official character because Nehru was the President of the Congress; after the Lucknow session, he was again elected President for the Faizpur session in December 1936. At Faizpur his speech was overcast by reference to 'the triumphant course of Fascism in Europe'. Apparently the session as a whole felt something of his concern, for Pattabhi writes in his *History of the Indian National Congress*, 'At Faizpur, as at Lucknow,

[1] Quoted in *Nehru – A Political Biography*, by Michael Brecher. Oxford Paperbacks 1961), p. 129.

we had the same thoughts of the World Peace Congress, the same apprehensions of a world war ... The Indian delegate attended the World Peace Congress.'

The Indian delegate was Krishna Menon. A new phase had begun in his career which was to have a profound influence on free India's history.

The World Peace Congress was held in Brussels in September 1936. It was an attempt to boost the shaky League of Nations and to counter the International Congress Against War, Fascism and Imperialism which was to be held in the same city a month later. The Congress Against War, organized by the International Bureau of Revolutionary Socialist Unity, was communist-inspired and vehemently critical of the 'capitalist-dominated League of Nations'. The Peace Congress, on the contrary, was almost subservient to the League.

The organizers of the Peace Congress were anxious that nationalist India should be represented at Brussels. They invited Krishna Menon and also some Indian students from the Y.M.C.A. in London. Menon knew the nature of the Congress and decided that it would be in the interest of Indian freedom to break into such a gathering rather than into an enthusiastically sympathetic assembly like the Congress Against War. But he was also particular that he should attend the Peace Congress only as an accredited representative of the Indian freedom movement. He informed Nehru that 'certain commissions will be set up, even on cultural matters, so the question of imperialism can be raised effectively though the gathering will be rather a mixed one'.

Nehru cabled back appointing Menon the official representative of the Indian National Congress for the Brussels conference. In a subsequent letter he sent his instructions as to what Menon was expected to do. In the light of India's post-independence foreign policy these instructions are quite illuminating. They throw light on the early attempts to give India a foreign affairs philosophy which was to become a source of controversy in course of time, a source of irritation to the West and of inspiration to Afro-Asia. As it happened, Menon was intimately connected with these beginnings and sometimes contributed even more than Nehru to the shaping of the policy. Nehru wrote,

As you know, our Congress has not got a clearly defined

foreign policy. But you are acquainted with the background of our work and policy and you should keep this in mind. As Congress representative, you will naturally endeavour to give expression to the Congress attitude and not do anything that you know goes beyond that attitude ... Generally we stand for the progressive forces ... without being committed to socialism.

The pattern of future collaboration on foreign policy was evolving. Nehru, indecisive about particulars but definite about the general line, would give broad indications of what he liked to have and Menon, quick of comprehension and precise in expression, would translate it into clearly identifiable planks of policy. The great partnership was being born.

Menon's appointment as Congress nominee for Brussels was widely welcomed in India. The *Congress Socialist* said editorially,

> The nomination ... is a well merited recognition of his long and devoted service to this country abroad. Krishna Menon is the Secretary of the India League and has for years been a familiar and popular figure in British political life ... It would be no exaggeration to say that Krishna Menon is the heart and soul of the League and has done more towards popularizing the Indian national cause in England than any other individual, Indian or English.

The editor of the *Congress Socialist* then was Asoka Mehta.

At Brussels Menon's only intention was to get the issue of imperialism raised; he aimed at having colonialism officially rejected by the Congress. His speech bears witness to the care he took then, as always, to raise a specific issue to the level of a general principle or, to put it the other way round, to have a principle approved in the first instance and then to apply it to a specific case. It was not India or British domination of India he was talking about, but the subjugation of some peoples by some others.

> Constructive peace calls for the release of social energies and their application to the creation of a more equitable and stable world equilibrium. Free peoples liberated from domination and thus themselves averse to conquests are the best guarantees of peace. Thus our struggle in India, whether it be in our opposition to war or for the liberation of our people

from imperialism, is one continuous endeavour in the cause of peace ... We the people of India in common with the countless millions of the rest of the Asian continent and peoples of Africa have no desire for aggression or conquest. To the progressive forces of the world our ready co-operation is always at hand and whatever the years to come may bring we shall continue to strive ceaselessly to make our contributions to world peace effective.

The year was 1936, but the words could well be from any United Nations debate of recent years.

Menon's performance at Brussels made Indian leaders sit up and take note for the first time. Ram Manohar Lohia, then the brilliant Secretary of the Foreign Department of the All-India Congress Committee, wrote to Menon, 'We all appreciated your speech so very much and I pray you to accept my hearty congratulations on such a creditable performance. I am sure you must have made a very good impression on the congress.'

The impression was indeed very good, but the effect was nil. The Congress had assembled with certain pre-determined inhibitions and, in the end, they deliberately sidestepped the two most important issues of the day: the Spanish and Ethiopian tragedies and the question of colonialism. The Congress set up special committees for even such subjects as the Church, arts, aviation and ex-servicemen, but it diligently avoided making any mention of imperialism. This could not have been otherwise because, firstly, one of the principles of the Congress was the recognition of the sanctity of treaty obligations, and secondly, its primary allegiance was to the League of Nations, which was in a mood to accept the territorial rights of empires without question.

The failure of the Congress to condemn colonialism did not embitter Menon. He believed that, despite what had happened at Brussels, India should establish a national committee for peace activities. He espoused the idea not because he thought it would help in getting the support of influential world opinion for Indian freedom as such, but because he knew that such support could be rallied for at least some demands that were important in the anti-imperialist struggle.

The pattern was set. Thereafter it became routine for Krishna Menon to attend every world gathering where the Indian cause needed pleading. Once Menon proved his ability in the role, Congress leaders began turning to him as a matter of course. In 1938 Dr Rajendra Prasad, Maulana Azad, Sardar Patel and Subhas Bose, in consultation with Gandhi, named Menon as the Congress delegate to the Peace and Empire Congress at Glasgow. Acharya Kripalani, then General Secretary of the Congress, was the man who wrote and informed Menon of the decision.

Neurosis overtook Krishna Menon in 1938. It had been building up for several years, the cold and the hostility of London acting as catalytic agents on his own highly strung temperament. The intensification of political activity by 1930 was a great drain on his physical resources. The academic work he was carrying on simultaneously made this worse. Contact with Nehru increased both the pace and the scope of his activities.

His system could have adapted itself had he looked after his health by taking a modicum of rest and nourishment. Caught between too much work on the one hand and too little money on the other, meal-times disappeared from his schedule. He took weak tea as a substitute for proteins – with inevitable results. By 1936 the first symptoms of a physical breakdown were visible.

His state of mind aggravated it. His father's death in 1935 had suddenly made him feel lonely and vaguely guilty. He knew he had caused considerable disappointment to his father by taking up politics. Although in course of time he became a barrister and thus fulfilled the dream his father had always cherished, the physical separation of years had been working unconsciously on his mind. A deeply affectionate man by nature, this separation from his family forced on him by idealism and circumstances constituted a crushing blow.

There were also emotional involvements in London. Menon has always had women admirers. He is a diabolically handsome man, and the uniqueness of his profile and the natural ruggedness of his ways, together with the brilliance of his intellect, always attracted women. They gathered about him, helped him with the running of the India League and lent a hand in the organization of public functions. Most of the women who stayed with the League were attracted more by the personality of Menon than by the cause he espoused. By and large Menon's own attitude to them was, as it continues to be, one of bemused tolerance. He enjoyed their company, but never had the patience to set himself up as a ladies' man. He was brusque and domineering, although those who worked with him long enough could see the underlying affection which characterized all his friendships. Once or twice he came perilously close to being conquered. Menon never had any ideological objections to matrimony but nothing came of it. He was in reality already married to India and the League.

The emotional interludes were not of a kind that could knock Krishna Menon out of circulation, but they might have contributed their share to the shattering of his health. He was entering his forties, and a decade of loneliness had left its mark upon him – loneliness and the almost unnatural devotion to work that he developed in its wake. Mannerisms developed, complexes became fixed. The breakdown was inevitable. As Mrs Frieda Laski says, 'It didn't help him not to be neurotic when he was living here on nothing.'

From 1936 onwards Krishna Menon was a sick man, medicines having supplemented tea and buns as his staple diet. By early 1938 he was bedridden.

Friends took weeks to trace him to the ramshackle garret in St Pancras where he had his home. There, in a dimly lit room, cold and inhospitable, Krishna Menon lay dying. There was no food around, nor any helping hands. Starvation had fanned the flames of the disease and Menon stayed in his corner, obstinately refusing to do anything to save himself. The whole thing was so macabre that legends began to spread. Some said that Menon was on a fast unto death for some mysterious reason. The fact was simply that Menon was paying for the overdrafts he had made on his mind and body. And when he fell seriously sick, he did not have the wherewithal to have himself looked after.

The hopeful turning point came when, one dismal day, Harold Laski and his wife went to St Pancras, climbed to the little garret and saw Krishna Menon. 'We expected him to die,' says Mrs Laski as she recalls the day now. But apparently the visit of the Laskis pulled Menon out of his suicidal mood and put him on the road to recovery. Within a few weeks he was out of danger and well on the way back to resuming his usual activities. But the breakdown left its permanent marks on him. When he rose from his bed he found it necessary to use a walking-stick. He has since become a habitual user of patent medicines.

This was the period when, far away in India, Jawaharlal Nehru was drifting farther and farther away from the entrenched conservatives of the Congress Party. After the Lucknow session of the Congress in 1936 he was, in the eyes of the conservatives, becoming a communist. In Nehru himself the cumulative result of the struggle between the conservatives and the radicals was a crushing sense of isolation.

International developments added to Nehru's discomfiture. Fascist crimes were marking the years in blood – Abyssinia in 1935, Spain in 1936, a new invasion of China by Japan in 1937. In 1938 Hitler marched into Austria. Nehru decided to make another trip to Europe. The proposal inspired Krishna Menon in London, just recovering from his near-fatal collapse. He heartily welcomed the opportunity to get away from London for a while and decided to accompany Nehru through Europe. When Nehru arrived in Marseilles in June, Menon was there to receive him. Nehru had some initial difficulty in getting his travel papers. It was Menon, with the help of his parliamentary contacts, who expedited the matter.

Their tour of the Spanish fronts lasted only five days, but the experience was a very significant one for at least three reasons. Firstly, the hypocrisy of the so-called democratic governments – of the United Kingdom in particular – made both Nehru and Menon very bitter about the democracies and their professions. Secondly, the cleverness with which the Soviet Union handled the problem won their admiration as it won the admiration of intellectuals everywhere at the time. Thirdly, the horrors they witnessed and the similarity of their reactions cemented the friendship between Nehru and Menon in a manner that was to stand the test of many years.

Few world events have shaken nationalist India as profoundly as did the tragedy of Spain. It was never seen as a civil war, but as a full-scale European war in which the forces of democracy were pitted against the forces of Fascism. What shocked India most was the attitude of Britain and France. They were openly helping the Fascist countries and adding to the difficulties of the Republic. The British Government, with its traditional gift for studied equivocation, set up a Non-Intervention Committee and admitted Germany and Italy as members, though they were helping Franco with sizeable armies, aeroplanes and pilots. Even when British ships carrying food to the Republic were sunk by Franco's forces, Chamberlain, the Prime Minister, defended Franco. At the instigation of the British the French Government closed the Pyrenean frontier, thus making sure that no supplies would get through to the Republic.

The bitterness felt by Indians was expressed by Nehru in his *Glimpses of World History*. He wrote,

> A Fascist Spain would be fatal for France, and would threaten both the British Mediterranean route to the East and the Cape route. Gibraltar would then be useless and the Suez Canal of no great value. Thus, even from the point of view of self-interest, if not from love of democracy, one would have expected England and France to give every legitimate aid to the Spanish Government to put down the rebellion. But here again we see how class interests move governments even at the cost of their national interests ... To such a pass has the British Government come in its fear of the spread of democracy.

In contrast to the Anglo-French stand, the attitude of Soviet Russia met with ready acclaim in India. Stalin's policy was of course not motivated by altruism; his principal concern was the advancement of communism. If he formulated his policies with the motive of strengthening communism, at least there was no question of hypocrisy or treachery involved. Indeed, Nehru went to the extent of observing that 'in Europe Soviet Russia remains the sole barrier to Fascism; if she were destroyed there would be a complete end of democracy in Europe, including France and England.'

What Nehru felt with considerable emotion, Krishna Menon felt with consuming anger. What he saw in Spain was painful in the extreme. From his hotel window in Barcelona he could see mortar fire mowing people down and aeroplanes strafing unsuspecting villagers. Italian and German aeroplanes were bombarding cities and the civilian population even on Franco's side of the fighting line so that no rebellion could rise against him.

The Indian visitors watched this from close quarters. In public life both Nehru and Menon have become famous for their personal courage in the face of physical danger. In Spain they went through the thick of battle, dodging flying shells and falling debris. They met the Prime Minister of the Republic, the Foreign Minister, General Lister who was in command of the sector and the legendary woman leader La Passionara. The experience of the trenches and the long discussions they had with the leaders of the Republic gave Nehru and Menon a unique opportunity to get to know each other well.

After his return from that unhappy country Menon kept Spanish relief high on his list of activities. He set up a committee in London to organize aid to Republican Spain. Whatever could be raised in India through Nehru's initiative was also sent through him to Spain. But what Menon could do was necessarily limited. He tried hard, for instance, to have the Indian National Congress send an ambulance to Spain in the name of the people of India, but the attempt had to be dropped after Nehru cabled to say 'Spanish ambulance impracticable.'

The Congress, however, relied on Menon's reports and advice for formulating its own policies over the Spanish war. In February 1939 he cabled angrily to Nehru saying, 'Request cable immediately London Government emphatic disassociation India recognition Franco. Betrayal Republic. R.U.P. calling worldwide protest Sunday.' Three days later the President of the Congress, Subhas Chandra Bose, cabled to 'Prime Minister, London. On behalf of Indian people we emphatically protest against recognition of Franco and betrayal of legally constituted Spanish republican government ... Consider such recognition violation of international law and morality.'

Spain touched the very vitals of Menon's being because he saw it as part of the same struggle in which India was engaged, the struggle between exploiter and exploited. The struggle against imperialism in India could not be something apart from the struggle against Fascism abroad. A great deal of Menon's activities in the 1930s were, in fact, directed against Fascism as such. He was an integral part of the growing international front against Fascism. When Mussolini was insisting on reforming the League of Nations, Menon held the view that 'the best we can hope for in this Dark Age is to prevent the forces of reaction from breaking up the present machine, with all its defects, and putting an international Fascist Grand Council in its place.'[1]

[1] In an article entitled 'The League at the Crossroads', *India League*, December 22nd, 1933.

The Nehru-Menon partnership was not confined to essentials of foreign affairs and political science. The time they spent together in Europe in 1938 was utilized for a free and leisurely exchange of views on a variety of subjects. Out of these discussions was born also a partnership in economic thought. Harold Laski and his London School of Economics had made Menon a qualified economist. Nehru had no academic qualification in the subject, but he was always aware of the fundamentals of economic laws and the basis of planning. He accepted Menon as a technical adviser as well as an ideological aide.

The Indian National Congress itself had just begun thinking in terms of economic planning for the first time. Under the Presidentship of Subhas Chandra Bose the Congress decided to draw on expert opinion and formulate an all-India plan for industrial progress so that the setback received by the national economy under British rule could be effectively faced. Subhas Bose was an all-out advocate of industrialization as distinct from mere industrial recovery. This was a welcome augury for the younger elements in the Congress. Menon saw in the move a laudable attempt by the Congress to tackle fundamentals.

But what kind of industrialization? Menon was not sure what orientation the industrial programme would receive under Subhas Bose. He knew Bose was a tough nut for conservative Congressmen to crack, but he could not be sure about the ideological basis of Bose's approach. At the same time he was absolutely certain about Nehru – and Nehru happened to be with him in Europe. The two men discussed at length the economic set-up of free India and the need to lay the foundations of it now that the Congress was contemplating action on this front. Menon felt, and so did Nehru, that to ensure the correctness of the foundation Nehru should be as closely associated with the deliberations as possible. They were happy when the Congress Working Committee cabled to Nehru asking him to be chairman of the new Planning Committee.

The apprehensions about Subhas Bose were soon to be proved justified. When Nehru returned from Europe after the Spanish tour he found himself in the midst of the internal war of the Congress which was to lead to the unedifying Tripuri crisis. The re-election of Subhas Bose as the Congress President against the wishes of Gandhi and the combined efforts of the powerful conservative wing was only the beginning of the crisis. Subhas, as President, was in a defiant mood and he began acting in a manner that appeared arbitrary even to his friends. Nehru, a man who began with great admiration for the dynamism and courage of Subhas Bose, was soon disillusioned by his tactics as President. Menon, watching from London, was flabbergasted by the frittering away of high talent on party feuds. Conscious of the need to present a united front to foreign observers, he was sensitive to any development that threatened this unity. All he could do from England was to write frequently to friends urging that differences among leaders should be confined to party conferences.

But the differences became public when, early in 1939, the Congress Working Committee resigned. This was the kind of rift that men like Nehru and Menon, who were conscious of the adverse impression such quarrels would make, were anxious to avoid. Nehru, trying desperately to follow a middle-of-the-way policy, issued a statement about his decision to stay away from any new working committee that might be formed. His mood was one of utter disgust, and as usual he wrote an explanatory letter to the one friend who would appreciate his feelings. Enclosing a copy of his public statement, Nehru wrote to Menon on February 22nd,

The statement might surprise you or even distress you. But after very full consideration I came to the conclusion that there was no other course left open to me. The statement is a long one and yet inevitably it cannot contain many important matters which have influenced me. Subhas has gone off the rails and has been behaving badly in many ways. His principal supporters are very irresponsible and unreliable people and it is quite impossible for me to join this motley group with whose viewpoints on national and international policies I do not agree ... Apart from principles and policies, Subhas's methods of work are difficult to put up with. He has paralysed the A.I.C.C.[1] office and passes orders over its head in all manner of election matters and local disputes ... For me this new development has far-reaching significance. I do not propose to join any working committee whoever forms it – subject to a crisis overtaking us. It is quite likely that Subhas

[1] All-India Congress Committee.

might not be able to carry on. If so the Old Guard might slip in. Even so I shall not join the working committee. I have had enough of this kind of thing.

Subhas soon gave up and the conservatives slipped in. But Nehru's plan to stay aloof in disgust was short-lived, for a crisis did overtake everybody. The war broke out on September 3rd, 1939.

14

War

THE Second World War was a challenge to Krishna Menon in more ways than one. Politically, it meant a whole new range of problems and opportunities for India. Locally, as member of the St Pancras Council, it meant standing up to the blitz and providing borough leadership. Personally, the very fact of living in London was a challenge.

Menon was totally unaware of personal danger. Many are the stories told in London about the courage he showed during the worst days of the blitz. It was as though he had some magical immunity to bombs.

His devoted secretary, Bridget Tunnard, remembers the day when she was called in at lunch time to handle an urgent typing job. Menon handed over the papers to her and went into the kitchen to prepare a cup of tea. Suddenly there was the shrill wail of sirens followed by the sound of explosions; a large bomb had burst near the India League. The building shook violently and every bit of glass was shattered to pieces. Bridget sat transfixed in horror. Presently Krishna Menon came out of his kitchen, splinters of glass sticking out of his mass of hair, tea in hand. He looked at the poor woman and said, 'I told you it was urgent. Why have you stopped typing?' She went to work as if in a trance while Menon dived into another mass of papers on his table. There was not a word about the explosions. The only indication that Menon knew there had been a bomb came when, as Bridget was about to leave, he gave her a broom and asked her to sweep up the broken glass.

Bridget was again part of a weird drama when the India League was moving into new premises. On the day of the move, Menon had a long and complicated Privy Council case to prepare and he was, as usual, late with it. Under the pressure of the deadline, he went on dictating page after page with amazing rapidity. Meanwhile the removers started taking away the furniture. With a great deal of noise and commotion they took away the cupboards, the cabinets, the files, the chairs. Menon seemed unaware of what was going on. When they moved the table in front of him, he merely leaned back on his chair and went on dictating. Finally all that was left in the room were the two chairs on which Menon and his secretary were sitting. There they sat while Menon dictated his case with complete concentration until he had finished. When it was all over, he quietly got up and asked, 'Where's the furniture?'

Menon could be frighteningly oblivious of the surroundings when he had a job in hand, but at the same time a bomb could rouse him to an overwhelming sense of duty. There was a time when the India League was situated close to the Government's own India House and when inhabitants of one would hardly look at inhabitants of the other. Once a bomb exploded in the vicinity and through his office window Menon saw India House shaking and its glass windows crashing down. He dropped everything and ran into the government premises to see if he could be of any help.

His own borough, St Pancras, remembers with awe and gratitude Menon's record during the war years. He became an air-raid warden in St Pancras and was on the job every night, the first to arrive and the last to leave. He never wore uniform, only a helmet. Through the Borough Council he put pressure on the authorities to improve the conditions in, and the safety standards of, air-raid shelters and wardens' posts. The local civil defence committee had recommended the construction of 'two-stage concrete shelters'; but the Government was sitting tight on the application. Seeing time being wasted, Menon moved a resolution in the council saying that

... in view of the great urgency of the question, the Council requests the Civil Defence Committee to wait in deputation on the Minister of Home Security at an early date to press for the necessary sanction in the matter. Further, pending the building of two-stage shelters, this Council requests the Civil Defence Committee and the controller to build only in mono-lithic concrete and not of brick as the latter has conclusively been proved unsafe.

The abandon with which Menon would throw himself into situations of personal danger has been described by Edward A. Nicholson, who was a fellow voluntary warden with Krishna Menon at Camden Square. He has written,

> Krishna Menon was on patrol with me more than with anyone else, and very often we were alone, just the two of us. He was a very hard worker and was always there when wanted. He was so keen that he used often to dig me out from my place, coming sometimes at 12.30 midnight. He was very serious about it. There was never a more serious man that I met in all my war work ... One night there was the black-out and we were coming down Camden Road. I saw what I thought was a mine dropping. I grabbed Krishna's hand telling him to drop. But it was a balloon and it dropped on to the trolley-bus wires and broke the cables. The cables were electrified and I had to pull Krishna away because he said he would fix them. He had no fear and he was a good scout.

Menon was often at the wardens' post till 4 a.m. He would sit there for long hours, pensive and with his head in his hands, thinking. He would roam about the roads, 'fixing' things up, meeting people who were in need of help, getting into shattered houses and sometimes finding himself in buildings that suddenly collapsed on him. His colleagues of the day, remembering those experiences, stress one factor more than anything else – Menon's total lack of fear.

War work was enough to keep any man excited for the best part of the day – and exhausted for the rest. The way Menon was throwing himself into the air-raid warden's job, one would have thought that he had suspended for the time being his main mission of agitating for Indian freedom. On the contrary, his political activity was accelerated in order to meet the new situation. The main issue thrown up by the war, the issue of freedom versus Fascism, provided an unassailable argument in India's favour. Two days after the declaration of war, the British Government declared India a belligerent. In a proclamation the Viceroy said that what faced the Allies was the duty of safeguarding principles vital to the future of humanity. He expressed his confidence that 'India will make her contribution on the side of human freedom as against the rule of force.'

These were words any Indian nationalist could have used to underline the reasons why the British should quit India. But Britain used them as though 'human freedom' meant British freedom. This attitude touched Indian leaders to the quick. The country had been committed to war without any consultation with any section of Indian opinion. Indeed, the Government had broken its own pledge to the Central Legislature that, without informing it first, Indian troops would not be moved out of India. The British Government's conduct was an affront to India, rendered worse by the fact that all dominions had been consulted by London before they were committed to war.

Indian leaders were particularly hurt because morally and emotionally they were on the side of Britain and would have voluntarily agreed to help in the war effort if they could have done so with honour. It is said that Gandhi, in the course of an interview with the Viceroy, broke down at the thought of enemy planes bombarding and destroying Westminster Abbey and the Houses of Parliament. But there was no question of being forced into the war by an overlord. The Congress therefore decided to oppose the war effort.

Krishna Menon's task in London was to hammer home to the British people the patent injustice of the situation vis-à-vis India. In speeches and pamphlets he argued the case with forceful lucidity. He understood the deep emotions of the British people, caught in the midst of a cruel war, and took pains to explain to them that Indian non-cooperation with the war effort was not because Indian leaders did not sympathize with the plight of Britain. 'At no time,' he said in one of the pamphlets he published at the time, 'has either the Congress or any other group in India adopted isolationism or indifference to the issue in the world struggle for liberty. This is a central factor that withstood the severities and the disillusionments that the incredibly stupid policy of the British Government imposed upon the country and particularly upon her leaders.' He argued that the Indian demand for a National Government was based on the assumption that popular leadership alone would be in a position to organize her defences, maintain the morale of her people by reasonably satisfactory administration and throw in her resources in the fight against Fascism.

In a tract called *India, Britain and Freedom*, he posed the issue directly to the people. After explaining at length the obdurate double standards of the British Government which had led to large-scale conflict in India, he said,

> Where do the people of Britain stand in this struggle? Their aims, their energies and their resources are pledged to the support of National Independence and to the victory over Nazi imperialism. They have proclaimed the unity of the forces of freedom and called to all peoples, conquered and subject, to join with them in the world battle for liberty.
>
> A free India is a potent ally. A subject India is a weak spot in Britain's moral armour and a weak link in the chain of the battlements of world freedom.
>
> The liberation of India is the strongest and most convincing appeal that Britain can make to the subject peoples of Europe to rise against their oppressors. The people of Britain must call upon the Government to apply to India the principles which they have proclaimed on their behalf.

He also took care to point out, characteristically, that Indian freedom against the background of the war was not an exclusively Indian concern; it was an international obligation. He wrote,

> The liberation of India from British imperialism will transform the nature of world imperialism and enlarge the area of world freedom. It will substitute the conception of free co-operation for enforced assistance. It will transform the power relations of other countries and cut at the root causes of international rivalry. Her emancipated people, with their passion for liberty won after ceaseless struggle, would prove by that token alone, ardent champions of freedom in the world. These are not India's gains alone.

The internationalist was being true to form.

By and large the war years represented a period of debate for India. Legal, constitutional and ethical points were heatedly discussed between Indian leaders on the one hand and British politicians on the other, as new responsibilities and anxieties were forced upon them by the war. Menon was in his element. Academic study and long years as a vigilant publicist had sharpened his argumentative faculties. He employed these talents fully to answer every charge that came up, to expose every bit of double-talk by the war cabinet vis-à-vis India and to explain the Indian viewpoint to the outside world.

Events were occurring in quick succession. The Labour Party entered the Government, speeches encouraging to Indian nationalists were heard, Lord Wavell was appointed Viceroy, United States pressure on Britain in favour of India was growing, Sir Stafford Cripps was sent on a mission to India.

Keeping pace with developments, Menon used his platforms to draw public attention to the contradictions and lapses in the British position on India. He was hurt by the failure of his friend, Sir Stafford Cripps, to achieve anything. It was generally believed at the time that Sir Stafford was soon restrained by conservative British influence and made to feel that if he came out for Indian independence, he would be repudiated.

It made Menon bitter. He pounded mercilessly at the Government and especially at Leo Amery, the Secretary of State for India. He emphasized that Amery was interested in maintaining a deadlock in India because negotiations with Indian leaders would be an essential first step in Amery's retreat or extinction. 'The deadlock is his protection,' Menon said, 'but it is our barrier which we must destroy.' He was at his most sarcastic when, in a pamphlet entitled *The Situation in India*, he presented 'the two sides of the conflict in India cast in their truthful roles'. He wrote,

> The Indian people and their national movement as the potential and anxious allies of democracy and unity against Fascism, whom neither Dr Goebbels nor Mr Amery either by propaganda or by provocation, can force into the camp of the enemies of mankind, stand on the one hand, and on the other are the dark forces over which Mr Amery presides, which at the moment have at their disposal the powerful forces of official propaganda, both in this country and in the United States of America, and unhappily find an ally in the comparative indifference – or more truly the lack of coherent and directed activity – of the British people.

As far as the British people were concerned, the campaign was productive. Across the length and breadth of the country groups began demanding negotiations with Indian leaders and unity with India against Fascism. Trade union branches and local councils, followed soon by the national organizations of all the more powerful and representative unions in the country, began passing resolution after resolution making the same demands upon the British Government. The British Council of Churches adopted the cause. A group of twenty-five missionaries who knew India also joined in. A meeting of one hundred liberals from all over the country called upon the India League to appeal to the liberals in the country and utilize liberal opinion for the policy it advocated. There were M.P.s, professional associations and local political groups echoing the cry.

Many people were won over to India by the very spirit of the man who was crusading for her. The way he persistently ignored personal dangers impressed them. In 1941, when he was addressing a meeting in Conway Hall, bombs started falling and panicky people began leaving the hall. The crowd dwindled and dwindled and finally but a dozen people were left. Menon, trying to make his voice heard above the din of the bombs, thundered away with his epigrams, satire and brilliance. Such incidents were frequent. Thousands of ordinary Britons felt that if a man could be so intensely dedicated to a cause that even bombs were unable to stop him, then that cause could only be a righteous one.

The tide of public opinion in favour of the Indian case was unexpected and impressive. It must be remembered that during the war years Government propaganda against the Indian freedom movement was total and vicious – and the Government had a monopoly of the propaganda channels. It was left to one man to break through this steel curtain and mobilize popular opinion in Britain against the Government's obstinate imperial policy.

For the duration of the war, however, public opinion could hardly compel action. Nothing but a stubborn refusal could be expected from the Government because, apart from the inflexible Mr Amery, the Government had at its helm none other than the great man who refused 'to preside over the liquidation of the British Empire'.

What was surprising to Krishna Menon, as to many in India, was that the leaders of the Labour Party were competing with their Tory counterparts in their war-time hostility towards the Indian freedom movement. Always unsympathetic to the Indian cause, in sharp contrast to the attitude of the rank and file, the Labour leadership completely failed to see the validity of India's stand regarding the war and her role in it. Under the strain of the war, it went out of its way to identify itself with the Government of the day and completely ignore its ideological obligations to the larger concept of human freedom. In the August of 1942, when India was trembling under the impact of its greatest mass upsurge, the leadership of the Labour Party wounded many hearts in India by justifying the arrest of Indian leaders as 'a timely and unavoidable precaution'.

Until the war Menon was steadily working among the trade unions and local party groups in the hope that pressure from the rank and file would eventually bring about a change in the higher echelons of the Party. With the war bringing the issue glaringly to the surface and simultaneously pushing the Party leadership into a position which was indistinguishable from that of traditional colonialists, the situation became different.

The official British line, which the Labour Party then acquiesced in, was that as long as any section of opinion in India objected to a constitution giving complete freedom to the country, Britain had no option but to stay on in order to avoid trouble and chaos in India. Since the large and fertile land of India always had groups, officials, vested interests and princes longing for the perpetuation of British rule, this was a line that suited the British genius admirably. That the Labour Party, despite the emergency created by the war, should compromise on principles and agree to a prevaricating policy was a fact that cut into the conscience of Krishna Menon and the many Indian friends of the Party.

Menon sought to make an issue of it at party conferences with the help of resolutions; he was rebuffed by the leadership. The war intensified official Labour disapproval of India's freedom movement just as it intensified Menon's campaign for India. A painful incompatibility arose between Menon and the Labour Party. This eventually led to a parting of the ways which, becoming as it did one of the principal pillars of the international propaganda against him, Krishna Menon was never to forget in later years.

15

Anatomy of a 'Communist'

IT was a month after the outbreak of war that the National Executive of the Labour Party endorsed Krishna Menon's Parliamentary candidature for Dundee, in Scotland. For six hectic months, despite his preoccupations with India and St Pancras, Menon conscientiously nursed the constituency. Then came the rift.

The Party leadership declared itself clearly against India. Krishna Menon accelerated his campaign for India and came into a head-on clash with the official Party line. The circumstances leading up to the final break were described in a letter, written by the Assistant National Agent of the Party in reply to an inquiry in 1958. He wrote,

> In May 1940 the National Executive Committee considered correspondence from Mr Krishna Menon regarding a decision of the Dundee Trades Council and Labour Party to cancel his Parliamentary candidature. An inquiry took place at which Mr Krishna Menon was present to investigate the circumstances which had led to the above decision. The opinion of the members of the National Executive Committee who conducted the inquiry was that the personal position of Mr Krishna Menon was difficult in view of the fact that he represented an important section of Indian public opinion and that his first loyalty appeared to lie in that direction. It was held that while his bona fides as a socialist need not necessarily be raised, it was questionable whether a person having a double loyalty was suitable as a prospective Parliamentary Labour candidate. After considering all the facts the National Executive Committee decided that the endorsement of Mr Krishna Menon's candidature for

Dundee be withdrawn. Mr Krishna Menon resigned from
the Labour Party in January 1941.

The false impression that Menon was 'expelled' from the
Labour Party because of his communist affiliations has persisted
through the years. This is obviously a distortion of facts. The
Labour Party's leadership did indeed often worry about where
Menon stood. But their real objection to him was based entirely
on the embarrassment he was causing to them on the India issue.

As a crusader for Indian independence, Menon employed the
tactics of sponsoring resolutions in local parties, trade union
branches, etc. These tactics succeeded with the spirited support of
the intellectuals, some trade unions and to a certain extent the
Communist Party. The Right-wing leadership, uninterested in
India as such, labelled Menon's efforts simply as part of the
communist effort to embarrass the conduct of the war.

This was the basic mistake of the Labour leadership. Menon's
aim was Indian freedom, and he would have been a fool to refuse
willing help from people who volunteered it, whether communists
or socialists. It no more proved him a communist than consorting
with Stalin made Churchill and Roosevelt communists. Nor did
his resignation from the Labour Party make him a communist
any more than actual expulsion by the Party made Cripps and
Bevan communist.

Labour leadership was convinced that Menon was a nuisance
before they began to whisper that he was a communist. As soon
as they realized that he was a thorn in their flesh and that they
would be better off without him, they began seeking the best
means of liquidation. Dubbing him a communist was the first
obvious thing to do. When Menon defended himself in a series of
letters to the Party, the leadership realized that they were getting
into deep waters. Then they changed tactics and said that it
would be better if an Indian did not make use of the Party to
enter Parliament. Menon wrote back asking whether there were
two classes of membership in the Party.

But there was little scope for logical argument. The Labour
leadership believed with the Tories that Indian freedom would
hamper the war effort and that the Indian on the spot had
therefore to be kept out of the picture. When they withdrew the
endorsement of his candidature, Menon did not look upon it as an

occasion to choose between membership of the British Parliament and work for India. He resigned from the Party rather than suspend his agitation for Indian freedom.

In his contacts with communists in Britain, which were regular and often intimate, Menon was sticking to the general pattern of the day. The London School of Economics had made him personally receptive to neo-Marxist ideas. But it was as a strategic necessity in his campaign for India that he took full advantage of communist leaders and communist-front organizations in Britain. The Communist Party was then the only party in Britain which unreservedly supported Indian independence. To Menon his cause alone mattered and anyone who was willing to support it was welcome on his platform. He was making good use of the communists. It is possible that the communists thought that they were making good use of him too. But if they did, they soon became wiser. Communist leaders both in Britain and in India are either confused or plainly derogatory when they are asked to give their opinion of Menon.

Many leading Labour M.P.s who worked closely with Menon agree that his views are incompatible with communism. According to Sidney Silverman, Menon had, 'like the rest of us', some sympathy for the Russian revolution. 'The reactionaries hate communists more for their triumphs than for their crimes. This we do not do. We sympathize with their triumphs but are not blind to their blunders. I don't think that Krishna Menon had ever been closer to communists than Nehru has been since.'

Reginald Sorensen put it most profoundly when he told the author, 'Krishna Menon will be one of the first martyrs if ever communism dominates India.'

These unequivocal views of men who knew Krishna Menon personally, and for many years, reflect an understanding of Menon's derision for any philosophy that seeks to overstep the bounds of constitutionalism and approves of extra-parliamentary methods as a means to achieve its objectives; his training and temperament render him singularly unsuited to acquiesce in such means. Menon had even opposed Gandhi's first non-co-operation movement because he agreed with Mrs Annie Besant that breaking the laws was wrong. The entire record of his crusading years and his public activities after 1947 underscore the man's predilection for the machinery of parliamentary democracy and his ability to use existing laws to create new laws that would defeat injustice. Among those who have understood this trait in him is Kingsley Martin, who told the author simply, 'Krishna is pro-Indian and pro-Krishna. He has no other allegiance.'

In a 1955 profile of Krishna Menon, Kingsley Martin's *New Statesman* referred to the Labour Party's position in the 'thirties and said,

> The official Labour leadership at this time naturally believed – or at any rate alleged – that Menon was in effect a communist. But this was not so. Like a great many other militant but non-communist Left-wingers at the time, he was associated *ad hoc* with all sorts of fellow-travelling activities and people. He was certainly a Marxist, but he has always been far too much of an individualist – and a Gandhi-ite too – to toe the Party line and probably no one who has ever known him personally, including even his opponents on the far right of the St Pancras Labour Party, has ever believed that he was anything other than a fiercely passionate and independent socialist with no use for money (which to this day he never carries on his person) or personal reward.

Menon himself gave early evidence of his disdain for communism in some letters he wrote as long ago as 1930. The Indian Labour Committee was just being set up by the India League and Menon wrote to *New India* of Madras: 'I hope that this Committee will be helped by Indian Labour to counteract some of the propaganda by the communist bodies here.' After the formation of the Committee he wrote in a personal letter to B. Shiva Rao, 'We would like you to put us in touch with all the trade unions in India. Of course I mean the trade unions, not just the communist unions.'

These views were expressed before the great purges in Russia, when it was the vogue among the intelligentsia to sing the praises of Soviet Russia and communism. The pages of the weekly *Congress Socialist* bear witness to the adoration with which such leading latter-day anti-communists as M. R. Masani and Asoka Mehta looked upon the Russian experiment in the 'thirties. It was at a time like this, when the Soviet Union and the British Communist Party were objects of admiration in India, that Menon wrote to his friends about the need to counteract communist propaganda, etc. It cannot be that Menon changed his views completely after 1940 when everyone else changed the other way about.

There is no doubt that with more tact and a better understanding of the importance of his public image, Krishna Menon could have effectively silenced all talk of his being a communist. During the war in particular, when communists were being freely called fifth columnists, Menon could have been more cautious about sharing platforms with them and participating in their processions. If he realized that open association was a liability to the cause he was expounding, he did not show any sign of it; he went on taking from all quarters whatever support he could muster for India.

This tactlessness continued during his years in the United Nations. The peculiar character of Indian diplomacy put him right in the centre of many bitter ideological wrangles and, although he has successfully solved some of the worst problems that have faced the United Nations, the frequent impression was that Menon was surreptitiously trying to promote Soviet objectives at the expense of the Western alliance.

In recent years, whenever the charge of being a disguised communist has been levelled against him, he has reacted with either poisoned invective or lordly contempt. He has never made any attempt at explanation, for he believes an explanation is an admission of guilt. When an interviewer once asked him whether he would deny the oft-repeated charge, Menon said, 'No. This is not a question of my ideology or my beliefs; it is a question of my honesty and bona fides ... I am not going to issue any contradiction. If I can masquerade as a crypto-communist, if I am dishonest, I can swear by the name of all the gods I know. Those who do not trust me will say that this contradiction is another piece of chicanery and double-dealing.'[1]

[1] The *Bharat Jyoti* (Bombay), February 18th, 1962.

16

An End and a Beginning

MENON'S break with the Labour Party lasted nearly four years, during which period he sat on the St Pancras Council as an independent member. The break only added strength to his campaign for India. The repression that followed the Quit India movement in August 1942 gave him powerful talking-points. In October, acting on a message received from Nehru earlier, he launched an India League drive to get the Allies to 'acknowledge the independence of India'. Efforts were made directly to persuade Roosevelt, Stalin and Chiang Kai-shek to urge such acknowledgment on Britain.

War produced a surge of American opinion in favour of India. The discordant notes that came from Washington and from certain publicists were drowned in the spirited speeches and writings of Wendell Willkie, Henry Wallace, Lin Yutang, Pearl Buck, Louis Fischer. Even *Life* magazine wrote an open letter to the British people saying, 'We Americans may have some disagreement among ourselves as to what we are fighting for, but one thing we are sure we are not fighting for is to hold the Empire together.' In Britain Harold Laski raised the same point when he said at the Labour Party conference in 1942, 'Mr Churchill has agreed that this is a people's war. We mean to win it, but we want from him a pledge that the people's war will issue in a people's peace. So far Mr Churchill has evaded that assurance. He has talked of victory in terms of the old world that is dying, not of the new world struggling to be born.'

To squeeze the maximum benefit out of the surge of American goodwill, Menon planned a trip to the United States. But before he could leave London there was a burst of hope on the Indian horizon.

In 1943 Lord Wavell was named Viceroy of India. Wavell had already kindled optimism in India by publicly stating that political progress in India was not debarred during the war. With his appointment as Viceroy, India expected a period of conciliation and political reform.

Menon saw in the developing situation encouraging portents for India. He stepped up intensive propaganda among the people and particularly inside the Labour Party. His theme was that the British Government's professed aims of freedom and justice were not being applied to India; practice was different from precept. The liberal-minded leaders of the Labour Party gave him stout support. Trade unions, study groups and local branches of the Party began feeling the impact of his constant pounding.

Some action followed. More than fourteen organizations submitted resolutions to be considered by the Party; they all criticized the leaders who were in the Government and demanded a fresh start in India. In July 1943 the India League headed the list of several non-party organizations that held meetings and demanded that Indian leaders be released from jail and invited to negotiations. Menon persuaded Lindsay Drummond to publish an 80-page booklet containing Gandhi's writings and speeches. This was the more effective for carrying no preface or comments; the readers knew that the purpose of the booklet was not propaganda but education. Eagerly watched and in some cases directly inspired by Menon, the Party's various wings began moving out of the shadow of the conservatives and putting out feelers towards a new policy on India. The net result was that at the Party conference towards the end of 1943 Arthur Greenwood gave a pledge that fresh consideration would be given by the Executive to the Indian problem.

Once he saw that the Executive was beginning to come round, Menon went all out to increase the pressure. The intensity of his lobbying broke all previous records. He worked particularly on the trade unions because that was where the greatest goodwill towards India existed. The response was immediate and encouraging. Many unions expressed strong disapproval of the prevaricating attitude adopted by Labour leaders in the Government and began to discuss what they could do about it.

The mood was perceptibly changing. Menon became anxious to ensure that this mood was canalized into some form of action. He felt it was necessary to clinch the issue at the next annual conference of the Party. Fortunately Harold Laski was now the

National Chairman of the Party. Menon, Reginald Sorensen and others met Laski and held discussions on the subject. They were agreed that the Indian question should somehow be brought up at the conference.

Laski succeeded. When the Party met in December 1944 there were two resolutions on India. Both came up for debate on the last day of the conference, December 15th. Behind the scenes Menon was both shrewd and tactful. On the one hand, men like Sorensen and Silverman who had been identified with the India League remained strictly in the background. On the other, a really powerful union was persuaded to table the first resolution.

C. Bridges, on behalf of the National Union of Railwaymen, moved a resolution affirming the conference's belief that 'the granting of freedom to the people of India to establish an independent Indian National Government will be a decisive factor in the fight against Fascism'. The resolution urged 'the immediate ending of the political deadlock by negotiation with all leaders of the Indian people with a view to the formation of a responsible National Government which will rally the entire population of India to the anti-Fascist cause'. As a necessary first step the resolution called for the release of all Indian political leaders.

J. Stanley of the Constructional Engineering Union followed with a resolution calling for early negotiations with India's popular leaders 'with the ultimate object of India being given a place in the British Commonwealth of Nations similar to that enjoyed by the other partners'.

A heated debate ensued. J. Walker on behalf of the Party Executive said that they were prepared to accept the second resolution, but asked the conference to reject the N.U.R. motion as going much farther than any previous resolution. It was, he said, equivalent to a demand that Britain should quit India tomorrow in spite of the Japanese menace. Would it not be irresponsible for Britain to wash her hands of India just when India was in trouble? If she did, would not Indians settle their differences 'in the one way it would be settled when people felt strongly'? The Executive, Walker promised in one final show of magnanimity, would be behind none in a desire to see agreement reached and an end to British rule in India at a very early date.

Then it was time for decision. The second resolution was put to the vote first. It was passed. The N.U.R. motion followed. It was carried by a large majority. The Labour Party stood strongly committed.

It was a moment of triumph for the India League. Two decades of intensive work had borne fruit. The sweat and the sacrifices, the agony and the tears were not in vain. Proudly, Krishna Menon returned to the Labour Party as a member.

The official Labour commitment could not have come at a more opportune moment. Weeks after the annual conference dispersed there began a quick succession of events – the end of the war in Europe, the collapse of the coalition in Britain, the General Election, the exit of Churchill. In July 1945 the Labour Party suddenly found itself in power.

Labour in power! And a Labour Party that had made a firm commitment to establish 'an independent Indian National Government'. This was the chance calculation on which Menon had begun his work in 1930. Often it had seemed a vain hope. But now it stood as a reality before the world. Would the Labour Government, with the eyes of the world now upon it, dare go against the mandate of its own members and stall Indian independence?

A month after taking office, the Labour Government announced a 'gift' to India – a general election to 'help India decide its own future'. But the Congress refused to be impressed. It said publicly that '[the new] proposals repeat, with unimportant variations, the offer made in 1942 by Sir Stafford Cripps. Neither the end of the war nor the change of Government in Great Britain appears to have resulted in any real change in British policy towards India.'

When he saw that the Labour Government was only trying to postpone action in India, Krishna Menon grew bitter. The bitterness was shared by many others. In order to provide a public outlet for these emotions, Menon organized a Nehru birthday-celebration meeting in November 1945 on a scale never attempted before. The venue was the St Pancras Town Hall and the principal speaker was Harold Laski. Menon spent long hours in discussions with Laski over the Government's perfidy and the all-round resentment its policies were creating. The speech Laski made at the meeting must be considered a landmark in the history of India's struggle for freedom.

Remarking that he had no desire to cause alarm and that he

was speaking for himself 'an English citizen and a citizen of the wider commonwealth beyond', Laski said,

> When are we going to realize our sense of responsibility towards the Indian people? ... Indian freedom is inevitable and inescapable, and what we have to decide is whether that freedom shall come gracefully by British co-operation or, instead, by British hostility. We have to decide whether we are capable as a Labour Party and a Labour movement of moving forward swiftly to the proud day when we can claim that we have assisted in the emancipation of a great civilization. We have to make up our minds ... A Labour Party which is unwilling to play its full part in the emancipation of India will, sooner or later, be unwilling to play its full part in the emancipation of the British working class. As a movement that is part of the international movement for human emancipation, a Labour Party which fails this test will pass from the historic scene, for the Indian problem is part of a much wider and more vital issue – the end of imperialism everywhere ... Freedom and democracy know no bar or colour, religion, class or birth, and unless we in this country are willing to play our full part on behalf of those people who until now have been bidden by us to hang their heads, we are not only betraying them and ourselves, but those men and women who in these past six years we asked to go out and die. Either we asked them to die for a dream we resolved to make true, or we asked them to die for a lie. That is the choice before this generation.

It was one of the most stirring speeches ever heard in St Pancras. A record audience had assembled and Laski's thrusts were frequently punctuated by enthusiastic cheers. Often the speaker had to take hold of the microphone to make himself heard above the din of applause.

Menon sat there enthralled. For once he felt overwhelmed. The sentiments were moving, the words expressing them powerful. His beloved teacher and friend had justified his expectations.

While the Congress strongly condemned the General Election 'gift' from London, it decided to fight the election 'in order to demonstrate the will of the people'. The nation went to the polls in November–December 1945. The Congress emerged with 91 per cent of the general seats (i.e. seats not reserved on a communal basis) in the Central Assembly. Later it obtained clear majorities in eight out of the eleven provinces. Britain's prolonged efforts to strengthen and protect the Muslim League also paid off; the League won all the 30 Muslim seats in the Central Legislature and 427 out of the 507 in the provinces. The 'will of the people' left the Congress and the League as the only parties that mattered.

Events were now pushing the Attlee Government forward. The criticism from party sources was mounting. The war had seriously depleted the British exchequer and Whitehall had found it necessary to write to Lord Wavell, the Viceroy, that 'England will not be able hereafter to spare one single man or one single farthing for the governance of India.'[1] On top of it had come the clear verdict of the Indian electorate which made it obligatory for the British Government to proceed to the next logical step. In February 1946 the Indian Navy mutinied and the British authorities became really nervous for the first time.

On February 19th, the day the naval mutiny broke out in Bombay, Mr Attlee announced the appointment of a Cabinet Mission 'to promote in conjunction with the leaders of Indian opinion the early realization of full self-government in India.'

With the appointment of the Cabinet Mission the Indian independence movement underwent a change, for it made clear that at last the British Government had decided to call it a day. The question was no longer how to wrest independence from unwilling hands, but what kind of independence to negotiate. It suddenly became important to have precise ideas on the legal and constitutional basis on which a subject nation could become free.

The agitator of the India League now became a negotiator. Without official position Menon greatly influenced the course of the negotiations by evolving formulas out of deadlocks and by suggesting practical methods to tide over legal difficulties. He was able to play this role because Jawaharlal Nehru was anxious to have Menon by his side during those crucial weeks.

Nehru had his reasons. The complicated character of the negotiations made him realize that two heads were better than

[1] *Political Memoirs*, by Dr N. B. Khare (Nagpur, 1959), p. 118. Dr Khare, a leader of the Hindu Mahasabha, was a Member of the Viceroy's Executive Council at the time.

one. Under the pressure of events, the top leaders of the Congress were drifting apart, even Gandhi becoming ultimately isolated from the Party. Nehru felt lonely. The future constitution of India and similar fundamentals were being discussed, many decisions being taken; Nehru could not do better than summon the friend who shared with him his basic beliefs. Besides, the discussions were often technical and called for a deep knowledge of the skill of British negotiators as well as of the mainsprings of British democratic thought. No one was better qualified to participate in such discussions than Menon. He began to travel back and forth between India and London.

A single-minded objective informed all Menon's actions in the months ahead – to avoid arguments and get power transferred without more ado. He was suspicious of any move from Britain to prolong the proceedings or, worse still, to transfer power in such a way as would take the glow out of freedom. He was even suspicious of the Cabinet Mission. Lord Pethwick-Lawrence, leader of the Mission, told the author, 'At first Menon was not impressed with our effort. But gradually he came to realize that we were doing some good work. Then he appreciated it readily.'

In May 1946 the Cabinet Mission published its plan. It was a plan that would have given the Indian Union a weak central government and enabled the Muslim-majority states to secede from the Union. But it had some attractive features. It formally rejected the plea for Pakistan. It proposed a Constituent Assembly to frame a constitution. It suggested an interim Government supported by all the parties to rule until the constitution was framed.

The League accepted the plan, for it thought that the right to secede in effect included Pakistan. For the same reason the Congress rejected the plan. Menon's advice to Nehru at the time was that the Cabinet Mission's recommendation with regard to the setting up of the Constituent Assembly should be accepted. It was his belief that once Indians framed a constitution of their own and once the foreign rulers left the scene, communal and other problems in the country could be contained. The Congress accepted the proposal to set up a Constituent Assembly.

Following the Congress decision not to participate in the interim Government, the Viceroy dropped the idea. This stung Jinnah, who was hoping to be called upon to form the Government. He withdrew his acceptance of the Cabinet Mission plan and threatened direct action.

Menon saw a new opportunity in the League's withdrawal of support to the Cabinet Mission plan. He thought it was an occasion for the Congress to change tactics. He sounded out Wavell as to whether a Congress offer to form the Government by itself would be accepted. On getting the green light from the Viceroy's House, he convinced Nehru of the tactical advantages of forming an interim Government. The important thing was to get power, to end the foreign rule. Once a Government was set up, other problems could be tackled effectively.

The Congress agreed. The Viceroy invited Nehru to set up an interim Government and on August 24th Nehru submitted a list of twelve names. On September 2nd the Government took office.

Krishna Menon was certain that the Muslim League had now lost the battle for good. The direct action called for by the League had taken place on August 16th, a day before Wavell reached final agreement with Nehru. The direct action had released a cyclone of communal rioting and in the gutters of Calcutta city alone some four thousand people lay dead. That Wavell still called upon the Congress to form the interim Government was interpreted by the Congress as an indication of his determination to ditch the Muslim League. Menon also made a note of the fact that London had clearly instructed Delhi to leave all future initiative to Nehru, the interim Prime Minister. This meant that the Congress and Nehru could carry on henceforth as a *de facto* sovereign government.

However, five weeks after the interim Government took office, Jinnah announced the Muslim League's decision to enter the Government after all. It actually did so on October 25th. Pyarelal, Gandhi's secretary, writes in his book *The Last Phase*:

> On the day the Muslim League was admitted into the interim Government on the Viceroy's initiative and invitation the battle of undivided India was irretrievably lost. His Majesty's Government had issued clear instructions that, Pandit Nehru having been asked to form the interim Government, further steps for bringing in the League should be left, on the analogy of the Cabinet system, entirely to him. Some members of the Cabinet Mission are reported to have

expressed surprise when they learned that the League had
been brought in by the Viceroy instead. How it happened
then and how the Congress acquiesced in such a procedure
are questions for the future historian to unravel.

It remains to be seen how far future historians will be able to
go without the co-operation of present history-makers. The
Congress leaders who are in a position to reveal the details of the
manœuvres that went on keep their lips sealed. For his part,
Menon will not go into any of the specific problems of the day,
saying simply that some of the crucial decisions were thrown at
him as faits accomplis. When he tried to point out the dangerous
implications of this or that decision, he was merely told that the
Congress had already committed itself.

It is possible that Nehru knew of Jinnah's intention to get
back into the interim Government and that, knowing it, he
acquiesced or was forced to acquiesce in it. It is possible also that
Whitehall, sensing that it was helping to liquidate its protégé,
instructed the Viceroy to go back on his word and ensure the
admission of the League. The acquiescence by the Congress was
one of those mistakes that slowly and inexorably built up the
foundations of Pakistan.

Meanwhile, the Congress was busy preparing itself for the
responsibility of Government. While negotiations went on on the
one side, on the other, the Congress set up various committees
to prepare reports which could become the basis of policy once it
assumed power. Many of these reports bear the personal stamp of
Krishna Menon. He wrote reports for Nehru and even for
Mountbatten.

One of the most important fields of study at this time was
defence. During the war, at the instance of Sir Stafford Cripps,
Menon had already made a study of military matters and written
a report on how India could be defended against Japan if the
Congress agreed to help the war effort. Now, on the eve of
independence, Indian defence problems had to be viewed from
a different angle. Again it was Menon who was entrusted with the
task, for already he had established a reputation in Britain as an
expert on defence.

For his report Menon made a thorough strategic study of

modern defence methods in the context of the developing cold war. He saw defence as essentially an element of foreign policy. The major point he made in his report then became, when he was Minister of Defence, a constant refrain in his speeches – that a country is not defended by its soldiers as much as by its national consciousness and the relative independence of its troops in equipment and supplies.

The Congress had set up an Expert Committee to prepare a draft constitution. Nehru wanted the committee to consult Menon, and Menon spent several days in August with its members. In his usual thorough manner, he prepared a 70-clause constitution which aimed at providing the benefits of an unwritten constitution along with the requirements of a written one. It envisaged power being vested in the people and not in the rulers. This would have meant the automatic integration into the Indian Union of the 554 princely states which later became Sardar Patel's primary problem. Menon had written into his constitution several basic principles aimed at transforming the Union into a socialist Welfare State. The Expert Committee, in no hurry for socialism or welfare, quietly spiked the draft. Menon remembers it today as 'an experiment that failed'.

In September Nehru commissioned Menon to write a report on the organization of the foreign service. He was also appointed Nehru's personal representative to tour world capitals to arrange for the establishment of diplomatic relations as soon as freedom dawned.

One of his activities which drew considerable attention at the time was a two-hour conference he had in Paris with the Soviet Foreign Minister, Molotov. In the Central Legislative Assembly later, Nehru explained that he had sent Menon to Paris to convey to Molotov 'the interim Government's greetings and also its request for food supplies from Russia' as well as to negotiate an exchange of diplomatic representatives. In October Menon went to the United States as alternate delegate to Lake Success where, in trusteeship meetings, he proved, in the words of the New York *Herald Tribune*, 'one of the most militant champions of colonial people'.

It was the beginning of the roving ambassador, the representative of Nehru, the negotiator, the militant voice at the United Nations.

As far as Nehru and Menon were concerned, this was the most natural thing to happen. They had known and understood each other from 1935. At international conferences Menon had already represented Nehru and the Congress, and Nehru knew how ably. When the first stirrings of freedom were felt in India, he had no difficulty in choosing the man he wanted. Nor did Menon have any difficulty in fitting into the new setting. To him, as to Nehru, it was merely the continuation of a relationship that had stood the test of time. But not all were happy. The sudden appearance in India of a man they had only vaguely heard about made many Indian leaders sceptical. When it became clear that he was exercising considerable influence on events, the scepticism developed into resentment. They knew little of Menon's long years of sacrifice in London or of his towering intellect. They felt therefore that Menon was usurping their right to be close to the Prime Minister. Unconsciously and perhaps inevitably the decks were being cleared for many a future feud over personalities.

But Menon was moving forward like a relentless force. Once the Muslim League was accepted into the Government, he realized that the game was up. The League had again become established in a bargaining position, League members were sabotaging the interim Government, and talk and more talk was going on. In London, Menon began putting pressure on friendly Labour leaders to ensure a decisive step forward. It is said that it was Menon who, through his Party contacts, first urged that the British Government should fix a definite date for transferring power. Such a move would not only establish British bona fides but also convince the feuding parties that they had no alternative but to arrive at some understanding or another.

On February 20th, 1947, Mr Attlee announced in the House of Commons that the Government had decided to transfer power by June 1948 whether or not an Indian constitution was ready by then. Simultaneously Earl Mountbatten was named Viceroy.

Mountbatten arrived in Delhi in March. He came in a hurry and began work in a hurry. The Hindu communal parties in the country interpreted the recall of Wavell and the appointment of Mountbatten as definite indications of Britain's decision to partition the country and to give Jinnah his pound of flesh. Mountbatten's hurry confirmed this impression.

By now Krishna Menon had established residence at the

Prime Minister's house in Delhi. He was in the forefront of discussions.

At the beginning Mountbatten was in a mood to consider any proposal that would make transfer of power possible without partition. The talks began with the Independent Sovereign Republic formula for which 'part of the original responsibility' was Menon's. Many were the breakfast meetings and informal discussions during which Menon explained to the Mountbatten entourage the origin of the Muslim League and its leadership, the role Britain had played in building up the Muslim demand, the sensitivity of Indians over the extent of freedom that would emerge from the talks under way, the historical perspective of it all. He talked about 'Indian desire for common citizenship but not Dominion Status. He wants what he calls reciprocity.'[1]

That was an unfamiliar word to most Indian leaders. In Menon's own case, it was an echo from the past. Mrs Annie Besant had, in 1917, introduced for the first time the principle of reciprocity between India and Great Britain. She had argued for it while simultaneously urging India to remain a part of the Commonwealth under the British Crown. It seemed a strange combination of ideas when Mrs Besant first put it forward, but history was now vindicating her. Ironically, her own disciple was one of the principal instruments chosen to do so.

The Independent Sovereign Republic idea was creating complications. The British Parliament was not competent to legislate a Republic into being. However, it was open to Parliament to create a Dominion. Once independence was accomplished, on whatever basis, India could move under her own steam and do what she liked. The overriding question at the moment was to achieve independence and to do it in a short time. In order to prevent a drift into costly controversy and with the legal problem well in mind, Menon suggested a speedy transfer of power on the basis of Dominion Status. This is what eventually brought freedom almost a year in advance of the date fixed by Attlee.

But Dominion Status was a phrase that aroused the suspicions of Indian leaders. The moment it became a point of discussion voices of protest rose in India. The Congress Socialist Party even organized a campaign against the move, pronouncing it reactionary.

[1] *Mission with Mountbatten*, by Alan Campbell-Johnson.

An End and a Beginning

This was a hangover of the 1930 battle against the idea of Dominion Status. At that time Menon himself had fought against it. But the legal and political context had changed. For one thing, the Statute of Westminster had come into force. For another, Menon had believed in the earlier years that if a person like Winston Churchill had accepted the idea of Dominion Status, it could not have been real freedom for India.

Menon produced the Statute of Westminster and argued that Dominion Status was nothing short of complete independence in practice. Under the dateline of May 10th, 1947, Campbell-Johnson writes in his book, 'At our staff meeting today Mountbatten reported on a breakfast meeting he had had with Krishna Menon. Dominion Status formula seems to be appealing increasingly to Congress leaders. Menon takes credit as the first man to suggest an early transfer of power to India on this basis.'

The formula was excellent as a legal basis for transferring power. But the political problem posed by the Muslim League proved insoluble. This became evident by April or May.

Lord Ismay, Mountbatten's Chief of Staff, had flown to London with a complete plan prepared within six weeks of the new Viceroy's arrival in New Delhi. Mountbatten, having shifted his residence to Simla for the summer, invited Nehru over for talks. Nehru, accompanied by Menon, went to Simla on May 8th. Two days later the plan came back from London with the British Government's suggested alterations. Mountbatten thought he would show it to Nehru.

When he saw the plan, Nehru's reaction was vehement. London had made drastic changes and visualized an India that would be hopelessly balkanized.

Nehru later sent a note to the Viceroy embodying his views. The note, in the drafting of which Menon had taken a leading part, throws significant light on the way he was approaching the negotiations as a whole. It called the plan a threat to future Indo-British relations, and said,

> Instead of producing any sense of certainty, security and stability, they [the proposals] would encourage disruptive tendencies everywhere and chaos and weakness. They would particularly endanger important strategic areas ... The proposal that each of the successor states should conclude

independent treaties, presumably also with His Majesty's Government, is likely to create many 'Ulsters' in India which will be looked upon as so many British bases on Indian soil ... The acquiescence on the part of the Congress in the splitting up of those areas which were predominantly League in their loyalty was in no wise an acquiescence in throwing overboard the all-India basis of future settlement.

London apparently was anxious to keep the League in the centre of things, Jinnah was being a master tactician, Mountbatten was concerned only with the time-factor and the Congress leaders were getting impatient. Gradually and inescapably thoughts were leading to partition.

It was during those days in Simla that Krishna Menon was finally convinced of the inevitability of partition. However, the partition he had thought of as a practical solution to the Congress-League rift was different from Jinnah's partition. What he envisaged was an India in which Muslim-majority areas would be constituted into autonomous units but the outer boundary of the country would be maintained as it was. He argued that the partition of provinces on communal lines was not at all inconsistent with an all-India union of both separated parts.

If the Congress had been firm on a partition of this kind, perhaps it could have accomplished it. But the Congress was anything but firm. And Jinnah was in no mood for nice formulas. He saw his quarry cornered and nothing but the final kill would satisfy him.

Bowing before the realities, Menon created a new slogan: Save As Much Of India As Possible. He pointed out that with partition only half of Bengal and Punjab would go, while on the basis of the British plan, the two provinces would be wholly lost. He was the one to propose the retention by India of the city of Calcutta in return for Chittagong's going to Pakistan.

Mountbatten went to London in the middle of May and when he returned towards the end of the month with an approved plan for partition and the new deadline of August 15th, 1947, he found all leaders accepting it – some with unconcealed joy, others sorrowfully.

Partition was a cruel solution to a cruel problem. The impatience of Congress leaders combined with an explosion of communal hatred to make it possible. Also at work was a certain cynicism on the part of Whitehall. It saw partition as a formula that would prevent communal violence and destruction in India. But the formula produced just the opposite of what might have been intended.

The deed was signed. A non-violent struggle reached a violent climax.

August 14th–15th, 1947. Krishna Menon was not in India to witness the great events of that night – or the great tragedies. It was only fitting that the moment of fulfilment should find him at the spot from which he had worked for just that end.

It was a memorable night at the India League – the little office off the Strand in London which had been command headquarters for two gruelling decades. A small crowd had assembled there, all devoted friends of India who had been labouring for the cause for many years. At the stroke of midnight a solemn stillness descended upon the group. One of the oldest workers unfurled a flag – the first Indian tricolour to flutter in the cold wind of London. Someone sang the 'Jana Gana Mana'.

17

Look back with Pride

IT was as a youth of twenty-eight that Krishna Menon landed in London. When his crusade ended with independence he was fifty-one.

It was a long innings. Twenty-three years! He had begun with health – and ended with a walking-stick. He had begun as a theosophist – and ended as a politician. He had begun with no hopes of accomplishing the mission in his generation – and suddenly the mission had ended in triumph.

From the threshold of old age he could look back upon a period of brilliant achievement. Besides being an agitator for Indian freedom, he had also been a student, a journalist, a borough councillor, a Labour Party leader, a publisher and a barrister. In the midst of it all, he had also been an errand-boy for all kinds of friends. An acquaintance from his home town of Calicut once sent Menon a bunch of poems in Malayalam with instructions that Menon should translate them into English and arrange to have them published in London. B. Shiva Rao, on a trip to Geneva, had sent his luggage on to London and wanted Menon to clear it at the customs, open one of the trunks, take out a few shirts and a suit and then forward the clothes to Geneva, holding the rest of the luggage in London for his arrival. Vijayalaxmi Pandit wrote to him in 1939 from Almora Hills, referring to her husband's nephew and niece who were going up to Cambridge, 'I'm writing this to ask if you will be a dear and keep an eye on these kids while they are in England ... Do "mother" them a bit.' Menon obliged them all.

He was rich in friends. One of them recalls that he was at once generous and 'expensive'.

When Menon had money it was everybody's property. He would spend it all on you. The moment it was exhausted, he

148

would ungrudgingly go into a period of abstemiousness. He could starve for many days without feeling the worse for it. But sometimes, when he was broke, he would invite an intimate friend to dinner in the best hotel. He would ask other guests too. After a good time was had by all, he would quietly arrange for the bill to go to the bewildered friend. We had to pay heavily for Menon's friendship!

He was a man with 'a terrific reputation among those of us who were Left', as several Englishmen remember. Even those who heard him only once cherish memories of the experience. A Dundee citizen recalls the day Menon journeyed to his city to address a public meeting.

> [At the railway station] I was surprised to see him walking with the aid of a stick. We didn't ask him what was wrong with his feet as he did not strike us as the type of person who would take kindly to personal inquiries about his health, nor desire sympathy ... Our chairman was a humble worker in the jute mills and it was to his council house that we were going for tea before the meeting. We wondered how our conversation would strike this talented, brilliant man who knew so much more than we did. We need not have worried. Krishna Menon, who appeared tired and not too well, fitted into the little sitting-room and talked to us and questioned us about problems in Dundee.

With good humour, patent sincerity and, of course, his sharp intellect, Menon was able to create a tremendous impression among the ordinary people of Britain. This was a significant aspect of his work in Britain, because over the years he developed an emotional link with the common man which has today become his principal source of inspiration.

One field where Menon met with little success in London was legal practice. His career as a barrister never went far. For one thing, most of the briefs he accepted were from impecunious Indian lascars who had found themselves in trouble in the United Kingdom. They neither brought him money, nor enhanced his professional reputation. He fought a couple of cases in the Privy Council in which some leading families of his native Malabar were involved. This probably sent his stock up a little in Malabar – but Malabar was far away. One leading M.P. told the author in London that colour prejudice was a serious factor that worked against Menon as a barrister. 'There is no use our trying to pretend that we were above all that.'

If failure was his fate as a lawyer, outstanding was his success as an editor and publisher. Ever since he joined the London School of Economics, he had been in close touch with publishers and writers. In 1932 the Bodley Head invited him to be one of their editors. For three years he worked in that capacity.

His most important contribution to the firm during the period was the concept and organization of what he called the Twentieth-Century Library. The plan was to bring out serious books dealing with problems of wide social interest 'in the context of a changing civilization'. The idea being Menon's, he strove hard to line up leading experts on various subjects and make them write the kind of books he wanted. In a couple of years the Twentieth-Century Library brought out such books as *Democracy* by J. A. Hobson, *The Jews* by Professor Norman Bentwich, *The Home* by Naomi Mitchison, *Art* by Eric Gill, *Property* by H. L. Beales, *The Black Races* by J. H. Drieberg, *The Theatre* by Theodore Komisarjevsky, *The Town* by David Glass, *Communism* by Ralph Fox and *Women* by Winifred Holtby.

For another firm of publishers, Selwyn and Blount, Menon edited a series called Topical Books. Among these were *My England* by George Lansbury, *Why Fascism?* by Ellen Wilkinson and Edward Conze, *Crisis in Europe* by Professor B. W. Maxwell and *I Will Not Rest* by Romain Rolland, translated by K. S. Shelvankar, a journalist and friend of Menon. It may be mentioned, by the way, that a U.S. magazine article once took great pains to establish Krishna Menon's communist loyalties and, as evidence, stated that Menon had inspired and published in London a book called 'Communism'.

The greatest monument to Krishna Menon's genius as a publisher, however, is the institution of Penguin-Pelicans. As a newcomer in London, avidly devouring books, Menon had been seized by a desire to flood the markets with cheap paperback editions of worthwhile books so that people with limited funds, people like him, could benefit from the best. He discussed his pet dream with many friends, among them a young colleague at the Bodley Head named Allen Lane.

Look back with Pride

In 1935 the two young men decided to quit the Bodley Head. With a hundred pounds as their capital they set up business in the crypt of the St Pancras Parish Church. There were born the fabulous birds. Lane edited the fiction under the name of Penguins while Menon looked after the non-fiction labelled Pelicans. Among the books Menon obtained for this series were the two-volume *The Intelligent Woman's Guide to Socialism, Capitalism, Sovietism, and Fascism* by Bernard Shaw, *A Short History of the World* by H. G. Wells and Sir James Jeans's *The Mysterious Universe.*

It was a partnership that would have made Krishna Menon wealthy. But it did not last. Lane often found Menon a strain on his patience. Sometimes he was too idealistic to appeal to Lane's business sense. One day Menon asked Lane to meet him at the Vigo restaurant in Soho. For an hour the Indian lectured the Englishman on grand schemes. Lane did not follow half of what Menon said; he was talking too fast and his voice was too low and muffled. In a moment of sheer exasperation, Lane called Menon a bottle-neck. The reaction was swift; Lane found himself sitting alone at the table. Thereafter he was alone in the business also.

This episode ended with a characteristic tailpiece. Menon had left the partnership with a payment of £125. The sum was sent through a solicitor. But the solicitor quietly absconded. Some London barristers who shared chambers with Menon tell how they urged him to prosecute the absconding solicitor and how Menon told them, 'That fellow has a wife and child and needs the money more than I do. I can't prosecute him.'

There can be no doubt whatsoever about the significance of the India League's work in London or its place in the history of the Indian freedom movement. Its scoreboard is impressive and in many ways unique. It was the only organization telling the British people of the sins that were being committed in India in their name. It was the only organization that became so integral a part of the Labour Party that the leadership of the party could not afford to ignore its voice. Many British M.P.s today concede that but for the League's persistent efforts 'from the bottom up and the top down and cross-wise around the country, the Labour Party's policy in regard to India and independence would have been as similar to that of the Conservatives as Tweedledum was to Tweedledee.'

It is easy enough to forget that one of the great factors of India's freedom struggle was the strength of the movement inside Britain. This was not only a strong movement but, in view of Britain's parliamentary traditions, a very significant one.

Among the very few in India who have understood the significance of the part played by the League is Jawaharlal Nehru; he was in touch with the League's work almost from its inception. This explains the persistence with which Prime Minister Nehru today ignores the professional Menon-baiters who question his allegiance and integrity.

If Menon was personally responsible for the unique achievements of the India League, his personality was also the cause of the League's shortcomings. These shortcomings flowed from the fact that Menon made the League a one-man show. If people called him autocratic, he called them worse names in turn. He was only interested in getting work done – and he had his own way of getting it done.

In the final analysis, London was a fulfilment. The twenty-three years he spent there were, in many ways, the best years of his life. In a sense, he was a man who missed his youth; the pursuits of the young held no attractions for him when he was himself young. He cannot enjoy small talk.

London was a home to him. It had been a battle arena for twenty-three years, but all through the battle he was developing a deep affection for his adopted home. When the battle was over, Menon saw freedom primarily as a new challenge. If one battle was over, another was beginning – for real social and economic freedom.

PART III

New Delhi

Is he imperious? Yes, but it
is the imperiousness of a man
who knows his job. Intolerant?
Perhaps. But it is the intoler-
ance of a man speeding up,
who finds his paths barred by
un-understanding associates.

YUSUF MEHERALLY
on Jawaharlal Nehru

18

High Commissioner

INDIA'S transition from servitude to sovereignty was sudden. It required a colossal amount of readjustment and reorientation. Apart from facing the problems thrown up by partition – and they were cruel – the new nation had also to take its bearings and set its course.

Krishna Menon had earned a right to be associated with the latter task. From the late 'thirties, he had been laying stress on the content of freedom as distinct from freedom itself. Controversies that struck many leaders in India as matters of the moment had sent Menon diving into the fundamentals. He had concerned himself with such matters as the economic direction, social needs and constitutional basis of free India. He had always acted with a live sense of history, seeing 'the present as a stage in the unfolding drama of the ages'.

But it was not as a policy-maker in New Delhi that freedom found Krishna Menon. He was named India's first High Commissioner in the United Kingdom.

In a way, this was natural. Foreign affairs was the field in which Menon had been the most widely recognized as an expert. And London was his real home. He knew the working of British democracy from within. He knew also the problems facing Indians in Britain. Besides, there was such a thing as poetic justice. For long years he was lampooned and attacked in London as a nuisance. It would be delightfully ironic if he were now to be the recognized representative of India at the Court of St James.

For just the same reason His Majesty's Government was none too pleased at the prospect. Mr Attlee made it known to Nehru that Menon would be an unhappy choice. Menon had been an agitator and had personally attacked Attlee when the latter sat on the Simon Commission. He had also been a major source of embarrassment to the Attlee Government between 1945 and the transfer of power in 1947. Sir Stafford Cripps also wrote to Nehru

155

advising him against Menon's appointment; a gulf had sprung up between Sir Stafford and Menon following the failure of the 1942 Cripps Mission and the Indian criticisms that came in its wake.

The objections only strengthened Menon's case. It became a matter of prestige for India to have as its representative in Britain the man who had been there for twenty years in the same capacity, though unofficially. Even Gandhi blessed the idea. When the British Government found the Indian attitude stiffening it agreed to the appointment. Soon Attlee was to develop a wholesome respect and regard for the erstwhile 'nuisance'.

As High Commissioner Krishna Menon was determined on two things. First, he wanted to make India's freedom felt. This desire led to the overhauling of the High Commission in a manner that became the talk of the town. Second, he wanted to place Indo-British relations on a new and model footing. This led to a historic chapter in the evolution of the Commonwealth theory.

For obvious reasons the High Commission in London had always been the biggest of India's foreign missions. But it was geared for bureaucratic administration. The bulk of the employees were British and the departments were organized with the sole purpose of facilitating the smooth functioning of a colonial Government.

Within four months of his taking office, Menon was back in India with detailed plans for a new Indian High Commission. The blueprint called for eighteen departments. The High Commissioner went from ministry to ministry in New Delhi explaining the need for the kind of reorganization he had planned and asking for approval of the scheme.

Soon the Indian High Commission became the biggest foreign mission in London. Its staff increased from 600 to 1,500. A fleet of limousines was bought and it included a Rolls-Royce. A palatial mansion in exclusive Kensington Palace Gardens was acquired as the High Commissioner's official residence. India House in Aldwych was refurnished and redecorated in grand style. The High Commissioner personally selected the hangings, the crockery and the furniture.

There was a touch of deliberate flamboyance in all this. Krishna Menon was proclaiming that India was no impecunious little country. Such a concept would not have fitted in with his notions of free India. There was need now to overcome the humiliations of the colonial era. It was necessary to create an impression. There might also have been a personal psychological element. His innate aristocracy was perhaps finding an outlet.

The High Commission's expenses were rising steeply. Yet Menon lived in a back room of India House, continuing his old diet of tea and biscuits. This routine was so incongruous in the new surroundings that people began wondering whether Menon was eating in the middle of the night for sheer survival. He never took any salary, and when his five-year term ended a sum of more than 200,000 rupees (approximately £16,000) went into India's account under that head. Not only would he not use official privileges, but he would not let his own niece, who was then studying at Oxford, stay with him on her visits to London. He would be charming to her – and put her up at the Y.W.C.A. He was at his desk at 7.30 every day and the lights used to burn till 2 and 3 o'clock in the morning. He would attend official functions in full regalia, Rolls-Royce and all, for the sake of the dignity of the office.

While returning from a formal party one evening, Menon saw an old cockney walking along the pavement in Aldwych.

'George!' shouted Krishna Menon.

George stopped and was aghast to see that the shout came from inside a Rolls-Royce. But the next moment old George beamed, for he saw emerging from the limousine Krishna Menon. George had been a janitor at the London School of Economics when Menon was a student. Menon put his arm around George and the two went up in the lift to the High Commissioner's office for tea and a gossip. The change from India League to India House meant no change at all in Menon's working and living habits.

In fact, the India League continued to engage Menon's attention. On the attainment of independence many said that the League had outlived its usefulness and that it should be wound up. Menon disagreed. As he saw it the League's real work was only beginning. It had to promote Indo-British understanding, continue 'the fight against the forces of reaction and the agencies of misrepresentation', interpret India's new aspirations and achievements to the British people and explain the British mind to India. 'Not less but more work for the India League,' agreed Prime Minister Nehru.

Menon reorganized the League. Reginald Sorensen became its

Chairman and Julius Silverman its secretary. Menon himself was President. He added new departments to the organization. The campaign against colonialism in other parts of the world where Indians were living was stepped up. 'Unity in the cause of freedom of peoples' became a living creed. Menon had always been interested in building up a community centre where Indians living in London could meet, and in 1957 Jawaharlal Nehru inaugurated the India Club. In the course of time an India Arts Society was added to the League, and Menon himself gave particular attention to the founding of a magazine *Envoy*, to be a bridge between East and West.

Indeed, the fervour with which Menon set about the task of cementing India's friendship with Britain was a surprise to many. They could hardly believe that a man whose life-mission was to expose Britain would overflow with such magnanimity in the hour of his triumph.

Appropriately enough, the most important policy matter that came up during Krishna Menon's tenure as High Commissioner was the constitutional basis of India's relationship with Britain. Independence in 1947 was on the basis of Dominion Status and an Englishman had continued as the Governor-General of India. The Constituent Assembly was finalizing the new nation's constitution and it was necessary to take a decision on the vital question of whether to remain in the Commonwealth.

Britain had already expressed the hope that India would not sever connections with the Commonwealth. Even in the speech announcing the appointment of the Cabinet Mission Mr Attlee had remarked, 'I hope the Indian people may elect to remain within the British Commonwealth. I am certain that India will find great advantages in doing so.'

But British Government leaders were not in the least optimistic that India would elect to remain in the family. In his *The Commonwealth*, far and away the most penetrating study of the evolution of this unusual political club, Patrick Gordon Walker refers to the Constituent Assembly's decision on January 22nd, 1947, to become a sovereign, independent republic and says, 'This was intended to dispose of all prospect of Indian membership of the Commonwealth.' In June the same year Burma announced her decision to leave the Commonwealth, and British leaders saw in this a further confirmation of their premonition about India, scheduled to be free only two months later. Detailing the odds against the Commonwealth, Gordon Walker even comments that 'India's independence leaders knew little of the Commonwealth'.

The basic assumption of the British leaders was not unjustified: there were difficulties in the way of India's becoming a member of the Commonwealth. But they went wrong in their observation of the trends that were visible in Indian political thinking at the time and in their analysis of the reasons that ultimately led to India's decision to stay on.

For example, the Constituent Assembly's decision in favour of a republic was not intended to dispose of all prospect of Indian membership of the Commonwealth. In his speech in the Assembly on January 22nd, 1947, Nehru said, 'At no time have we ever thought in terms of isolating ourselves in this part of the world from other countries or of being hostile to countries which have dominated over us. We want to be friendly with the British people and the British Commonwealth of Nations.'

The reasons attributed by Gordon Walker and other Western commentators for India's final decision in favour of the Commonwealth are generally vague and occasionally wrong. Among these reasons are the selflessness with which a relatively small number of British officials worked with Indians as devoted servants of the Indian State during the holocaust that followed partition (this convinced Indians, as Gordon Walker says, that 'when Britain said independence she meant it: and that complete independence did not mean the end of help and co-operation in need'); India's realization that isolation might be dangerous against the background of Russian designs and communist uprising in Malaya in July 1948; Asian Prime Ministers' participation in the Commonwealth Conference of October 1948 and their consequent realization that the Commonwealth was an association of equals.

Only a lack of understanding of the Indian mind will make one believe that the selflessness of British officials at a time of communal massacres or the threat of communism in Malaya could have driven India into political alliance with the West. These points were probably not even noticed by Indian leaders at the time.

The most important reason for India's Commonwealth membership was that a few individuals at the top were politically convinced of the advantages of such membership and personally sentimental about it. These individuals were mostly at the top of the administrative cadre, advising the new ministers. Two were politicians and leaders themselves, Jawaharlal Nehru and Krishna Menon.

Early in the freedom struggle Nehru had expressed himself against Indian membership of the Commonwealth, but by the time independence was in sight he was quite in favour of India's maintaining a link with Britain and the Commonwealth. Menon had all along been in favour of such a link. He saw that association of nations was going to be the order of the day in the post-war world. He knew as well as any British Labour leader the changed and changing character of the Commonwealth and how, even economically, India could benefit from an alliance with the 'club'.

The most important predisposing factor as far as Menon was concerned, however, must have been the lingering influence of Mrs Annie Besant. The idea she had planted in him, the idea of a Commonwealth based on the principle of reciprocity, had never lost its appeal. True, he had opposed Dominion Status in 1930; but that was when the legal frame-work of the phrase had not yet been devised. In 1947, with circumstances changed, he was the first to advocate Dominion Status as a basis of transferring power. Personal intimacy with English life may have later strengthened the sentiment first imparted to him by Mrs Besant. When the time for decision came, he had no hesitation in taking the stand he did.

The British notion that India's national leaders knew little of the Commonwealth applied to the generality of the leadership; they equated the Commonwealth with Britain and Britain with colonialism. But Nehru and Menon were prominent exceptions, and as it happened, the exceptions influenced the ultimate decision. It might be said that India's membership of the Commonwealth was the work of two individuals.

The two were swimming against a strong current of public opinion. The communists were vehemently opposed to the idea, seeing in the proposed link a lingering symbol of slavery. The non-communist Leftists were also prejudiced against any association with imperialist Britain. As for Congressmen, they were either ignorant or uninterested. They were content to let Nehru have his way.

Nehru had his way at the Jaipur session of the Congress in December 1948. A resolution was passed expressing the Party's support for India's free association with the Commonwealth. The move had the full support of Right-wing Congress leaders and business magnates on the periphery of the Congress Party.

But how was this resolution to be reduced to the practical level of legal terms? India had already decided to constitute herself a republic. A republic was the antithesis of a monarchy, and the lynch-pin of the Commonwealth was allegiance to the Crown. It was in the solution of this constitutional problem that Menon played his most significant part in the evolution of the Commonwealth. In the process the Commonwealth itself was transformed into a completely new concept.

The Commonwealth had hitherto been an all-white affair. India was opening a new chapter of Asian membership. Indian officials put forth the idea of an 'associated' status whereby India could have the best of both worlds. For a while the suggestion was seriously considered both in London and in New Delhi. The phrase 'India that is Bharat' had just been coined by the constitution-makers. Menon thought that if there could be an 'India that is Bharat', there might as well be a republic that was in the Commonwealth. In other words, it was pointed out that the desire for a phraseological rationalization need not push India into 'associated' membership.

Besides, Menon was operating on the basis of reciprocity, the charmed word bequeathed by Mrs Besant. This meant not a restricted membership, as 'associated' status was bound to be, but complete equality. Finally, reciprocity was accepted as the basis, with equal obligations among members on all matters from citizenship to policy consultations. It was full membership.

In April 1949 the Commonwealth Prime Ministers met in London for the specific purpose of deciding upon India's membership. Menon, as the Indian High Commissioner in London, assisted Prime Minister Nehru at the talks. New ideas and new phrases emerged.

The status of the monarch was the biggest problem. Some suggested that the King be nominated King of the Commonwealth. Some wanted the President of India to be nominally appointed by the King. Mountbatten wanted the Crown put on the Indian flag. All these ideas were rejected by India. Finally the simple designation 'Head of the Commonwealth' found unanimous approval. More than one negotiator present at the talks has claimed credit for this particular phrase. However, credit may be given to Menon for the definition that accompanied the phrase, if not the phrase itself. In order to avoid any impression of the King having any real authority as Head of the Commonwealth, he defined the King 'as the symbol of the free association of the Commonwealth's independent member nations and as such the Head of the Commonwealth'.

This vital definition and indeed the whole of the Prime Ministers' Declaration was accepted in the teeth of opposition from lawyers in the Foreign Office who insisted that a republic was incompatible with a monarchy-based Commonwealth. But statesmanship won the day. Ingenuity combined with diplomacy to defeat bureaucracy. Even Churchill hailed the solution as a magnanimous gesture on India's part. Attlee wrote years later, 'Had this precedent been set earlier, both Burma and Eire would have remained in the Commonwealth'.

For his part, Menon considers his role in the evolution of the new Commonwealth as one of the most important achievements of his career. He told a public meeting in St Pancras in January 1955, 'In the great Commonwealth there is reciprocity of relationship and we have found in it a pattern which may become a great contribution to world civilization.'

As a diplomat and promoter of Indo-British friendship Menon was a signal success. He ran into trouble, however, as an administrator.

During her 150 years of subjection, India had developed the habit of going to Britain for practically all her requirements. One of the principal activities of the Indian High Commission in London, therefore, was shopping on behalf of India. Stores and supplies worth large sums used to be bought by the High Commission every year for shipment to India. Menon, unused to the proper channels of government and unhappy over the ways of bureaucracy, attempted his own methods of arranging purchases and shipments.

Naturally there was criticism. In Menon's case the number of those interested in criticism was steadily increasing. He was rubbing many people up the wrong way, at home and in England. He was also alienating many who expected a share of freedom's spoils. The stage was set for a series of scandals. The most notorious of these turned out to be the 'jeep case'.

In India the 'jeep scandal' has become a legend. The prosecution and defence have produced masses of literature on it. The episode is so much part of current Government history that a biographer cannot hope to cover new ground in an effort either to prove or disprove what is already known. All that can be attempted is a résumé of the available facts and an objective analysis.

In 1948 the Government of India was in urgent need of military equipment for operations in Kashmir and Hyderabad. More than 2,000 jeeps were required in Hyderabad. Urgent messages went to the Indian High Commission in London, the usual agency for procuring all materials. The High Commissioner, according to the prosecution, ignored the traditional channels of supply and placed a contract with a company called Antimistantes, floated by one E. H. Potter. In August the firm was given an advance payment of £81,000. The firm said the vehicles would be reconditioned ones, but that spares would be sent along with them. A contract was signed. The firm itself arranged for the inspection of the jeeps, allegedly by unreliable agents. By the end of the year the firm wanted another advance to complete the terms of the contract. This was agreed to and made the total of the two advances approximately £172,000.

In March 1949, a shipment of 155 jeeps reached Madras where they were inspected by Defence Ministry experts and rejected as being unserviceable. It was also discovered that no spares had arrived. Subsequently the Ministry cancelled the remainder of the order. A loss of £143,162 resulted from the transaction.

The case for the defence begins by stressing the urgency with which the Government needed the jeeps. The military situation in India was so serious that the Government wanted the High Commission to get the jeeps at any cost. The High Commissioner found Britain in an unsympathetic mood; the Press was whipping up an anti-Indian campaign and Whitehall was plainly hostile, so that he found it impossible to get jeeps from official sources. The Indian Defence Ministry's financial adviser was at the time in London. With his concurrence the High Commissioner accepted an offer from Antimistantes to supply reconditioned jeeps. The price quoted was £250 per vehicle, half the price of a new jeep. The jeeps were in Italy, but the Ministry of Defence in New Delhi said that it would not send its experts to Italy to inspect the vehicles. Thereupon it was arranged to have them inspected by Lloyds. One thousand vehicles were certified by Lloyds and on these sixty per cent of the price was paid to the firm as per contract.

When the first consignment of 155 jeeps arrived in Madras, army inspectors certified them as unfit for use. The Defence Ministry ordered the stoppage of further shipments, although it was known that advance payment on 1,000 certified vehicles had been made. The High Commissioner personally tried to reduce the Government's loss, but it was of no avail.

Had considerations of the 'jeep scandal' not been influenced by strong prejudices against Krishna Menon, it would have been possible to see the lack of orthodoxy in this particular deal. In the first place, the firm had been recommended to the Indian High Commission by high British Government sources. It was the British Consul in Rome who later wrote to the High Commission certifying that the goods were in Italy, thus fulfilling the contractual condition for payment on site of half the agreed price. Again, the entire negotiations in London were conducted by the financial adviser to the Indian Defence Ministry. The High Commissioner entered the picture only in the final stages when trouble had arisen. And then the financial adviser's files on the negotiations were found to have been destroyed. Most important of all, certain top Defence Ministry officials were backing some influential industrialists in India who were interested in another make of vehicle. But the 155 jeeps which were officially condemned on arrival in India were not bad at all. These same vehicles, after being abandoned in defence depots in Avadi, near Madras, exposed to sun and rain and pilferers for as long as two years, were brought into use in 1951 after some minor repairs, and gave excellent service till 1960. Had the Government of India not panicked following the hullabaloo raised by interested politicians in Parliament, and had all the 1,000 jeeps been accepted, there would have been no 'jeep scandal'.

While Krishna Menon's lapses were loudly broadcast, his achievements were hardly mentioned. The Government had also placed a large order for rifles with the people who were connected with the jeep transaction. Subsequently Krishna Menon was able to persuade the British Government to make some supplies available; new British rifles were marked as disposals and sold to India at a cut rate. Not only did Menon get this done but, when the previous contract with the private party became consequently unnecessary, he succeeded in getting that contract cancelled without having to pay a penny in compensation. The vast sums of money India saved in this transaction caught no one's eye.

It is clear that the scandals were blown up out of all proportion by those who had already begun to look upon Menon as a marked enemy. The spotlight of accusers was focused on him, although many others were directly involved. Characteristically, Menon took the full rap of the scandal, when he could easily have got out of it by naming names.

The scandals put Krishna Menon under a cloud towards the end of his term as High Commissioner. A new High Commissioner assumed charge in London before Menon's term expired. The new man was B. G. Kher, a former Chief Minister of Bombay. Menon wanted to stay on till August 15th, 1952. Kher, however, said that he had completed arrangements to proceed to London and would not like any postponement. Menon thereupon had no alternative but to hand over charge to his successor on June 13th, two months before completion of his full term.

Menon decided to stay on in London. This made matters worse for him. The new High Commissioner lost no opportunity to display his animosity towards the old. At the many parties held by the High Commissioner during the first days of his term, Menon was conspicuously absent. Even for the Independence Day celebration at the High Commission on August 15th, no invitation went to him. On this occasion, however, Menon went, as an Indian citizen, to attend the public meeting held in the morning. Quietly and alone, he stood at the back of the hall leaning against the wall. After a little while a High Commission clerk noticed his former boss standing forlorn in a corner and insisted on leading Menon to the dais. Rather than create a scene, Menon went. Old English friends who had toiled with him for Indian independence were on the dais and they welcomed him with warmth. But the new High Commissioner remained cold.

Some friends suggested that Menon should go away somewhere for a short holiday. But he would do nothing of the sort. The plain fact was that, having taken no salary during the years of office, he was without money. Once again he was seen in bus queues and Tube stations.

Menon spent long hours in agonizing solitude. He even thought of forgetting all about public life and making a fresh start. He prepared to set up practice in London and entered the chambers of the noted Sir Frank Soskice, a former Attorney-General in the Labour Government. He also registered himself as a senior advocate in the Supreme Court of India.

Menon was in the wilderness from June 13th until early September. It seemed for a moment that his gifts, taken for granted, would be forgotten, and that his failures, providing sensation, would be remembered.

Strangely, though perhaps fittingly, Britain provided the only silver lining in the dark clouds of these months. Top British leaders, both Labour and Conservative, jointly offered Menon a place in British public life. They had misjudged the man in the earlier years, but his ability and his affection for Britain had impressed them during the first years of Indian freedom. They wanted to make him a gesture of goodwill and sent out feelers in order to make use of him in high positions in Britain.[1] The offer came as a tonic to Krishna Menon, but in another sense it accentuated his agony, for it emphasized his apparent rejection by India.

Walking absent-mindedly along the street one day, Menon was struck by a speeding taxi. Crowds collected and he was recognized. He was in no position to get up, for he was badly hurt. He lay in a hospital for several days on the danger list.

While in hospital, he thought of Delhi's inexplicable silence. Nehru had told him that after the High Commissionership he would be wanted as leader of the Indian delegation to the United Nations. But there was no word from India. Finally the newspapers brought the news – and the news was that Mrs Vijayalaxmi Pandit had been nominated leader of the Indian delegation. Menon's name appeared in the list as deputy to Mrs Pandit.

He accepted the Delhi decision and decided to go to the United Nations. When he arrived in New York, bruised both in body and in spirit, he was so sick that he had to be carried out of the aircraft. He had two walking-sticks, one in each hand. Extreme mental depression combined with the accident made him a pathetic invalid. Doctors examined him – and gave him six months to live. Why had India, asked New York, sent this decrepit old invalid to the United Nations?

But neither the doctors nor New York knew the calibre of this invalid. Like the phoenix, Menon rose again.

---

[1] The British leaders who were concerned with these offers are still alive and the author has been requested not to go into details of this episode.

19

'Formula Menon'

THE United Kingdom High Commissionership was a false start to Krishna Menon's official career. He was simply too big to be confined to one diplomatic mission where there was too little diplomacy and too much administration. The United Nations, on the contrary, suited his own genius. Here he found opportunities that stimulated him and brought out the best in him. The world became his arena, and the world saw the birth of a new concept of diplomacy and of a new vocabulary in which to express international relations.

From the personal angle, however, 1952 was a muffled beginning for Krishna Menon in the United Nations. He was number two in the Indian delegation and he was hardly used to such a role. He had already crossed swords with his chief, Mrs Vijayalaxmi Pandit.

The estrangement continued to affect the relationship between the leader and deputy leader of the Indian delegation. In fact it became a favourite topic of gossip in the United Nations, the usual gibe beginning, 'They are so good at finding solutions to world problems. Why don't they find a solution to the problem of their own mutual relations?'

A year later a satisfactory solution was found by other members of the General Assembly. They elected Mrs Pandit President, thus leaving the field clear for Menon.

Menon's way of dealing with the personality problem was to forget that it existed. There was no better way of achieving this end than by burying himself in work. The thorniest problem then facing the United Nations was Korea. He adopted Korea as his special interest.

The war in Korea had raged relentlessly for a year with no hopes of a military or political settlement when Russia's Jacob

Malik dramatically announced that a cease-fire could be negotiated. Two weeks later, in July 1951, the opposing sides began armistice negotiations in Panmunjom. But complications arose almost immediately and the talks became protracted and tortuous. After several frustrating months, during which each side tried to score propaganda points, a general agreement was reached on all aspects except one. The stumbling block was the disposal of prisoners of war. Negotiations over this apparently innocuous subjecstt arted in January 1952 and produced so much heat that the United Nations Command suspended the talks on two separate occasions for periods totalling nine months.

In no previous peace talks had prisoners of war become the crucial issue. In the Korean war this happened for various reasons. The United Nations held nearly 140,000 prisoners at the start of the negotiations, but the communist side declined to give any information regarding the number or condition of the prisoners in their hands. The United Nations command discovered that a large number of their prisoners did not wish to be repatriated after the armistice. This was too great an opportunity to be missed by the United States, which practically constituted the United Nations command. The United Nations therefore laid down the principle that all prisoners should be allowed to decide for themselves whether or not they wished to be returned.

The same reasons that prompted the United Nations Command to adopt an inflexible attitude on this matter made China and North Korea determined to ensure that all prisoners were repatriated whether they liked it or not. They had in their favour the letter of the Geneva convention of 1949 which said that 'prisoners of war shall be released and repatriated without delay after the cessation of hostilities' (Article 118) and that 'prisoners of war may in no circumstances renounce in part or in entirety the rights secured to them by the present convention' (Article 7). A complete deadlock arose, and when the truce talks were suspended for the second time in October 1952, there was the danger of hostilities breaking out all over again.

The development of the impasse almost coincided with Krishna Menon's arrival in the United Nations. He saw the Korean war as essentially an Asian problem in which Asian nations should have a decisive say. His method of work was different from that of the rest. At a time when contact between the two blocs was almost non-existent, he began mixing freely with everyone. He would spend hours with the leader of a communist delegation, and then hours with the leader of a Western delegation. Private man-to-man conferences became the order of the day. For more than a month activity went on at a feverish pitch. Everyone knew that the Indian delegation was working on a secret plan. The way in which Menon was going about his business aroused tremendous curiosity. The general anxiety about the Indian plan became more acute as other solutions proposed by Mexico, Israel and Pakistan found little favour in the General Assembly. On November 17th the long-awaited Indian resolution was tabled.

It is the habit of mediocrity to complicate a simple issue; it is the way of genius to simplify a complex one. Menon's 17-point solution to the Korean deadlock was very simple. He merely suggested that all prisoners should be repatriated under the supervision of a Neutral Nations Repatriation Commission composed of two from the communist side and two from the West. The repatriation, the resolution said, should be in accordance with the Geneva convention, the well-established principles and practice of international law and the relevant provisions of the Draft Armistice Agreement. It was also stipulated that force was not to be used against the prisoners either to prevent or to effect their return to their homelands. Menon explained that the resolution sought to reconcile the two divergent points of view not by a surrender of principle on either side, but by fitting them into the general pattern of a solution. 'The Indian proposals,' Menon said, 'are not a solution but a way to a solution.'

So indeed they proved to be. Britain approved of the plan as being 'timely and constructive', but the United States unofficially expressed strong opposition. The United States Press howled with anger and said that Menon was smuggling China into the civilized world in the name of peace. But the worst cut came from Russia's Vishinsky. Delivering one of his bitterest speeches in the United Nations, Vishinsky attacked the Indian plan as a 'rotten solution' and hurled personal abuse at Krishna Menon.

This was an unexpected let-down. Menon had personally discussed the various points with Vishinsky before the resolution was tabled and had received the impression that they were broadly acceptable to the communists. China had also expressed general approval of the proposals. The sudden change of tune was an indication of the inscrutable ways of the cold war. Vishinsky had suddenly realized that a small newcomer was assuming too much importance in an arena meant primarily for the giants. It served communist purposes then to hold India up as a stooge of the Americans – and Vishinsky did just that.

The West has forgotten all about this incident. Vishinsky's stand gave the United States a god-sent opportunity to win the confidence and sympathy of Asia. But the United States, gone Republican on November 4th, did not even make an effort not to miss the bus. John Foster Dulles began bullying and blackguarding India, which, providing a characteristic sidelight on the cold war, made the Soviet Union re-examine its own policy and quickly readjust its attitudes towards India and Asia.

Vishinsky's unexpected opposition to the Menon plan inspired the United States to re-consider its initial opposition; taking advantage of some amendments Menon offered after the debate, the United States announced its full support for the Indian plan. (Dulles still continued to refer disparagingly to the plan, thereby proving that the belated United States support was meant only to avoid being in the same bracket with the Soviet Union.)

But the Soviet attack remained, leaving Menon in the lurch. The tragedy was the greater because the reasonableness and workability of the formula had been recognized publicly by many, privately by all. In the face of this painful setback, Menon could only say feebly that the Indian delegation would continue to explore possibilities of getting the communists to agree to its plan.

The full Assembly of the United Nations passed the Indian resolution on December 3rd. But the Soviet bloc had voted against it, which meant that the resolution had failed in its primary objective of bringing the two warring sides together. And yet it was only a case of delayed triumph. Menon persisted with his efforts to win over the communists. Six months later, at Panmunjom, the two truce teams signed a final agreement on prisoners of war. Clause by clause it was the same plan that Krishna Menon had tabled in the General Assembly. The only significant change was that India was nominated Chairman and 'umpire' of the Neutral Nations Repatriation Commission. It was recognition at last.

The successful conclusion of the truce talks made Menon something of a hero in the United Nations. He came to be ad-

miringly called 'Formula Menon', a phrase coined by Frank
Graham, the American university professor who was United
Nations representative in Kashmir in 1951. The West was
generous with its acknowledgment. Sir Anthony Eden said in the
House of Commons, 'It is only fair that I should add a tribute to
the Indian delegation and Mr Krishna Menon in particular for
their wise statesmanship.' Mr Dean Acheson, speaking in the
General Assembly, said that 'No one who had listened to the
brilliant speech of Mr Krishna Menon would have failed to be
moved by his deep dedication to peace. We respect and welcome
the statesmanship of the resolution which he produced.'

The end of the Korean crisis signalled the beginning of a new
epoch in Indian foreign policy. India was no longer merely a
go-between. She had a definite programme of her own which
she would pursue no matter what the two blocs said. The starting
point of this programme was that the under-developed world
could not be taken for granted. As Nehru said, 'The countries of
Asia, however weak they might be, do not propose to be ignored,
by-passed and sat upon.' It fell to Menon to give shape to this
new policy and thereby mobilize African and Asian opinion as a
new and decisive force in international affairs.

New Delhi was prompt in its appreciation. In 1953 Krishna
Menon was asked to lead the Indian delegation to the United
Nations. Always conscious of the exceptional abilities of Krishna
Menon, Nehru wanted also to pave the way for the eventual
absorption of Menon into the Cabinet, and in the same year the
Madras unit of the Congress Party elected Menon to the Upper
House of India's Parliament.

It is Krishna Menon's misfortune that the good he does is often
obliterated by the publicity given to the bad. Even as the world
was paying tributes to his contribution to Korean peace, a lobby
was forming against him.

This lobby had three faces – the American, the British and
the Indian. While certain features were common to all, each
face had its own distinguishing marks. The lobby began in each
country for different reasons; later they dovetailed into each
other, the American and Indian lobbies in particular.

The growth of the anti-Menon propaganda in the United
States must be considered in the context of Indo-American

relations. These relations started in the modern sense in 1947. The cold war had begun and soon McCarthyism raised its head. The United States began to see everything in black and white; grey disappeared from her vision.

India entered this scene in a garment that was decidedly grey. For reasons valid from her own historical, geographical and economic standpoints, India projected the idea of non-alignment. The United States found this an immoral view-point and one that interfered with her notions of national security. But the United States also found India determined.

The American attitude to India thus began on a schizophrenic note. On the one hand the United States hated India for being a symbol of the non-acceptability of United States leadership in the cold war. On the other, it realized that without India democracy had no chance in Asia. This contradiction has determined the main course of Indo-American relations from 1947 up to the present time. Realization of the importance of helping Indian democracy to succeed in turn accentuated American anger at Indian leaders' rejection of American political concepts. The United States found it necessary to put pressure on India to give up her non-alignment and simultaneously to do everything to ensure the healthy growth of the Indian economy.

On the political level, American policies created the opposite results. The idea of putting pressure assumed, under the dynamism of John Foster Dulles, the proportions of plain bullying. This offended Indian sentiment. At the same time, it often threw the United States into postures of hostility towards India. Acting on the assumption that political pressure would force India to change course in self-interest, the United States threw her weight against India every time an opportunity presented itself. On Kashmir, South Africa, Goa and even on the general question of colonialism, the United States worked actively against India. Only lately have anti-colonial forces gained in momentum in the United Nations and so only now has the United States reversed its stand on colonialism; in the earlier years it voted invariably in favour of its colonial allies.

This persistent United States opposition to India in turn inspired the Soviet Union to appear to support India with equal persistence. Especially in matters which touched the deeper emotions of the Indian people, like Kashmir and Goa, the

Russians vociferously backed India, sometimes saving India with their vote. Unwittingly the United States Government was playing into the hands of its adversaries. If the Americans had been shrewder and more understanding, perhaps the nuances of Indian foreign policy would have been different today.

Krishna Menon's appearance on the United Nations stage had coincided with the election of General Eisenhower to the Presidency of the United States. Dulles, as Eisenhower's Secretary of State, obsessed with his own notions on the containment of communism, was incapable of appreciating any other motivating force in the world. Menon, obsessed with the Indian revolution and the need for a climate of peace in Afro-Asia, was incapable of appreciating anti-communism as a motivating force at all. Their simultaneous entry on the world stage had a profound and far-reaching influence on Asia's political evolution as well as on Indo-American relations.

From the very beginning an image of Menon as a villain was projected to the American people. All through the years, the general run of American newspapers have consistently suppressed the friendly statements and speeches of Menon, while every word he has uttered in support of communist policies has been played up.

In Britain the anti-Menon lobby came into existence for totally different reasons. Though concerned with the cold war and India's attitude towards it, they were more concerned in the late 'forties and early 'fifties with the fate of the Empire. The British Government and conservatives generally found in Indian independence the beginning of the end of Empire. And it was the India League and Krishna Menon who had mobilized British public opinion for Indian independence. Besides, Menon had become tremendously popular among the Afro-Asian nations. He not only took India out of the Empire but was now helping others to get out too.

Nor did British Empire-lovers like the change in the character of the Commonwealth. It had always been the 'British Commonwealth' until India joined the family as a republic. Though Britain appreciated India's staying within the Commonwealth, the royalists were disappointed at the way the British Commonwealth was republicanized. They saw Menon's hand behind the change.

After Menon became India's spokesman in the United Nations, there were many occasions when he had to criticize the British Government. The greatest wound was inflicted at the time of the Suez invasion. Indian criticism hurt Britain as much as the lack of American support did. It was again Menon who was seen as the principal villain. To a section of Britons he represented all that was unpleasant about Indian policies.

Let it be mentioned at once that an equally significant section of Englishmen has appreciated Menon and his attitudes without reservation. Menon is understood in England better than anywhere else if only because he has lived and worked there longer than anywhere else. Generally, therefore, Britain is free from the malice and viciousness associated with the anti-Menon lobbies in the United States and in India.

In India the growth of the lobby has been due mostly to fear. His socialist convictions as much as his efficiency and political importance filled influential sections of Indian opinion with fear for their survival.

This must be traced to the polarization, early in the era of freedom, of political forces in India. Independence had found Gandhi politically in the back seat; up in front Jawaharlal Nehru and Sardar Patel constituted a duumvirate. It was an uneasy partnership, for the two men were diametrically opposite in background, beliefs and temperament. Patel was a strong man with an unchallengeable hold on the Congress Party machinery. Equally unchallengeable was Nehru's hold on the masses. As soon as the bloodshed and carnage that came in the wake of partition subsided, the differences between the two came to the fore. Generally speaking Patel represented conservative opinion, while Nehru symbolized more progressive views. There was an unseen mobilization of forces behind each.

In this battle of ideas and personalities Krishna Menon was identified as a 'Nehru man'. Although he was not in the country, the conservatives marked him out as a man in the opposite camp. Soon he began moving to the centre of the controversy. The sizzling stories coming out of the Indian High Commission in London were too good to be left unexploited. Once the process began, it gathered rapid momentum for Krishna Menon proved to be an ideal image around which to build legends. This was due partly to the fact that he was comparatively unknown in India.

Even the very important role he played during the days of the transfer of power was behind the scenes, so that his name was seldom in the headlines. Only after independence did he become a public personality. This put the country in a mood to accept unquestioningly anything that was said of him.

Menon had accumulated many enemies at home. His apparent roughness of behaviour had antagonized many who felt insulted or ignored. And the veteran patriots, who had faced lathi charges and spent years in British jails, did not welcome a man who did not have even one arrest to his credit. He was also hated by the business world. To them he was a comparatively unknown quantity, but he lost no time in revealing what he thought of them. Although he could count among his most intimate friends some leading capitalists, as a class they aroused the crusader in him. The last category of anti-Menonites were merely men who were opposed to Jawaharlal Nehru but had not the courage to come out in the open. Nehru was too much of a hero and mass magician to be effectively attacked in public, so they attacked him by proxy – and the proxy was Krishna Menon.

Menon himself perhaps deliberately pushed people into the lobby that was growing against him. He never minded being in the centre of a storm. He never yields to bullying, and the growth of the lobby in fact increased his obstinacy. The lobby and the man strengthened each other. At home Menon began to attack his detractors without restraint. Abroad, for a few years from 1953 onwards, as will be seen later, he went out of his way to be unpleasant towards Western nations and delegates in the United Nations. The result was that a movement that might have been at worst a right-left tug-of-war in New Delhi became an international campaign of revenge and personal vendetta.

'The Tremendous Representative'

THE distaste the West developed for Krishna Menon was in reality a distaste for India; Menon merely happened to be in the front line of attack.

Western antipathy to India was inevitable because there was a direct clash of interests between the United States and India. The first concern of the Indian Government was economic regeneration. It had drawn up a development plan and was bent on making it a success. But success was dependent on a period of peace in the world and stability at home. India's stake in real peace was therefore one hundred per cent genuine. The policies that followed were not a moralistic posture, but an economic necessity. (The over-selling of the moral side was a blunder.) It was basically in her own interest that India began interfering in situations that threatened a drift towards war. As Menon has repeatedly said, 'There is nothing foreign about our foreign policy. It is the extension of our national policies in international relations.' Coexistence became a condition of survival for India.

And coexistence was 'treason' in Eisenhower's America. The clash was as fundamental as it was unavoidable.

Krishna Menon went to the United Nations with two obsessions, both directly related to India's national ambitions. He wanted to prevent the United Nations from splitting into two hostile camps and thereby becoming a mere instrument in the cold war, unable ever to settle a dispute by negotiations. For, he believed, the United Nations was the best agency to ensure a climate of peace in the world if only it was made to serve the purposes for which it was founded. At the same time he wanted to get the individuality of Afro-Asia recognized by the West.

All Menon's work in the United Nations reflected these twin objectives. Korea was an excellent opportunity. It helped him prove the ability and political maturity of the hitherto neglected

176

countries of Afro-Asia. More important, it showed that peaceful settlement of disputes was possible and uncommitted countries could play a pivotal role in it. More efforts in the same direction and more results in the field of practical diplomacy were obviously what India needed.

After Korea it was Indo-China. But the two situations were quite different. The Korean conflict was between two sovereign states enjoying legal and international standing. In Indo-China sovereignty itself was in dispute. This question was therefore taken out of the arena of the United Nations and handed over to a nine-nation group holding its sessions in Geneva from May 1954.

India was not one of the nine nations. The non-aligned nations had been kept strictly out. The inevitable happened. Soon after the conference opened the United States withdrew from the conference and began talking in terms of 'intervention' and 'united action in Indo-China'. An uneasy standstill followed. Every bit of hope threatened to vanish while Britain tried to find a way out.

At this explosive moment, Krishna Menon landed in Geneva. The United States Press at once called him an intruder, for it was Dulles who had taken the initiative earlier to prevent a two-thirds vote in favour of India's participation. Menon himself was aware of his unofficial status. 'I am an old fool,' he told reporters, 'here only as a tourist, a bystander.' It was obvious, however, that Menon was no ordinary tourist. India had realized that she could not any longer remain in the background as far as the Indo-China war was concerned. Since the opposition to French colonialism was being led almost exclusively by the communists in Indo-China the United States had begun plans to internationalize the war. Indo-China was about to become another Korea – and Indo-China was again in Asia. If the war spread, it could again threaten India's progress as well as the progress of other Afro-Asian countries. India had entered the picture a month before the Geneva conference opened. She had put forward what was known as 'the Nehru Plan' calling for an international agreement for non-intervention in Indo-China so that the belligerents could negotiate directly. It was very much a Menon plan and, as with the Korean formula, its theme was again big power co-operation for peace and cessation of hostilities.

Menon reached Geneva without any precise mission. The trip had not even been planned. He was en route to New York, and hours before leaving New Delhi he had discussed with the Prime Minister that he should call in at Geneva in order to keep himself posted with developments there. On landing in Cairo, Menon wrote to Sir Anthony Eden in Geneva suggesting a meeting. That was the signal for the world Press to explode into a blaze of headlines saying that Nehru was moving into the impasse at Geneva, that Menon was carrying a secret formula, etc.

As it turned out, Menon became the focus of attention within hours of his arrival in Geneva. The basic difficulty there was the absence of a non-aligned power. The committee could not carry on fruitful talks for any length of time because each suspected the other's motives and there was no one to explain the difficulties of one side to the other. By filling up this vacuum Menon became an important, almost a decisive, influence in Geneva.

He remained completely in the background. But the official delegations looked to him to do a great many things that they could not do in the circumstances. Reporters computed that during the first phase of the conference Menon had sixteen conferences with Eden, eight with Chou En-lai, five with Molotov, five with Pham van Dong of the Vietminh régime, six with the United States representative and two with the French, while representatives from Canada, West Germany, Norway, Sweden, Colombia and Indonesia called on him regularly.

By offering himself as a bridge between the opposing camps, Menon revivified the conference. During the final phase of the conference, he was the one who interpreted each side to the other, cleared up misunderstandings and effectively persuaded the one party to take into account the problems facing the other.

The formula he produced at the end of his long round of talks accommodated all points of view and suggested a solution on the basis of mutual tolerance. When, on July 21st, a joint declaration signed by all the powers except the United States brought to a close the eight-year war in Indo-China, the key role of 'tourist' Menon was acknowledged by spokesmen of many governments.

The work Menon did was his own. He accepted it as another occasion to prove that the supposedly insurmountable barrier between the East and the West were not as insurmountable as all that, that negotiation could end quarrels, that Asia had potentialities of its own.

One of the by-products of Menon's work in Geneva was his acquaintance with Chou En-lai. He spent long hours with the Chinese Premier discussing, besides the immediate issue of Indo-China, the long-term problems facing Asia in general. Menon's theme was the goodwill and mutual respect that should govern the relationship between Afro-Asian countries. It struck a chord in Chou En-lai at the time, for China was shrewdly trying to build up her prestige in the Afro-Asian region as a counter to the United-States-sponsored ostracism of the Peking Government following the Korean war. Together they went over some points that they thought should form the basis of the relationship between two sovereign states. Menon informed Nehru of these talks and the Prime Minister promptly invited his Chinese counterpart to visit Delhi on his way back to Peking from Geneva. It was at their subsequent meeting that Nehru fashioned the philosophy of 'Panch Shila'.[1] Hardly did anyone know then that Chou En-lai would soon betray the principles and stab India and Asia in the back.

A direct outcome of these contacts was the Bandung conference of Asian-African nations in April 1955. Provoked by frustrations in Korea and Indo-China and angered by the rising 'immoral' tide of non-alignment, Dulles had brought into being the South-East Asia Treaty Organization. This had created considerable resentment in Asia. In order to canalize these emotions along constructive lines, Menon and Nehru together thought up a geographical conference of Asian and African countries. The aim of the conference was, in Nehru's words, not to create any separate bloc of world Powers, but to bring countries in Asia and Africa together for as large a measure of co-operation as possible in strengthening the cause of peace.

Krishna Menon's responsibility for what happened at Bandung was great. The conference had begun with a good deal of mutual suspicion and antagonism. Menon played a leading role in keeping these tendencies at bay. His greatest contribution was in

---

[1] *Panch Shila*, literally meaning the five pillars, formed the preamble to an India-China treaty on Tibet signed in April 1954. It said that the treaty was based on five principles – mutual respect for each other's territorial integrity and sovereignty, mutual non-aggression, mutual non-interference in each other's internal affairs, equality and mutual benefit, and peaceful coexistence.

emphasizing that the conference was in no way a rival to the United Nations. His aim was to get the Afro-Asian statesmen to endorse the United Nations and thus gain, for what it was worth, a moral victory over those big Powers who were objecting to the admission of some Asian and African nations to the United Nations. As a result, every major decision and resolution at Bandung was related to the United Nations. Later, at the United Nation's tenth anniversary commemorative session in June, Menon said, 'It was not without importance that those nations which had been badly treated by the United Nations did not give it back in that kind.' Explaining the observation, he said that China was a charter member of the United Nations and the charter was as much hers as anybody else's. He also pointed out that Ceylon, which was not represented at the United Nations, had expressed her enthusiasm for the United Nations.

Apart from directing the deliberations at Bandung along purposive lines, Menon's principal task was to keep an eye on what was going into the records of history. He was the one who did all the drafting. The joint communiqué issued at the end of the conference swore by the United Nations in almost every other clause. It urged 'respect for human rights and for the United Nations Charter' and 'the right of any nation to defend itself singly or collectively under the United Nations Charter'. The readiness with which nations that were outside the United Nations gave unreserved support to it was the major achievement of the Bandung conference. In his first public speech on returning to India, Menon noted how Bandung had established the 'Personality of Asia and Africa'. He stressed that Afro-Asia had achieved this 'without isolating itself from the rest of the world'.

Korea, Indo-China, Bandung – Krishna Menon was no longer a politician; he was a statesman and a world figure.

In 1955 Krishna Menon rose to full stature in the United Nations. That year's index of the *Asian Recorder* under the title of 'Menon, V. K. Krishna' reads like a chronicle of the year's world events.

In New York – Confers with British Premier – Meets Canadian High Commissioner in London – Meets Canadian Premier – Meets Dag Hammarskjöld – Meets Dulles – Meets Eisenhower – Meets Molotov – Meets Soviet Envoy in

'The Tremendous Representative'

London – On admission of 16 nations to U.N. – On 'Big
Four' talks – On China-U.S. relations – On China – On
Czech arms for Egypt – On disarmament – On distribution
of U.N. jobs – On elections to U.N. Security Council – On
18-nation atomic energy agency resolution – On Formosa
– On French attitude re Algeria and Morocco – On Goa – On
India's foreign policy – On Indians and Africans in South
Africa – On Indo-China – On Korea – On proposal for
International Atomic Energy Agency – On release of U.S.
airmen – On Soviet atomic tests – On peace and Soviet
Union – On South Africa in U.N. – On Turco-Iraqi Pact –
On U.N. resolution re re-unification of Korea – On Viet-
nam's attitude towards Geneva agreement – On Western
disarmament proposals – On withdrawal of South Africa
from U.N. – Tribute to Dr José Masa – Proposal re study of
atomic radiation – Praise for – Supports Soviet resolution re
China – visit to China.

Here was high-pitched activity, one man doing the work of
many, one trend of thought trying to string together divergent
views, service beyond the call of duty. Menon once explained the
philosophy behind work of this kind. 'The purpose of people like
us,' he told a news conference in New Delhi in May 1955, 'who
are neither mediators nor busybodies, is that we allow ourselves
to be utilized – or we utilize ourselves – in order to contribute
towards harmony. This is part of our domestic and foreign
outlook.'
This outlook and the success of his earlier efforts at peace-
making inspired him to pitch his hopes higher. The greatest
gamble he took was in trying to bring the United States and
Communist China to an understanding. Formosa had staged one
of its periodic entries to the world stage and Menon felt that if
this problem could be satisfactorily solved, it would mean the
elimination of the biggest threat to peace in Asia. It would mean,
he knew, the recognition by the U.S.A. of the Communist
Government in China. But such recognition would in turn mean
a pinning down of China within the framework of the United
Nations, the creation of unprecedented goodwill between the
West and the Communist bloc and a bright new hope for peace
everywhere. There were a few encouraging signs. At the time of

the Indo-China conference, the United States had already sat down with the China it did not recognize. British recognition of Peking was a fact too. The immense hatred Washington felt towards Peking, however, could not be ignored. Perhaps, thought Menon, this hatred could be reduced through some gesture of goodwill by China. Could he persuade China to co-operate?

Chou En-lai was now a friend. They had done good work together both at Geneva and at Bandung. He had received the impression that the Chinese were anxious to join the United Nations. At Bandung Chou En-lai had even offered to negotiate directly with the United States on the question of lessening tension in the Far East. Menon felt confident that a frank talk with the Chinese Premier would produce results. On May 8th he flew to China.

China was then holding prisoner a group of American airmen, shot down near the Chinese coast and condemned as spies. This had become a highly emotional issue in the United States. The United Nations had passed a resolution condemning the imprisonment and in the first week of January the United Nations Secretary-General, Hammarskjöld, had gone to Peking and held discussions with the Chinese Government on the matter. Here was a situation where Peking could make an essentially humanitarian gesture that was bound to have a profound impact on American public opinion as well as on the United Nations.

Menon talked to Chou En-lai as one Asian to another. This had its effect in the atmosphere of Asian solidarity generated by the Bandung conference. It yielded results. On May 30th, one week after he returned from China, Menon was able to announce at a Press conference in Delhi that the Chinese Government would be releasing four American airmen 'in the next few hours'. This was in contrast to the Press conference held by Dag Hammarskjöld when he returned to New York from Peking. He could then say no more than that 'the door has been opened and can be kept open, given restraint on all sides'.

At the end of his visit to China, Menon said in a statement to the Chinese Press, 'It is a great deal in these days to feel that political and social endeavours are useful: that is to say, to see the ground is not sterile right in front of you, and to look forward with hope.'

Menon began looking forward with renewed hope. With the

first act in the drama completed by the release of the United States airmen, he took off for New York immediately, on June 1st.

What followed was an unprecedented series of high-level talks. Appointments were so crowded that he drove directly from London airport to No. 10 Downing Street. Great names flickered from the pages of his diary ... Sir Anthony Eden, Harold Macmillan, Jacob Malik, John Foster Dulles, Dag Hammarskjöld, Molotov. Each day, as Menon himself remarked, was a new element.

On the specific issue of Formosa, however, the talks produced no solution. By July the attention of the world had turned to something far more dramatic – the conference of the Big Four heads of states in Geneva. But Menon's initiative had very definitely contributed to a general lessening of tension in the world. His personal dynamism and that special brand of diplomacy now being referred to as 'Menonism' captured the imagination of many. Harold Macmillan, then Britain's Foreign Secretary, said in the Commons that he would like to 'pay a special tribute to V. K. Krishna Menon's services in the cause of world peace'. Menon's prestige as a statesman had become so great that the tenth session of the United Nations General Assembly, which began in September 1955, became known as the 'Menon session'.

The Afro-Asian countries lost no time in setting the mood of the tenth session. They wanted old favourites like Algeria and Morocco to be placed on the agenda. A letter signed by fourteen Afro-Asian countries and requesting the inclusion of Algeria on the agenda was voted down by the General Committee. Afro-Asian nations thereupon had the motion passed by the General Assembly with a one-vote majority. In a huff the French delegation walked out.

Krishna Menon was all for the consideration of colonial questions by the United Nations. But the technique he had developed to achieve results rested on the goodwill of all who were parties to a dispute. If one party walked out, he argued, there was nothing that could be achieved by those who stayed behind.

The French walk-out convinced Menon that over-enthusiasm on the part of Afro-Asia would take them nowhere. Discretion had to be recognized as the better part of valour. Publicly Menon spoke in the Assembly with a view to making the metropolitan

Powers understand Afro-Asian sentiments. 'With the ushering in of the Atomic Revolution,' he said, 'Asian nations were becoming vigilant lest they again became part of colonial exploitation as they had after the Industrial Revolution.' Privately, however, Menon began a new exercise in lobbying, and conferred with Afro-Asian delegates night after night over the desirable versus the attainable. Two months after the General Assembly vote, he drafted a resolution and had it sponsored by a Latin-American delegation. The resolution said that the General Assembly had decided not to consider further the item of Algeria. When it was passed as per previous arrangements, what had threatened to be insoluble crisis was settled, to everyone's relief. Menon was demonstrating, in his own peculiar way, that half a loaf was better than no bread.

Even after the tenth session Menon continued to exercise a sobering influence on the more emotional Afro-Asian delegations. He made India stick to a very strict principle: that no resolution should be couched in condemnatory language.

At the next session this principle was put to a severe test. Fifteen Afro-Asian nations signed a letter again asking for the inclusion of Algeria in the agenda. Despite the previous year's experience, they had attached an 'explanatory memorandum' that was severely worded and angry in tone. Menon felt passionately on Algeria. He also knew that if he dissociated himself from the letter-writers, India would be jeopardizing her position in the Afro-Asian group. But India had chosen a principle and that was that. He refused to sign the letter.

The performance was repeated in 1957 when the letter had eighteen Afro-Asian signatures. Menon still kept out. By the 12th Session, however, the ebullient Afro-Asians realized that nothing was coming out of their annual routine. This time they drafted a letter without any recriminatory passages. Menon was one of the twenty-one delegates who signed it.

The fight to preserve the integrity of the United Nations was a continuing one. As soon as the Afro-Asians cooled down, the free world and the communist bloc warmed up. A serious situation arose over the admission of new members to the United Nations.

The two blocs had always been trying to add to their respective numerical strength in the United Nations. The one side had invariably frustrated the attempts of the other and the only outcome was a great deal of bitterness. The impasse lasted so long that when the Soviet Union suggested a package deal for the wholesale admission of eighteen nations during the 10th Session, everyone accepted it as a sensible compromise. The eighteen included five communist and thirteen non-communist nations. Everything looked promising until voting time came and Kuomintang China cast an unexpected veto to scuttle the admission of Outer Mongolia. In a flash of retaliation, the Soviet delegate vetoed all the non-communist applicants.

Krishna Menon stepped into the crisis because he found the United Nations actually being turned into a battleground by cold-war propagandists. It was important to end this and restore the United Nations' capacity to be positive. He evolved a compromise formula according to which both the communist bloc and the non-communist bloc would drop one candidate each; Outer Mongolia was balanced with Japan from among the non-communist applicants.

Again both sides accepted the proposal and proceeded to vote. Then, all of a sudden, the Soviet Union backed out and a fresh deadlock developed. This time even Krishna Menon could think of no new proposals. The only possibility was to put pressure upon the Russians and make them lift their opposition.

The Soviet Prime Minister Marshal Bulganin was just then in New Delhi on a State visit. That gave Menon an idea. What transpired thereafter was described by the General Assembly's President, Dr José Masa, who told reporters,

After the Security Council meeting practically all representatives were discouraged ... Then that night Prime Minister Nehru's great gesture came – that very evening. There were continuous movements of telegrams, telephone calls, radio messages, coded messages back and forth. Prime Minister Nehru, following the inspiration of Krishna Menon, this tremendous representative representing India here, whose capacity is unique and extraordinary, whose intelligence is awe-inspiring and who has great common sense, according to his inspiration that night the negotiations were carried out ... The next day we were all astounded that the Soviet Union proposed the admission of sixteen countries.

A Cult is born

I N the process of building up Afro-Asia, Krishna Menon built up
himself. He became an institution that compelled attention –
grudging on the part of some, no doubt, but attention all the
same.

For Menon the political objective of pushing India and the
rest of Afro-Asia to the forefront was something that conditioned
everything, including personal behaviour. He became aggressive,
sometimes even offensive, as a matter of policy.

He wanted India and other Afro-Asian countries to have a
say in everything that came up before the United Nations, however important. This was a frustrating business in the first few
months when he was only the deputy leader of the Indian delegation and when the leader had her own ideas on what the delegation should and should not do. Whenever he saw a big-Power
delegate lording it over the General Assembly, he would grow
impatient and prod the leader of the delegation to stand up and
call the bluff. 'Don't let them get away with it,' he would say.
But no one would get up. The leader of the delegation preferred
courtesy and tradition to aggressiveness.

When he became leader, Menon began employing his method
with vigour. From 1953 to 1957 there was hardly a subject discussed by the United Nations on which Menon did not speak. He
ignored the usual custom of delegation leaders speaking only on
political matters. Instead he began addressing all committees of
the Assembly. He never paused to think whether the subject was
important enough to merit his personal presence. He was everywhere. When the Administrative Committee scheduled a discussion on catering arrangements in the United Nations building,
Menon announced that he would speak on the United Nations'
catering service. The Indian delegation already had a member on

the Administrative Committee and Menon was informed that this member could do the talking in the routine way. But Menon disagreed. Who would listen, he asked, if an ordinary member made an ordinary speech?

Menon kept striking. He looked round the offices of the United Nations and came up with a serious allegation. A few Western countries, he said, were monopolizing the jobs in the United Nations. It was an insult to geography, an insult to the basic concept of the United Nations and, Menon demanded, it must be remedied immediately by giving to the Afro-Asian countries the representation that was their right. It was the first time anyone had brought up the subject and, the moment he said it, everyone realized how true his charge was and how strong his case.

Menon also hit out at Western delegates whenever he thought they were trying to be patronizing or supercilious in their attitude to Afro-Asia. Many were the representatives of Western nations who tried to score a point over the Indian leader and in return got the whiplash of the Indian's tongue. During a debate on the admission of Communist China to the United Nations, the United States Senator, William Knowland, made the mistake of calling India 'a floor-leader for the Soviet drive to bring Red China into the United Nations'. At the best of times the Senator would have irritated Menon; the 'floor-leader' epithet incensed him. When he rose next, Menon unleashed a fury of words upon the Senator. He began by putting the whole thing on a high plane, saying how unfortunate it was for one delegation to question the integrity of another, how such accusations could do a disservice to international friendship, how his relationship with top United States leaders prevented him from taking the Senator's views as those of the United States Government. Then he referred to the Senator's statement that he had been shocked at India's position. 'As for being shocked,' spat out Menon, 'that is a question of state of mind and the thing to do is to go to a doctor or to a psychiatrist about it.' Knowland squirmed, but the Assembly was amused.

This aggressiveness was a cultivated pose. It was his way of saying that Afro-Asia was no longer willing to be sat upon.

A certain glamour became attached to his name in the process. His mannerisms combined with his gaunt appearance to add to the mystical appeal of his personality. His very arrival in the United Nations building became an event. A few minutes before Assembly time a gleaming Cadillac would come to a halt before the delegates' entrance. In the front seat beside the liveried chauffeur would be the Indian chief delegate, an open magazine held to his face. He would sit there intently reading, unmindful of the fact that the car had come to a stop. Presently the chauffeur would step over to the other side and hold the door open. The Indian leader would slip out, walking-stick dangling from the crook of his arm, the magazine still holding his attention. As though in a trance he would move towards the escalator, eyes still glued to the magazine. Many visitors standing around the porches would nudge one another. Hearing nothing, seeing nothing, Krishna Menon would reach the foot of the escalator and his legs would mechanically catch one of the moving steps. Still reading with fierce concentration, he would ascend. At the top, the legs would again move mechanically, the magazine still in place. Forward he would go, reading all the while, and subconsciously slip into a chair in the lounge, still reading. Minutes later, as though jerked by a sudden contact with electricity, he would come alive, drop the magazine at last, and busy himself.

There was no doubt that Menon dramatized the fundamental changes that were taking place in the character and composition of the United Nations. He made the West realize that the climate had changed.

His approach to the 'domestic jurisdiction' theory is an example of the knack he had of beating the West at its own game. Whenever a discussion on colonies was sought to be raised in the United Nations it was the custom for metropolitan Powers to thwart all efforts by citing Article 2, Paragraph 7 of the Charter, which prohibited the United Nations from intervening in 'matters which are essentially within the domestic jurisdiction of any State'.

Menon watched this routine at the 7th Session when the question of Morocco came up. He then introduced a new interpretation of the relevant article arguing that as long as the action of the Assembly was not condemnatory or punitive, consideration of and resolutions on a subject could not be called intervention. In 1954 when the Assembly was considering the treatment of Indians in South Africa, he said, 'India is not asking the United Nations to intervene in the Union of South Africa. It is merely

A Cult is born

asking the United Nations to express an opinion, to make an appeal.' Next year when stiff resistance was being mounted against putting Algeria on the agenda, Menon used the very phraseology of the Charter to drive his point home. He said, ' "Nothing in the Charter shall authorize the United Nations to intervene ... Let us take first the words "authorize to intervene". No authority is being sought at the present moment to intervene. The discussion of an item is not intervention. If there were a motion before the United Nations to take collective action or to impose sanctions, then it could be argued as a matter of intervention.' He said further that while Article 2, Paragraph 7 was not 'attracted' by such items, other articles were. He cited Article 14 and emphasized the words 'the General Assembly may recommend measures for the peaceful adjustment of any situation regardless of origin'. His argument, of course, centred on the words 'regardless of origin'. He developed his position with such thoroughness and put forth arguments that were so logical that the jurisdiction plea lost all its potency in subsequent wrangles between colonial powers and Afro-Asia.

On the question of Cyprus again it was Menon's freshness of approach that won the day. Greece had brought the issue to the United Nations on the basis of *enosis* – union with Greece. Turkey had made counter-claims on the basis of the Ottoman Empire background. The imperial solution as usual was on the basis of partition.

Menon gave a new dimension to the controversy. Saying that the position taken by Greece and Turkey would not contribute to a solution of the problem, Menon put forth ideas which at once changed the character of the whole problem.

Nationhood, he said, was territorial. The fact that in a particular territory people were of one ethnic group or another did not constitute a claim to that territory by nations from which such groups originated. There was such a thing as Cypriotic entity. Greeks or Turks, the people of Cyprus were Cypriots. If Iceland with a smaller population could be a sovereign State, why could not Cyprus be Cyprus?

Even Cypriot leaders had not looked at their problem from this angle. As soon as Menon projected the idea of an independent Cyprus, it became the main topic of discussion. The ultimate solution of the problem of Cyprus was based on this theory and

Archbishop Makarios lost no time in expressing his gratitude to India and to Krishna Menon.

The reputation he achieved as an orator was due also to his knack of driving a point home through wit and satire. Talking on nuclear tests, he once said, ' ... These refinements in atomic weapons – it's like asking a man whether he would like to be run over by a Chevrolet or by a Cadillac.' During a debate on Kashmir he looked at the Pakistani delegate and said with affected innocence, 'Aggression is not the function of a neighbouring state.' Once he referred to Pakistan-occupied 'Azad (free) Kashmir' and remarked parenthetically: 'Names do not mean anything. You can call a man with a weak arm Armstrong.' Speaking of the free world's professions of democracy vis-à-vis its possession of colonies, he said in a speech in 1956, 'We used to hear about democratic imperialism in the old days. There can no more be democratic imperialism than there can be a vegetarian tiger.'

His debating skill and intellectual brilliance as much as his faith in the United Nations, his anxiety to act as a link between hostile blocs and his determination to see that small nations were recognized, combined to make Menon a power in world politics. 'Menonism' became a byword. This was a philosophy that had its roots in the Indian tradition of synthesis. It was a technique that grew out of India's diplomatic intimacy with nations of diverse political hues. It represented a set of values that India could pursue because of its non-involvement in the cold war. The distinguishing feature of 'Menonism' was a moderation born of respect for the other person's point of view. With all his superficial explosiveness, Menon was capable of great tact and tolerance in his handling of difficult problems. He would not only counsel patience to young countries whose tendency was to go to extremes, but also be great enough to compliment his opponents when compliment was due. At the United Nations commemorative session in June 1955 he was warm in his tribute to the late Field-Marshal Smuts of South Africa, and called him 'a great man who served his country and the whole world – a gallant adversary'. The reference caused what newspapers termed 'audible expressions of surprise' among his listeners, for they knew only too well how deeply and profoundly India abhorred South Africa's racialism. In 1956 when a debate on Togoland had aroused anti-colonial passions in the United Nations and when its successful conclusion had sent Afro-Asian delegates into a mood of jubilation, Menon gave unstinted praise to Britain and said, 'Here is an imperial country, to a very large extent steeped in the attributes of Empire, but also imbued with the traditions of liberal administration, coming forward for the first time and saying "We want to release from tutelage these people whom we have governed as a colonial power and afterwards as custodians." '

These qualities – the ability to feel passionately but act with a sense of balance, to hate a system but praise many individuals connected with the system, to relate the problems of one to the problems of all and the security of all to the security of one, to know with his heart but think with his mind – are seemingly contradictory. And yet they are essential parts of Krishna Menon's complex personality.

22

Storm over Hungary

THE fires of controversy raged in India as Krishna Menon rearranged ideas and alignments in the United Nations. His election to the Rajya Sabha, the Upper House of Parliament, in 1953 had been taken by the conservative lobby as a danger signal. Their fears proved correct when the following year the Prime Minister proposed him for the Cabinet. At once powerful institutions and individuals began putting pressure on Nehru to drop the idea. Some of Nehru's closest lieutenants in the Cabinet supported the plea. A controversial character like Menon, they told him, would be a liability in the Cabinet.

Nehru yielded – but only for a moment. Menon's international stature rose during the following months with his visit to China, the high-level talks in Western capitals and the great record of the 'Menon Session'. Nehru seized the opportunity created by this eminence to press his point again. This time the critics could not harp on the liability argument. A man of Menon's acknowledged standing in the world, Nehru told them, would be an asset to the Cabinet.

Nehru won. On February 3rd, 1956, Menon was named Cabinet Minister without Portfolio. He was three months to the day short of sixty.

As a Minister of the Union Cabinet Menon looked after the Health Portfolio for a while, and was associated with the Secondary Education Committee. He also began airing ideas privately about the Indian economy, social programmes and political directions. But it was not yet the time for him to put his teeth into New Delhi's politics. By and large Menon confined himself to foreign policy issues, assisting the Prime Minister who was also Minister for External Affairs.

There was plenty to keep him busy. As it turned out, 1956

drew to a close to the accompaniment of a series of crises – it was the year of the Suez invasion and the Hungarian revolution. India herself was embroiled in a bitter United Nations battle over Kashmir.

The Suez crisis was one more occasion when he put to constructive use the position of influence he had built up for himself and for India among the Afro-Asian nations. Egypt's nationalization of the Canal on July 26th, 1956, sent Britain and France into a paroxysm of anger. Statesmen of the world, realizing the explosiveness of the situation, moved in swiftly with proposals for a settlement. There were conferences in London in which Krishna Menon participated. Finally Britain and France took the problem to the Security Council. The first debates were fruitless and the Security Council decided to go into secret session. It was already October.

At this juncture Krishna Menon arrived in New York. As he had already established close contact with President Nasser, he became the focal point of the private talks going on between the representatives of France, Britain, the United States, Egypt and the Secretary-General of the United Nations. All except Menon were talking around a resolution Britain and France had jointly tabled. Menon was working out his own scheme.

The first part of the Anglo-French resolution laid down six principles upon which any settlement of the Suez problem was to be based. The principles included recognition of Egyptian sovereignty over the Canal Zone and the need to guarantee free and open passage through the Canal. This part was unanimously adopted. The second and operative part, however, enjoined Egypt to accept the recommendations of an earlier London conference which Cairo had rejected. The Soviet Union vetoed this part. It was again an impasse.

It was then, on October 24th, that Menon's formula was officially announced. It envisaged, as a basis of discussion, a revision of the 1888 convention with a view to giving Egypt the responsibility for maintaining and developing the Canal, co-operation between Canal users and Egyptian authorities, arbitration in case of complaints of discrimination and United Nations association with the Canal Authority for a few years.

As usual, Menon had obtained prior consent of the parties concerned before he made his proposal public. A basis for discussion having been agreed upon, the Secretary-General suggested provisionally that on October 29th the informal talks might be resumed in Geneva.

On October 29th Israel struck. Two days later British planes were bombing Egypt.

Menon's plans foundered on the rocks of Anglo-French reck-lessness. The marathon efforts of the earlier London conferences were buried and forgotten. The whole process of peace-making had to begin from the beginning all over again. Menon, who had returned to India after announcing his October 24th formula, was now back in New York helping United Nations efforts to stop the fighting. It was hard going for the United Nations, however, for London and Paris were smarting under a sense of humilia-tion.

The fighting stopped soon enough, thanks to American criticism of the Anglo-French action, a Russian threat to enter the fray, a grave danger to sterling and an unprecedented tide of Afro-Asian opinion against 'imperialistic cussedness'. But troop withdrawal proved a more difficult problem. Along with eighteen Afro-Asian nations Menon moved two resolutions in the United Nations on withdrawal and five others on post-withdrawal arrangements in Egypt.

Menon's significant contribution to the solution of the crisis was in preventing the Afro-Asian nations from becoming too emotional. The audacious invasion had touched every Afro-Asian nation on a tender spot. Menon spent hours with the Afro-Asian and particularly the Arab delegations convincing them of the futility of being merely angry. He told them that real achieve-ments could come only if they maintained a sense of balance in the face of provocation. It was a personal victory for Menon that the Afro-Asians did not move a single resolution in the United Nations condemning the Anglo-French-Israeli aggression.

The Suez episode underlined one other characteristic of Menon: his ability to see beyond the crisis of the moment and pave the way for a settlement of traditional feuds. The roots of the Suez war really lay in the enmity between Arabs and Jews. Menon sought to tackle this basic issue when crisis brewed in the wake of the nationalization of the Canal.

In his October 24th formula Menon had envisaged Egyptian co-operation with Canal users and arbitration in case of complaints against discrimination. In persuading Egypt to agree to these principles, he was playing a delicate and shrewdly statesmanlike game.

It was under a unilateral declaration of a 'state of war' with Israel that Egypt had always denied passage through the Suez Canal to Israeli ships. Menon's plan was to have the dispute referred to the International Court of Justice. Even during the first London conference in August he had said, 'We would be the first to say that if the verdict of the World Court goes against the Egyptian Government they ought to abide by it.' Menon personally impressed upon President Nasser the importance of complete allegiance to the United Nations Charter and international law. Nasser was statesman enough to see the validity of Menon's argument. He agreed to submit to arbitration if a dispute arose over the Suez Canal.

If Israel had brought Egypt to the World Court, it would have meant automatic abandonment by Egypt of her right to unilateral action. The presence of an international arbitration authority would have compelled Egypt to drop any discriminatory policy that did not have the sanction of law behind it. This in turn would have made it possible for other friendly nations to enter the field and suggest ways to end the most complicated feud in West Asia. But the Israeli Government never took the issue to the World Court, perhaps because it feared that the Court might uphold Egypt's claim of a state of war.

The most unfortunate offshoot of the Suez crisis was that it affected attitudes and judgments vis-à-vis the Hungarian crisis which flared up simultaneously. The Russians used Suez to divert world attention from their violent actions in Hungary. The West tried to use Hungary to divert attention from its own embarrassment in Suez. The worst sufferers in the bargain were the uncommitted nations and particularly Krishna Menon.

The Hungarian national revolt broke out during the night of October 23rd–24th. On November 4th the Soviet army launched a massive attack with tanks and infantry to crush the uprising. Brutalities followed. Tens of thousands of civilians were killed. There were deportations of Hungarian youths, a 'hunger blockade' of the capital city, a mass exodus of refugees.

Krishna Menon was in his native Calicut on October 31st, the day Britain mounted her air attack on Egypt. On November 3rd he left for New York to attend the General Assembly. The Soviet attack on Hungary took place while Menon was airborne. On November 5th, a day after the Soviet action began, a tired and drawn-faced Menon landed at Idlewild airport.

An American businessman sauntered up to the Indian diplomat. He was indignant. Why, he demanded, had not India condemned the Soviet aggression in Hungary?

Menon flew into a fit of temper. He brandished his cane at the accusing American and began shouting at the top of his voice.

'This will be answered in the right places,' cried Menon. 'I am not accountable to your country. I'm tired of being bullied by you.'

Reporters ran to the spot, but Indian officials put Menon in a car and drove off before the Press could get at him.

It was a warning of the storm that was gathering.

The storm broke on November 9th when India cast her votes on three separate resolutions before the General Assembly. The first was a Five-Power motion proposing free elections in Hungary under United Nations auspices. Menon voted against this. The second resolution was tabled by the United States. Its operative part was concerned with emergency assistance to the people of Hungary, but the burden of the resolution was condemnation of the Soviet Union. Menon abstained on this. The third resolution, sponsored by Austria, urged, without condemning any power, measures to render aid to the Hungarian people. Menon voted for this motion.

There was uproar everywhere. The cry was that Menon opposed free elections on the one hand and on the other refused to condemn the Russians. The West condemned India in general and Krishna Menon in particular for practising double standards.

In India some newspapers and political leaders mounted a powerful attack against Menon. Jayaprakash Narayan demanded 'the removal of Mr Krishna Menon from the political scene'. Asoka Mehta said Menon did not truly represent the Indian people. It was freely alleged that Menon had acted against the instructions of the Prime Minister. Suggestions for his recall or dismissal were made from many platforms.

To see the controversy in perspective, one must remember that to India there was no comparison between Suez and Hungary. There is no use pretending that India approached both problems impartially. Like other Afro-Asian countries, India was quite subjective in her emotions over the invasion of Egypt, while towards Hungary she was objective. There is no need to be apologetic about this vital difference. In Afro-Asia, for obvious reasons, communism is not half as hated as is colonialism, and anyone who expects Afro-Asian peoples to show the same intensity of feeling against communist as well as colonialist aggressions is living in a fools' world. Significantly, Indian opposition to Krishna Menon's actions came almost entirely from the organized Right. For the rest, even those who were enlightened enough to feel bitterly against the Soviet aggression in Hungary unreservedly supported the Indian votes in the United Nations.

The votes were strictly in the spirit of India's traditions and past policies. It is quite possible that the fact of his being an Indian affected Menon's personal reactions to the Suez and the Hungarian issues differently. It is possible, too, that the Government of India could have handled the Hungarian problem in a better way. But the votes cast by Menon were consistent with his own previous record in the United Nations, from the Korean crisis right up to Suez. There was no deviation from principles.

The principles, as applied to the specific issue and placed by Menon before the United Nations, were first, that the object of the United Nations was concern for the interests of the Hungarian people; second, that irrespective of the character of any government that might happen to exist in any country, the existence of a sovereign State should not be ignored; and third, that since the aim was to help the people of Hungary, the approach to the question should be such as would lead to concrete help; the whole machinery of the United Nations must be used for conciliation and for obtaining a settlement. These principles governed Menon's voting pattern all through the nine weeks of United Nations debate on Hungary.

The most controversial vote was the 'nay' that was cast against the idea of United Nation-supervised elections in Hungary. Menon objected to it on the ground that he could not subscribe to

> phraseology or proposals before the Assembly which disregard the sovereignty of states represented here. For example, we cannot say that a sovereign member of the Assembly can be called upon to submit its elections and everything else to

the United Nations without its agreement. Any approach we make as though this were a colonial country which is not represented here at the United Nations is not in accordance with the facts or law of the position.

Apart from the basic principle involved, Menon had an added reason for emphasizing this carefully chosen stand. There were already under-the-counter moves in the West to hold a United Nations-sponsored plebiscite in Kashmir. Had India agreed to the principle of United Nations elections in sovereign States, New Delhi would have been committed to a policy which Indian public opinion would have repudiated.

Menon's abstention on those resolutions which sought to condemn the Soviet Union was again typically Indian, however reprehensible the West might have found it. All through the years, conciliation as distinct from condemnation was the core of Indian diplomacy in the United Nations. It was through strict adherence to this principle that India had been able in the past to maintain her capacity to act as a bridge between opposing camps.

His votes stole the thunder from the strong denunciation of communist repression which Menon made subsequently. Speaking in the United Nations, he endorsed 'the right of the Hungarian people to choose the form of government they desired'. He said, 'We make no distinctions about repression, whether perpetuated by one Government or another. We make no distinctions whether tragic events take place in one country or another.' On December 3rd he attacked both the Hungarian and Soviet Governments for disregarding United Nations resolutions, said India did not agree that the Hungarian question fell exclusively within domestic jurisdiction, reiterated 'India's sympathies with the Hungarian national movement' and repeated that Russia's non-compliance with United Nations resolutions was deplorable. But there was no condemnation for the sake of condemnation. Having counselled the Arabs not to condemn Britain and France for invading Egypt, he could not possibly support any move to condemn the Soviet Union over Hungary.

Hungary is one of those topics that belong to the heart rather than to the mind. There is little scope here for a rational understanding of one another's attitudes. The West may continue to believe that Menon played a sinister role during the debates on Hungary. But at least it should be possible to concede that he was faithfully adhering to the Government of India's policy. It was a week after the November 9th votes that Nehru paid Menon his greatest compliment by saying that 'Menon is the best man in international affairs after Vishinsky.'

23

The Hero of Kashmir

IN the best of times India's neutralism was anathema to Western statesmen. Her appeals to rationality, they thought, were inadequate to meet the challenge of an anti-rational menace. Her attitude on Hungary proved to them what they had always suspected: that India was neutral in favour of Soviet Russia and communism. Western wrath found a natural target in Krishna Menon, the man who was said to have done everything on his own initiative, the man who was justifying his position spiritedly despite the avalanche of criticism he had run into.

Just then the Foreign Minister of Pakistan sent a letter to the Security Council asking for an early meeting to discuss the Kashmir question. The letter was dated January 2nd, 1957. The wounds inflicted by India on Britain and France over the Suez issue and on the United States over Hungary were still raw. What followed were the most trying days in Krishna Menon's United Nations career.

The Kashmir case was born with India and Pakistan in 1947. When the two nations were created it was stipulated that the princely states would have the option to join one or the other. The Hindu Maharajah of Muslim-majority Kashmir wavered over a decision. Mountbatten went from New Delhi to Kashmir to assure the Maharajah, on behalf of the Indian leaders, that if he decided to join Pakistan India would not take it as an unfriendly act. The Maharajah still hesitated. Fearing that Kashmir might eventually opt for India, Pakistan's Jinnah ordered a military operation.

With the first shot fired across the boundary, the Maharajah of Kashmir appealed to India for urgent military assistance. He also expressed a desire to accede to India legally. The Indian Cabinet decided to wait until the Maharajah signed the Instrument of Accession making Kashmir, like other princely States that had welcomed the Instrument of Accession, part of India. Thereupon Indian troops were airlifted to Kashmir and they landed just in time to save the capital city of Srinagar.

At the time of accepting the accession of Kashmir, Prime Minister Nehru had said that he would like to give an occasion to the people of Kashmir to decide the future of their State 'as soon as the invader had been driven from Kashmir soil'. Nehru repeated this voluntary assurance when he wrote to the Pakistani Government in November 1947 about the aggression in Kashmir and its consequences. Anxious to keep India's record clean and above suspicion, Nehru also took the matter to the United Nations in 1948. The United Nations set up a Commission for India and Pakistan, sent teams of observers to supervise the cease-fire, appointed several mediators and passed a string of resolutions. Years went by.

The Kashmir problem of 1957 was not the Kashmir problem of 1948. When India first referred it to the United Nations, it was a simple case of aggression by Pakistan's armed forces. There was a plaintiff and a defendant. One of the United Nations' own mediators, Sir Owen Dixon, studied the evidence and judged Pakistan an aggressor.

In nine years, however, the situation had changed. There was no longer any talk of aggression by anybody against anybody else. The distinction between the plaintiff and the defendant had disappeared. The roles were in fact reversed, and the original plaintiff appeared to be the guilty party. The idea of a plebiscite, put forth initially by India in good faith, was thrown back at her. It was made out that India had gone back on an international commitment.

The cold war was the chief agent that brought about this transformation. Pakistan had identified herself with the Western pattern of defence and security, while India had kept out of it. Indeed, India was influencing other Afro-Asian nations against Western military pacts. The West naturally became interested in propping up Pakistan and putting pressure on India. Kashmir became the focal point of this cold-war game.

Krishna Menon's achievement in 1957 was that he succeeded in the almost hopeless task of restoring the perspective on Kashmir. As he put it, 'So many trees have grown and a very considerable amount of undergrowth, that it is impossible to see the wood properly and it will be my endeavour to present it as best we can.' He did this by reiterating the basic facts, examining who was who in the case and driving his points home with the aid of wit, logic and his own unique phraseology.

Menon's opening speech, which set a record for the United Nations in terms of length, was subsequently called an instance of filibuster. It was and it wasn't. There was nothing India stood to gain politically by holding up the proceedings of the Security Council. Pakistan had injected a sense of urgency into the debate by saying that on January 26th Kashmir was going to be annexed and merged finally into the Indian Constitution. The 'annexation' had already taken place, for, weeks before the Pakistani letter was sent to the Security Council, the Kashmir Constituent Assembly had finally resolved to merge into India; the Kashmir Constituent Assembly was a sovereign elected body. All that was going to happen on January 26th was that at midnight the Constituent Assembly would cease to exist. It was a matter outside the jurisdiction of the Security Council and there was no political attraction for India to stall the Council's work.

But a resolution by the Council expressing disapproval of the Kashmir Constituent Assembly's decision would have been a propaganda embarrassment for India on January 26th when the nation would be celebrating its Republic Day. Perhaps this was at the back of Menon's mind when he began to speak on January 23rd with only two days to go.

The debate found Menon unusually vigilant. For days he studied his brief and collected his arguments. He drove his staff to exhaustion point in his search for data. During the speech he brought out points that earlier representatives of India had not stressed. The story had a new look as he presented it.

Menon's advocacy of India's case over Kashmir rested on three principal points. Firstly, he maintained that throughout the debate the Security Council had failed to address itself to the basic issue, which was aggression by Pakistan. By so doing, he said, the Council was legalizing aggression. Secondly, Kashmir's accession to India had never been conditional. It was final and binding. Thirdly, the 1948 United Nations resolution was no longer a basis for talks between India and Pakistan because conditions had changed on both sides. In 1957 India was not

The Hero of Kashmir

prepared to sacrifice her national integrity or to welcome arbitration on matters affecting her sovereignty. The idea of a plebiscite, therefore, was no longer acceptable. By taking a tough and clear-cut line (which, incidentally, he had been advocating privately in New Delhi even before), Menon changed India's position from one of being on the defensive to one of insistence on basic rights under the United Nations Charter.

India, said Menon, took the matter to the Security Council under Article 35 of the Charter as 'a situation – I emphasize situation – the continuation of which was likely to endanger international peace. This was no dispute about territory. The Security Council, under the Charter, would be incompetent to deal with it as such because that would be either a political or a juridical question. So we brought here a situation, not a dispute.'

Referring to the basic issue involved, he said, 'We are here on a complaint of aggression. That complaint of aggression has not been resolved. So long as there are foreign forces in a place where they have no right to be, irrespective of our right, then I think the Security Council is called upon under the Charter to act accordingly.'

It was the plebiscite idea that had turned out to be the most embarrassing to India. On August 13th, 1948, the United Nations Commission for India and Pakistan had passed a resolution that proposed, as Part I, a cease-fire order; as Part II, a truce agreement and withdrawal of Pakistani troops from Kashmir; and, as Part III, that

the Government of India and the Government of Pakistan reaffirm their wish that the future status of the State of Jammu and Kashmir shall be determined in accordance with the will of the people and to that end, upon acceptance of the truce Agreement, both Governments agree to enter into consultations with the Commission with a view to determining fair and equitable conditions whereby such free expression will be assured.

The conditions laid down for determining the will of the people were clear, but they were ignored in subsequent attacks on India for not honouring an international commitment.

Krishna Menon denied that India had entered into any commitment that she was not honouring. The commitment was

203

not one to hold a plebiscite but to enter into consultations. The idea was not that the two countries should march on to a plebiscite, but that they should first fulfil two conditions and then start consultations for a plebiscite. Besides, he said, an offer that remained unaccepted could not be held over the people's heads for generations and generations. India had made many offers to Pakistan. Some might be considered when the time came. But it could not be said that if an offer were made and not accepted within a certain time, that offer could stand for ever. He pointed out in detail how Pakistan's military aid agreement with the United States and her entry into the South-East Asia Defence Organization and the Baghdad Pact had materially altered the situation since the 1948 resolution. This was a new point. Menon added another when he said that once the Kashmir Constituent Assembly voted to make the State constitutionally a part of India, the whole issue entered the realm of sovereignty. Sovereignty, he said, could never be subject to arbitration. So questions of plebiscite and arbitration no longer arose.

It was a strong case as Krishna Menon built it up. Some said it was legal hair-splitting. But legalities were so deeply involved in the Kashmir case that none dared challenge him. To throw in a non-legal argument, he said that secular India would resist accepting the principle of territorial division on the basis of religion. India claimed Islam as one of its own religions. There were fifty million Muslims in India, and if they accepted the view that if people were Muslims they belonged to another State, 'I ask you what would happen to the Muslim community in our country?' India was the third largest Muslim nation in the world, and proud of it, said Menon.

No one had thought of putting it quite that way before. When Menon did, it seemed to knock the bottom out of Pakistan's case; nobody in the Security Council would have the courage to say openly that religion was a valid basis for deciding sovereignty. Even in India people who had been confused till then suddenly realized what a powerful case theirs was. Menon had helped India out of a difficult situation legally and convincingly. Of course it made no difference to the manœuvres of his adversaries. But in India itself, it boosted his reputation more than any other single performance had done till then.

The Kashmir speech, spread over two days, was a performance

that brought out the great faculties of the man – his penetrating intellect, his quick-wittedness, his mastery of parliamentary procedure, his withering sarcasm, his ability to marshal facts, his doggedness, his sheer power of endurance.

Opposition provokes Krishna Menon – and he is at his best when provoked. Perhaps it was the formidable opposition he faced in the Security Council that roused him. The Council was then composed of Britain, the United States, Australia, France, Kuomintang China, the Philippines, Cuba, Colombia, Sweden, Iraq and the U.S.S.R., with Carlos Romulo of the Philippines in the chair. There were no more than one or two delegates from whom India could expect sympathy in that aftermath of the Hungary votes. At one stage, Menon remarked, 'I look round this table and I know I have got to fight my battles.'

He fought as he had never fought before.

It must be remembered that Menon was suffering from ill health during this period. The strain of both Suez and Hungary had made great inroads into his reserves of energy. The travelling involved had added considerably to his fatigue. Besides, general elections were scheduled in India for early March and he was standing in Bombay for his first popular election in India. This was weighing heavily on him, far as he was from the scene of the campaign. The tension had proved too exacting and he had been resorting more and more to energy-giving pills. In a personal letter to a friend in Bombay he referred to 'the terrible stress of things here' and said, 'I fear by the end of this one would not be of much use for anything.'

The Kashmir debate was a physical ordeal. It began on January 23rd. The morning session went off smoothly. When the Council met in the afternoon, the first signs of a 'stop Menon' campaign began to appear. Towards the close of the day, at the end of what Menon called 'this instalment', the President asked how much time he would require to finish his statement. Menon said one more meeting would be sufficient. The President then suggested that the Council stay for another hour. Menon discouraged the idea by saying that he would need 'two to two and a half hours, even if I condense everything. The whole of the argument in this case remains.' He then added in a tired drawl, 'I have no desire to prolong these proceedings. I would have a considerable personal difficulty in carrying on for another two hours.'

But the President was not moved. He proposed a night meeting. The Soviet delegate thereupon intervened to draw the President's attention to 'the very anguished condition of the representative of India' and to say that the Council had better meet the next day.

Undaunted, the President went on to ask 'the pleasure of the Council' about a night session. Menon, trying hard to control himself, asked whether he was entitled to speak on this point. The President looked at him and said, 'I think this is a decision to be made by the Council.'

Menon was touched to the quick. 'Under Article 32 of the Charter,' he shouted, 'when I am asked to participate in this discussion, if the Council desires to hear the views of the Government of India, that must be physically possible.'

There was an instant transformation in the President, who said, 'The President will listen to your views.'

Menon let him have his views. The Cuban representative followed, saying that there was no need to insist on an extraordinary session. The President finally gave in and fixed the meeting for 10 o'clock the next morning.

Menon began the next day with a caustic reference to 'the President's impatience'. But he soon discovered that many more than the President were determined to be impatient that day. The members of the Security Council knew that the only success they could score was on the propaganda front. For this it was necessary to put their resolution before January 26th.

When the Council met that morning, the delegates found before them copies of a resolution tabled overnight by the United States, Britain, Australia, Cuba and Colombia. It opened with the remark, 'Having heard the representative of India ... ', although the representative of India had stated at the end of the previous day that 'the whole of the argument in this case remains'.

Menon prefaced his statement of the day with the remark that he was going to speak without any reference to the resolution, 'and the reason – I want this to go on record – is that I want the people of my country to know that this resolution has been put down by five sponsors before they have heard the statement of India'.

The people of his country had another occasion to know of the undercurrents in the Security Council as Menon's speech progressed. The Pakistani representative had referred, in his opening speech, to certain private conversations among the Commonwealth Prime Ministers. Menon asked for a ruling on whether private conversations could be quoted in a public debate and, if they could be so quoted, whether India could also refer to those private documents in order to tell the full story. The President had said that 'the representative of India has the right to make reply as he chooses and to make such statements as he may make'.

Menon began quoting from the Government of India's record of the Commonwealth Prime Ministers' talks. When he was half way through, Britain's Sir Pierson Dixon raised a point of order. He said how unfortunate it was that such confidential papers should be so publicly quoted, what a wonderful institution the Commonwealth was and how they all had to be more discreet in handling its affairs. The representative of Australia then added his own views on the sanctity of the Commonwealth.

Menon was stung. He had been elaborate in his reference to the situation created by the Pakistani delegate's first allusions to the documents. He had even gone to the extent of saying that if those allusions were struck off the record, he would consider the episode closed and not himself quote from the talks. At that time, as at the time when Pakistan was quoting from the Commonwealth documents, the British and Australian delegates had held their peace.

Menon turned upon his Commonwealth colleagues. For a moment he was calm. 'I can only conclude,' he said, 'that because of the general fatigue caused by listening to me, they could not have heard the point I raised with you, Mr President.' Then he suddenly roared, 'I yield to no one in my desire to maintain Commonwealth relations and I suppose in my time I have contributed as much to this as anyone else at this table ... One way to preserve Commonwealth relations is to appreciate that it is a two-way relationship ... I will make an appeal to Sir Pierson Dixon to exercise some degree of fair play in dealing with different members of the Commonwealth – at least in public.' Sir Pierson was silent.

What began on January 23rd stretched into February. The mounting fatigue kept Menon's colleagues on the Indian delegation and his physicians worried. But it had no effect on his own sarcasm and alertness. The encomiums from home were a source of great inspiration.

On February 15th, a new resolution was tabled in the Council by Britain, Australia, the United States, and Cuba. It suggested the stationing of United Nations troops in Kashmir. This incensed India, for it implied aggression by India and openly equated the accuser with the accused.

Menon was growing paler day by day. The frequency with which he took energy pills had increased alarmingly. The doctors insisted upon rest, and rest was not possible for more than two or three hours a day.

Mobilizing his failing faculties with great effort on February 16th, he spoke on the Four-Power resolution which he called a 'poison pill'.

Why is it that we have never heard voices in connection with the freedom of people under the suppression and tyranny of Pakistani authorities on the other side of the cease-fire line? Why is it that we have not heard here that in ten years these people have not seen a ballot paper? With what voice can either the Security Council or anyone coming before it demand a plebiscite for a people on our side who exercise their franchise, who have freedom of speech, who function under a hundred local bodies?

The hoarse voice of the speaker was quivering by now. In a rising crescendo, he said,

Our country will not tolerate threats. If it came to that we would perform our duty under the Charter, that is defend our country's soil.

Steel fingers gripped the edge of the desk. There was a gasp for breath. Then Menon cried,

My country has deliberately chosen the path of an independent foreign policy. No pressures will elbow us into an alignment in one direction or another.

There was a sudden thud and Menon fell back on his seat. Anxious aides sent for help. A hush fell on the Security Council. Presently, there was movement. A weak and completely worn-out figure lumbered up from the seat. Without a glance at anyone, without a word, a shadow of Krishna Menon limped out of the chamber.

The Hero of Kashmir

The angriest man that day was Dr W. H. Hitzig, Menon's personal physician in New York. He had warned that Menon was at that moment fit for nothing except a total rest. The collapse made Hitzig really anxious.

The good doctor's consternation knew no bounds when Menon woke up the next day and started for Washington for a nation-wide TV broadcast. He was miserably sick, but he not only disobeyed doctor's orders but also threw all kinds of gibes at him.

It was the TV talk in which he spoke the now-famous sentence, 'Aggressors must not be allowed to reap the fruits of aggression.' After the broadcast, he drove back to New York running a temperature of 106 degrees. His blood-pressure was below 80 and still falling. Hitzig described the condition as 'an extreme state of collapse' and his one hope rested in the fact that his patient was scheduled to leave for India the following day. He knew that in escaping from the mad tensions of New York lay the chance of this impossible patient's survival.

But the patient did not leave. He received urgent instructions from New Delhi asking him to stay on. A dramatic situation had developed in India. The External Affairs Ministry announced a grave new development on the Kashmir front. It summoned twenty-three foreign envoys in New Delhi for an urgent briefing. Hours later, Ministers electioneering in various parts of the country were called back to Delhi where an extraordinary Cabinet meeting was held. This was followed by an emergency session of the Defence Sub-committee of the Cabinet. Something ominous had developed, but there was no indication as to its precise character apart from the announcement that the Indian representative would make an important statement in the Security Council on February 20th.

But the Indian representative was suffering from acute postural hypertension which made it essential for him to lie down so as to maintain blood-pressure at a safe level. He was unable to eat and was being fed intravenously. The doctor pronounced him incapable of standing.

As the day of his speech dawned, Menon had no ear for doctors. When he was finally convinced that he was physically unable to deliver a speech, he devised his own solution. He ordered the doctor to inject a stimulant into his arm.

The doctor refused point blank to comply with such a request.

Menon promptly got hold of a junior doctor. After taking the first shot, he bared his other arm and demanded another one. The doctor was horrified. But the order was so peremptory that he obeyed before he knew what was happening.

Life rushed into Krishna Menon. Like a man possessed, he walked into the Security Council, a wry smile on his lips. The Council, having known how dangerous was Menon's condition, was seized with an unusual fear.

Menon made his statement. It was a disclosure of war preparations in Pakistan's half of Kashmir. He listed details of how American arms were being massed by Pakistan along the cease-fire line and of the diplomatic activities that were going on in Karachi. It was a bitter, devastating speech lasting two hours. When it came to a close, Menon flashed his famous sardonic smile. But it was only for a fleeting second. The next moment he slumped forward on his desk. The effects of the drug had passed off, and now a cold numbness set in.

Head resting on the table, Menon lay still. Sensing danger, Arthur Lall, India's permanent representative to the United Nations, motioned to Dr Hitzig. The doctor took a seat behind what appeared to be the lifeless form of Menon. He slowly stretched his hand to take the patient's pulse. The touch sent Menon shooting back to life. He violently pushed the doctor's hand away, grunting. He made an effort to sit up. But the time for such bravado was over. As the Council was being adjourned for lunch, he fell back on his chair and passed out again. Arthur Lall sent for a wheel-chair, while dismayed delegates waited around. Minutes passed and then Menon slowly opened his eyes. The first thing he saw was a United Nations guard pushing a wheel-chair towards him. Menon frowned and motioned it away. 'I can walk,' he said and the voice came as a distant whisper. Summoning up that superhuman will again he walked out of the Chamber leaning heavily on his stick and dragging both his feet.

Sedatives lulled him into a light sleep in the United Nations clinic. But it was a short respite, for he had already told the outraged Dr Hitzig that he intended to attend the afternoon session.

Not only that afternoon but also the next day, this despair of medical men was at his post. Back at home, a grateful India wept – in the pages of newspapers, in the speeches of Nehru.

But Dr Hitzig was incensed. On February 21st, he decided to be frank with the public. 'I am displeased with Menon's actions,' he told the Press. 'Yesterday he promised to talk for only half an hour in the morning, and he spoke for two hours. He promised to speak only ten minutes in the evening and he actually spoke for fifty-five minutes. I begged him to stay in bed. But he insists on going back. He believes he has a mission and he says that God is with him and will protect him ... This man needs a period of convalescence. I have told him that if he persists in disobeying my instructions, I cannot be responsible for what happens. He was very emotional yesterday. But he made a beautiful speech. It was a delight to listen to him. It has compensated for all my anguish about his condition. This condition is provoked by the fact that he will not eat properly, keeps himself short of protein foods and absorbs too much liquid. Never before have I seen a man who drinks thirty cups of tea a day.'

Menon had in fact defied every known principle of medical science during this week of extreme danger. If he still survived, the explanation did not lie within the realm of reason.

On February 21st the Security Council passed a revised resolution, the earlier 'poison pill' having been vetoed by the Soviet Union. The new resolution asked for the dispatch of another United Nations representative to India and Pakistan to evolve a solution to the problem. One of the stormiest debates in United Nations history was at last over. Menon was ready to leave for India the same day, but this time the doctor counselled a couple of days' rest in New York and for once he had his way.

Or did he? Menon did not seem to have rested. Lying in bed, he became involved in a new West-Asian crisis caused by the Arab demand in the General Assembly for sanctions against Israel. For good measure he also threw himself into the Cyprus debate.

Dr Hitzig's day of deliverance came when Krishna Menon left New York for India on March 2nd.

24

The Adoption

THE leaders of the West knew, as well as India, the tremendous implications of what Krishna Menon had achieved through the Kashmir debate. He had stood up to pressure tactics the like of which the United Nations had seldom witnessed before. He had displayed a political toughness which had no parallel in other non-Western delegates. He had shown an amazing capacity to fight his way through past mistakes and omissions and emerge in a position of strength. Kashmir was no longer India's political graveyard; Kashmir was now a glaring example of Western perfidy towards India. By turning the tables on the West, Menon showed that he was a match for their combined might.

An immediate advantage that flowed from the Kashmir debate was that it more than compensated for his absence from India at election time. The West made a tactical mistake in picking this particular debate for a concentrated attack on Menon. Instead of crushing him, the debate all but deified him. In the first place Kashmir was the wrong subject. It caught the Indian people in too emotional a mood. The open discrimination shown by the West against India during the debate gave Menon the prestige of a victim. His illness completed the picture. Menon became a martyr in the eyes of Indians.

For a change, praising Krishna Menon became the rule in India. Newspapers gave full coverage to the Security Council proceedings. Pictures of him were all over the land. Newsreel shots showed him fighting doggedly against heavy odds. Menon's heroism became the talk of the nation. The Prime Minister summed up the national mood when he told a mass meeting in Madras,

There are some people in this country and some people in other countries too whose job in life appears to be to run down Mr Krishna Menon because he is cleverer than these people and because his record of service for Indian freedom is far longer than theirs and because he has worn himself out in the service of India. We do not run away from criticism. Mr Krishna Menon's handling of the Kashmir case in the Security Council and the line he took there fully reflect our views on the subject. Mr Menon has done his work brilliantly and most effectively.

Krishna Menon could not hope for a more favourable mood in which to fight an election. By enabling him to become a national saviour, the West had inadvertently ensured his electoral victory.

This was clear when Menon landed at Bombay's Santacruz Airport on March 6th. It was ten o'clock at night, yet a crowd of 3,000 was at the airport to cheer the home-coming hero. As many as 200 garlands were put round his neck. From the airport he drove straight to an election meeting where 10,000 men and women were waiting for him, despite the late hour. There were only four days left before polling day.

Menon had been anxious to fight a popular election. He had spent the best years of his life away from India, but 1947 had sent him to the forefront of the country's public life. After 1947 his importance had steadily increased. He was handling more and more responsible tasks. In the capitals of the world as much as in the United Nations he was always speaking in the name of the people of India. If he was to do this with authority and confidence, he thought, it was necessary for him to receive a direct mandate from the people. He had been elected in 1953 to the Upper House of Parliament, but that was not a popular vote, only the members of the legislature having participated in the election.

There was also the 'stranger complex' in the back of his mind. Was he really part of life in India? The Prime Minister, of course, knew about his long record of service for Indian freedom. His enemies were already saying that Menon was what he was solely by courtesy of the Prime Minister. This was damaging gossip, for it made him appear all the more removed from the main currents of India's public life. 'The more I have thought about it,' he wrote to a Congress Party friend in Bombay in November 1956, 'the more I consider it the necessary thing to do. At least it gives one the feeling of being wanted in the place. I have also been thinking that if some such thing does not come off it would be logical for me to give up the present position, as quite obviously the country is not interested.'

Krishna Menon felt strongly on the matter, but it was not easy to obtain party backing. Influential sections of the Congress were not enthusiastic about the prospect. The lobby that had opposed him from the very beginning and thwarted the 1954 attempt of the Prime Minister to take him into the Cabinet was busy campaigning against putting Menon up as a candidate. Menon was by then too important a personality for them to condemn him as an unwanted man. They therefore took the line that he was too useful a man to be exposed to the tender mercies of the electorate. He was told, 'It seems that the top people do not like you to fight an election. There is no risk from their point of view but they do not wish to take any chances in your case ... I have been asked to write to you and find out whether you still prefer to fight an election.'[1]

The suggestion, of course, was repugnant to Krishna Menon. He left no doubts in the minds of the top people that he still preferred and would always prefer to fight an election.

He had been returned to the Rajya Sabha for Madras. The Chief Minister of Madras and Congress strong man, Mr Kamaraj, announced that he was reserving a seat for Menon. He also told the Congress that he would personally conduct the campaign in the absence of Menon.

With Kamaraj to conduct the fight, Menon would have had a walk-over. The idea left Menon cold. If he was to obtain a safe seat, he could see no point in fighting at all. Some friends suggested Bombay. Bombay was an urban constituency. It had a stirring history. It was also one of the most politically conscious constituencies in the country. It was a cosmopolitan city, a miniature India, and a verdict from Bombay was the nearest thing to an all-India verdict. Bombay also happened to be at that time the centre of a strong parochial movement. The Marathi-speaking people of western India had been demanding a separate linguistic state with Bombay city as capital. The Government of India had refused and this had led to the formation of a powerful United

---

[1] From a letter written by a Bombay Congress official. (For political reasons, I have thought it better to omit here names of individuals when quoting from personal correspondence which was kindly made available to me from several sources. – Author.)

Maharashtra 'Samiti', a combination of all opposition parties pitted against the Congress. The emotional appeal of their platform was great and the Congress position was shaky in the Marathi-speaking areas. Here was an opposition strong enough to merit the attention of Krishna Menon. The challenge inspired him.

It was not easy to persuade the Congress Party to give Menon one of Bombay's four parliamentary candidatures. The Prime Minister was anxious not to issue a *Diktat* lest it be said that he was favouring a particular candidate, however useful that candidate might be. He had also been told of linguistic and other difficulties if Menon stood for Bombay and of the certainty of a strong contest. However, a few influential Congress leaders in Bombay were keen to have Menon elected, and so he was adopted by North Bombay.

The hottest months of the campaign were January and February. Even gratitude for Krishna Menon's performance in the United Nations did not make it a walk-over for the Congress Party. So strong was the opposition that there were some areas in North Bombay where Congress workers could not go. There was also systematic personal propaganda against Menon. As usual, birds of many feathers were flocking round him. They included communists and 'persons known to be associated with communists'. This gave a good opportunity to the opposition to attempt to pin the charge of communism on Menon. The Catholic Bishops' Conference of India issued a directive to all Catholics not to vote for candidates who 'maintain the principles of atheistic communism'. This was being effectively used by the opposition to alienate the Catholic vote from Menon and the process was helped by the fact that the opposition candidate was a Catholic.

While the charge of communism was freely levelled against Menon, the Communist Party itself was actively opposed to him. It was the principal constituent of the united Samiti party which was opposing the Congress and Menon. Its leader, S. A. Dange, was the Chairman of the Samiti. When the Party saw that several of its members were campaigning for Krishna Menon, Dange summoned some of them privately and admonished them. He said he did not want any communist to stand in the way of the Samiti candidate. In a public statement he said that even though the Party supported Nehru's foreign policy and therefore was willing to support Krishna Menon who was its symbol, foreign policy was not the issue in North Bombay. The linguistic issue was much more important and Dange wanted to leave no doubt about the significance his Party attached to the victory of the Samiti nominee. To make matters worse, the General Secretary of the Party, Ajoy Ghosh, issued a statement strongly denouncing the Congress. A vote for Menon in North Bombay, he said, would be a vote against Maharashtra. In the atmosphere of heightened parochial passions then prevalent in Bombay, this appeal of the Communist Party boss did much harm to the Congress candidate.

But in the end the election was decided on the issue of foreign policy. Menon was held up as a symbol of Indian individuality in international affairs. In a special appeal Nehru said,

> We have asked Mr Krishna Menon to stand from Bombay City so that the citizens of Bombay may have an opportunity to give their verdict on the major international policies of the Congress and the Government of India ... We felt that it was right that the voters of Bombay, which is in many ways the political nerve-centre of India, should pronounce on them and give their verdict generally on the policy of non-alignment which India has followed. Mr Krishna Menon represents this policy in the fullest measure ...

Perhaps it was C. Rajagopalachari, comrade-in-arms of Gandhi and India's elder statesman, who expressed the mood of the nation most succinctly.

> Not even Jawaharlal Nehru's return is so important as Mr Krishna Menon's victory in the Bombay elections. After his brave and single-handed fight in the Council of the United Nations, united in their hostility to India, if he should by any chance or mishap fail to be returned in Bombay, what would be left of the prestige of India before the world?

That sentiment finally prevailed. On March 11th, Menon polled 171,708 votes, giving him a majority of 47,741.

The significance of Menon's 1957 victory is likely to be forgotten in the light of the more spectacular victory he scored five years later. In 1962 there was an organized all-out bid to get rid of him. It was essentially a personal war and the eventual victory was a personal victory. In 1957, however, Menon was fighting an unusually powerful local political movement. The results proclaimed the strength of the movement. Although the candidate put up by the Samiti was a small-time local leader, he polled almost forty-three per cent of the total votes cast. And although Kashmir had made a hero of Menon, his majority was small. The significance of the 1962 victory was that he won with a record majority; the significance of the 1957 victory was that he won at all.

With the results announced, new horizons opened up before Krishna Menon. For the first time he had received from the people of India an unmistakable sign of their approval. With typical single-mindedness he began evolving possible cures for the social and economic ills afflicting India. His devotion to these objectives created problems for him personally in so far as it brought him into conflict with important people. But it was not in him to change. The lack of personal motives, on the other hand, helped him to influence Indian socio-economic thinking significantly. Krishna Menon became a serious political factor in India only after the 1957 election.

After a life-time abroad and now in his sixty-first year, it was not easy for Menon to fit into India. He was long out of touch with his mother tongue, the only Indian language he knew. And he knew nothing at all about the peculiar political ways of Congress leaders. There was, of course, no question of his compromising with the high principles he had learned and practised in the past.

Inside the Congress Party there was already dissatisfaction about his ways. The open support he had received in the election from persons known to be associated with communists made many people hostile. Some Congress candidates contesting the elections to the State Assembly from the same area had protested against non-Congressmen working for Menon while ignoring all the other Congress nominees and even the Party.

Menon's personal antipathy to several Congressmen in high positions was another problem. The criticisms he had encountered during his High Commissionership and later during the United Nations debate on Hungary made him react strongly against those he suspected of being his enemies. There was never any thought of making it up with them or of winning them over. On the contrary he made no bones about his contempt for them. Sentiments against him grew in the process. Powerful business interests, which meant also powerful sections of the Press, became more and more vicious in their attacks.

Menon was aware of the problems, but did not wait to find neat solutions to them all. His election gave Nehru an opportunity to give him a senior Cabinet post. In April 1957 Nehru named him Minister for Defence.

Ideologically Menon brought a new element into the Cabinet. The Congress as a party was committed to a socialistic pattern of society, but the Cabinet contained no one, barring of course the Prime Minister, who was in earnest about it. Menon was articulate and influential enough to make socialism felt. On the one hand he gave Nehru the ideological support he needed. On the other, he provided a natural rallying point to those socialists in the Congress Party who had been languishing for want of leadership.

25

Minister for Defence

THE first years of freedom had shown that Krishna Menon was not at his best when confined to too small a field. The Defence Ministry was a big enough challenge.

An efficient army had been inherited from the British, but India had not formulated a proper defence policy of her own. This was natural. The governmental pattern of free India was a continuation of the leadership pattern that obtained during the struggle for freedom. The struggle was carried on by men who had spent years developing a particular philosophy of life and a particular frame of mind. The business of warfare had no place in this philosophy. The result was that when India attained independence there was no attempt to build up an adequate defence system.

The Prime Minister was aware of the importance of the subject. But the problems that faced him in the aftermath of partition were so pressing that he never found it possible to give to defence the same attention he gave to economic planning, foreign affairs or social legislation. The approach of Menon's predecessors at the Ministry was anything but technical. The defence forces had been 'Indianized'. But the concept of Indianization covered only the personnel. At the time of independence the three commanders-in-chief were British and so were most senior staff officers. The early Defence Ministers arranged for the retirement of these officers and for their replacement by senior Indian officers. Beyond this, initiative gave place to old traditions. Perhaps it was thought that India, committed to non-violence and peace, would never require a military force in the modern sense.

Some of the senior generals were happy with this state of affairs. Trained at Sandhurst, they were too attached to British military thinking to suggest or welcome any changes. But the younger officers were dissatisfied. They saw in the Government's approach

to defence matters a lack of imagination that was incompatible
with the needs of a modern State.

Menon had precise ideas about military matters. He had made
a thorough study of defence, submitted several papers on it to
various authorities and become recognized, particularly on the
Left in Britain, as something of a military genius.

India's mood had also undergone a change. On the west
Pakistan was growing militarily strong through various security
pacts. On the north-east the Nagas were restive. Most unexpected of
all, China had turned inexplicably belligerent. She began her de-
predations in 1954–5 (though the Government of India knew about
it only later and the people later still), and by 1957 the traditional
frontier of the Himalayas lay breached at half a dozen points.

Krishna Menon started with a definite set of views. It was, in
historical terms, a late start and this fact was to leave its mark on
his programme. He tried his best according to his lights to make up
for lost time.

Menon saw a three-fold basis for any programme of modernization. First of all, the armed forces should be reorganized along
lines suited to Indian strategic needs and economic realities.
Efficiency in organization could even make up sometimes for
deficiency in equipment. Secondly, he believed that a national
defence system must have its own national industrial basis. It
should not be dependent in times of crises on other nations for
essential armament and other supplies. Thirdly, Menon put great
emphasis on welfare programmes for the troops.

The new Defence Minister was conscious of India's economic
limitations. He insisted on building up strength from below.
During several defence debates in Parliament, he repeatedly said
that defence could not be separated from either the economic or
the social policy of the country. It would be tantamount to acting
in panic, he would say, to earmark money for building up the
fighting forces at the cost of national planning and developmental
schemes. He would say that the per capita income in the United
States was 9,200Rs., in the United Kingdom 3,980Rs. and in
India 252Rs. (13.6 rupees equal one pound sterling) and that
therefore India could not think of large forces.

We can have forces that are qualitatively efficient. The
morale of our people, the quality of our equipment, the

brains our officers use in learning strategy and in using imagination, the capacity for adaptation and improvisation, the lack of blind adherence to past formulae and at the same time the lack of blind fanaticism to a rejection of past formulae – these are things that have to make up for the lack of our material resources.[1]

A revealing development was the Chinese activity on the Himalayan frontier. In July 1954, almost simultaneously with the signing of the nobly-worded Panch Shila agreement on peaceful coexistence, China had protested to Delhi about the presence of Indian troops in Barahoti – the first instance of a Chinese claim to Indian territory. In September 1955, five months after the grand conference at Bandung, Chinese soldiers had intruded ten miles across the border into India at Damzan. The greatest surprise of all, the Aksai Chin road in Ladakh, was completed by the Chinese in September 1957.

Menon had differed from his Prime Minister, in the very first years of freedom, over India's China policy. Nehru had been advised by the Indian ambassador to Peking that there was no possibility of any clash of interests between India and China and the policy towards Peking had been formulated on this assumption. Menon questioned the assumption then, but had no evidence to put forward in support of his suspicions. He identified himself with the policy and tried to establish genuine friendship between New Delhi and Peking.

For a while he was taken in by the cunning of the Chinese. Chou En-lai's sweet reasonableness during the Indo-China conference, his generous spirit at Bandung and his goodwill gesture in accepting India's request on behalf of the American airmen in 1956 gave the impression that the Indian policy was the right one.

After Aksai Chin, however, Menon's early instincts came again to the fore, though he still found it difficult to carry the rest of the Cabinet with him. Fighting his way through temperamental, ideological and financial obstructions, he launched a crash programme of road-building, mountain-warfare training and armament manufacture. It was for the first time in history that India was turning its attention to building up defences in the

---

[1] Speech in Parliament, July 25th, 1957, four months after taking over the Defence portfolio.

inhospitable Himalayas. But again it was a late start. Menon's programme turned out to be not fast enough, for the Chinese forestalled him and moved in too massively and too soon. For what happened when they did, though, others also must share responsibility.

The new Defence Minister found millions of rupees' worth of stores and equipment lying idle in open military depots. He launched a huge programme of recovery and reconstruction. Condemned vehicles, tens of thousands of them, were repaired and put into service. Covered accommodation was extended to hundreds of acres of land. Existing maintenance depots were streamlined and new ones added. Old notions of organization were reassessed and an all-out effort made to achieve co-ordination between the three services, and between the services collectively and the Ministry. There was greater insistence on improvement in the quality of training. The latest methods of work study were introduced. An integrated programme to raise the educational level of the armed forces became part of the general training. Simultaneously welfare programmes for the services were expanded. The scope of death gratuities and family pensions was extended. Pay scales were revised upwards. Pensions were improved. The troops' ration allowance, which had been abolished, was restored. Junior commissioned officers and their families were permitted to have their baggage carried free while on transfer. Large-scale housing programmes were carried out. New areas of technology were explored and new targets set. The Defence Minister's Research and Development Committee was set up to mobilize scientific and technical skill. The number of civilian scientists working for the armed forces was increased, their status enhanced. Scientific planning was insisted upon in every field of activity. Out of the war-time maintenance depots, fully equipped production factories bloomed. Nothing was held too difficult for these factories to attempt. They began producing not only armament, but also trucks and aeroplanes, cooking utensils and milk evaporators.

The services grew in strength and quality. Mobility, which had always been a frustrating problem for the army, became one of its strong points. After one year in office, Menon was able to announce that the army was capable of much quicker movement than ever before. An unprecedented degree of inter-services operational co-ordination was also achieved. The swiftness with which the Goa operation was completed in December 1961 was an indication of the measure of these achievements.

Also evident was a new spirit in the services. There was a great urge to produce results, a great pride in what was being done. This upsurge of enthusiasm was a direct result of Krishna Menon's personal leadership. He began his term by short-circuiting usual channels and making direct contact with the men who were doing the jobs. Formerly, bureaucracy had held sway in the Ministry and generals had to wait their turn to get an interview with the Secretary to the Ministry; an interview with the Defence Minister himself had been a rarity. The new Defence Minister was accessible to all. Before 1957 the administrative chain was too long for the officers to put forward their ideas effectively; with Menon's arrival it became possible for an officer with a new idea to discuss it personally with the Minister himself.

The services also realized that for the first time they had a civilian chief who knew a great deal about what were supposed to be technical defence subjects. On matters of strategy and logistics, Krishna Menon proved to be equal to any general. On the scientific front, his knowledge was superior.

Menon's most important contribution to the defence system in India was in the field of defence production. He would make no compromise over his belief that the essential pre-requisite of any effective national security was availability of all defence requirements within the borders of the country. 'It is not merely a matter of money,' he told Parliament in April 1959. 'It gives our people a sense of self-esteem; it gives our people a belief that our defence power is not dependent upon the nature or upon the goodwill or the technique of another country. There is a kind of moral, inferior factor coming into things when someone else has to help you in these matters.'

Menon vastly expanded the research and development programme. He made a clear distinction between planning and production. In 1958 he merged all existing research establishments into a new Defence Research and Development Organization.

Menon's habit was to pose a problem and ask his men to provide a solution. It created an inquiring spirit in those manning the research and production units. It helped increase their self-confidence. It sharpened their interest in modern technology.

But his policy frightened private industry. He ended the purchasing of army trucks from private manufacturers, and the Defence Ministry's factories even produced pressure cookers. The Indian Press took up the cudgels on behalf of the private sector. Questions were asked in Parliament. It was said that the Defence Minister was acting with malice towards private industry and that he was forcing the ordnance factories to waste their capacity on non-defence programmes.

Menon answered this criticism in his own way. Replying to questions asked by a millionaire industrialist in Parliament, he said in April 1960,

> We are told by Mr R. R. Morarka that a great deal of capacity is misused by the making of hair-clippers, pressure cookers, etc. These are two of the items that are required. It is a matter of very great importance because, even though the Defence Minister does not probably clip his hair as often as he should, the army must have its hair clipped, and the Ministry of Commerce and Industry, in its wisdom, decided to prohibit the import of clippers. Now, are our soldiers to go like sadhus with long hair, or are they to use hair-clippers? Therefore, the ordnance factories and the service headquarters used their initiative, ingenuity and everything else and produced hair-clippers which are as good as any imported hair-clippers. That is the answer.
>
> The second is with regard to pressure cookers. I do not know why anybody is so worried about pressure cookers being made here. There may be a reason or may not. The fact is we have troops at heights where water does not boil properly without a pressure cooker, and they are entitled to cook food. And the Commerce and Industry Ministry, again in its wisdom, prohibited the import of pressure cookers. Therefore we made the pressure cookers and they are giving good service. Incidentally we discovered that these pressure cookers probably cost only one-fourth of what we have been paying for them. There is no objection to saving government money so far as I can understand, and therefore we saved it. That is the position.

Some of the officers close to Menon were excited, just before he resigned, about a new idea he had thrown at them. This was to help develop a scientific temper in the country by bringing out cheap booklets on scientific subjects on the one hand, and by manufacturing mechanical toys on the other. Toys being Menon's own hobby, the idea had a special appeal to him. Although mechanical toys are a big industry and a popular pastime in advanced countries, they are rare in India. What is available is prohibitively expensive. Menon wanted to flood the country with working models of the HF 24 supersonic fighter, Shaktiman trucks, patrol boats and all the rest of them. He had already held an exhibition of toys in Delhi. He then began putting pressure on his men to produce little electric motors that would power models, and to set up a central organization for the distribution of the products. It was a project which, if implemented, could have helped Indian children to catch up with a dream-world they had been missing. It was also a project which reflected Menon's all-embracing reformist outlook; under him even a military organiza-tion had to be ever conscious of its social obligations to the country.

On the whole, what one may call the creative period in Krishna Menon's career began with his appointment as Defence Minister. Before 1957 he was essentially a foreign affairs man. In that field his speciality was negotiation rather than initiation of policy. He was the builder, while Nehru was the architect. As Defence Minister, Krishna Menon began to visualize and initiate as well as implement policies. He became both architect and builder.

It is a pity that before he could complete his building pro-gramme, the country was plunged into a full-scale though un-declared war. The 'Yellow Peril' cast a shadow on Menon's defence policies. Like a half-finished masterpiece they stood exposed to the spotlight in bare outline.

26

The Gathering Clouds

O<small>NE</small> unfortunate effect of Krishna Menon's taking over the Defence portfolio was that it brought India's fighting forces into the centre of public controversy and newspaper gossip. Menon is fond of saying that he never goes after controversy but that controversy chases him. The problem really is that a stage has been reached where there can hardly be a controversy in India without Krishna Menon figuring in it, and Krishna Menon cannot take one step without creating controversy. It afflicts everything he does. Even the defence forces were not spared. A disgruntled officer would speak to an editor on the quiet, and a fresh scandal broke out. A young officer had an affair with a girl, and the next day's headlines described how the Defence Minister was encouraging immorality and indiscipline in the services.

The critics were not content with attacking Menon in their speeches and writing. They considered practical ways of 'liquidating' him. They had a moment of triumph on September 1st, 1959, when news of resignations by the chiefs of the three Armed Services burst upon the world.

In fact only the Army Chief, General Thimayya, had sent in a letter of resignation. It was said that the two other service chiefs were about to follow suit. The Navy's Katari, who was in Delhi at the time, maintained silence on the matter, while the Air Force's Mukherjee, in London on a visit, said he was surprised at the news.

The Thimayya drama opened with a meeting between him and the Prime Minister in the last week of August. The general spoke at length about the bottle-necks other ministries were creating in the working of the Defence Ministry, about the growing difficulties of 'processing' defence proposals through the various economic ministries. This lack of co-ordination between the ministries was hampering the work of the Defence Ministry, he said.

Subsequently Nehru conveyed to Menon the gist of General Thimayya's complaints. On a matter of principle, Menon took objection to the general's conduct. He told the Prime Minister and later the general himself that it was not the business of a soldier to go over the head of his Minister and talk to the Prime Minister about inter-ministerial troubles. As Minister he was aware of these problems and it was his job to inform the Prime Minister of them. The right thing for the Army Chief to do, if he felt so strongly about the matter, was to discuss it with the Defence Minister.

The general said that he realized that he had done something wrong, and that since it appeared that he had lost the confidence of his Minister he would resign. Menon pointed out that there was no question of a resignation and that as long as they understood what was right and what was wrong, they could carry on as usual. It should be said that hitherto Krishna Menon and General Thimayya were on very friendly and close personal terms.

After this conversation Thimayya must have fallen under political influence. He had been in touch with certain senior members of the Government, as well as with some leading opposition M.P.s It is likely that they got wind of what was going on and rushed in with their advice. Despite the conversation he had had with his Minister, General Thimayya sent in a letter of resignation to the Prime Minister.

This was about mid-day on August 31st. In the evening Nehru sent for Thimayya, said that his resignation was completely wrong and asked him to withdraw the letter in order to avoid further unpleasantness. Without protest, General Thimayya withdrew his resignation.

The news of the resignation leaked *after* this withdrawal. In the evening of August 31st there was a cocktail party at one of the embassies in New Delhi. General Thimayya was there, and so were some leading newspaper correspondents. A close associate of the general took the political correspondent of the *Statesman*, one of India's foremost newspapers, aside and told him that Thimayya had resigned and that the other service chiefs were doing the same. The correspondent left the party and went straight to his office.

The Editor of the *Statesman* of course believed his correspondent's story, but insisted on confirmation. A telephone call was put through to the residence of the general and a female voice, when questioned, replied that he had resigned.

The news was splashed across the front page the next morning. The Prime Minister was at a loss to know how this confidential item of news, not disclosed by him even to the Cabinet, had leaked to the Press.

When Parliament assembled on September 1st, there was a spate of adjournment motions in both Houses. Sentiment was unmistakably against the Minister and in favour of the general. Thimayya was an officer of great reputation and his performance as Chairman of the Neutral Nations Repatriation Commission in Korea had enhanced his prestige greatly both at home and abroad. Even the Congress Party benches gave him their sympathy.

By the next day, however, the tide had turned. Sympathies that were with the Army Chief the previous day were now with the Defence Minister. Many members realized, as they reflected on the crisis, that the fundamental issue of civilian over military authority was involved. The reason for Thimayya's resignation as given in his letter to the Prime Minister was said to have been his differences with the Minister over a top appointment in the army. Members saw that even if the Government was wrong in the matter of an appointment, its right to control the appointment could not be challenged by the service chiefs.

Nehru in a long statement on what had happened described the reasons given by Thimayya for his step as trivial, and said he would not condone the action. He explained how the promotion that was said to have provoked the Army Chief had been decided upon, and added that Thimayya himself had put forward the name of the officer concerned. It was important, he said, to leave no doubt about the supremacy of civilian authority over military. He also said, 'I don't have a resignation in my hand'. That made people realize that there was something strange in the sequence of events – the news appearing after the resignation had been withdrawn and the chapter closed.

The Thimayya scandal was a political manœuvre and had been shrewdly timed. Krishna Menon was just packing his bags to go to the United Nations. The country had also just realized for the first time how serious was the Himalayan border problem created by China. It was an attempt to discredit Menon personally and show how he had demoralized the services just when the nation faced a military threat.

The episode caused considerable damage to Menon's position. The opposition took full advantage of his predicament. They succeeded in creating a popular impression that there was discontent in the services, because of his autocratic methods of administration. The repercussions inside the army were more serious, for Thimayya was extremely popular.

Menon personally felt upset by the experience. His friends say that they had never seen him looking older. He was wounded and disillusioned.

The speeches he delivered in Bombay soon after the incident reflected this sense of hurt. He made frequent references to his own public position – an indulgence which he rarely permitted himself. He said, 'Attempts are being made to pull me down in public esteem, but I am not going to go about with my card of patriotism to convince them.' He said that the crisis had been timed in such a way as to cause him embarrassment when he stood before the United Nations as the spokesman of India. In other countries, he said, even when a member of the opposition party was chosen by the Government to represent it at international gatherings, he was not stabbed in the back by some of his countrymen. 'Beware of those who stab you in the back and play into the hands of the opposite side.' In a low voice of unusual humility, he concluded a speech with the sentence, 'I hope you will go home with the conviction that your Defence Minister is not undermining the defences of your country.' Perhaps the audience realized the anguish of the man; he received a prolonged standing ovation.

Menon's opponents were undaunted by the petering out of the Thimayya affair. They took up with renewed energy the question Thimayya had raised – promotions in the army. It was said that Menon was promoting his favourites; that he was driving many able men to frustration; that seniority was being ignored and only friendship and political allegiance were being honoured; that morale was being destroyed.

Menon's declaration in April 1959, 'I do not hesitate to have supersessions and there will be supersessions if the armed forces of this country are to be efficient', did not help the situation. It was even suggested by his enemies that the Defence Minister was preparing the ground for a military coup.

There were, in fact, hand-picked promotions and 'supersessions'. But the public concern generated by the first accusations subsided as information became available about the procedure for promotion in the services. It was a subject about which people knew very little and informing the public was the method devised by Krishna Menon to answer his critics.

It proved effective because the public came to realize that 'supersessions' were the rule in the army. Up to the rank of lieutenant-colonel an officer got promotion by seniority. Above that rank all posts were filled by selection. The Army Head-quarters operating through two selection boards considered the various cases, reconciled the differences if there were any and forwarded their recommendations to the Minister for approval. A Cabinet sub-committee consisting of the Prime Minister, the Home Minister and the Defence Minister made the final appoint-ment. In this set-up, plainly, a Defence Minister could not do things arbitrarily and get away with it.

Of course Menon did pick his 'cronies' for handling various defence projects he initiated. Without tampering with the ranks of officers, he nominated those he thought efficient to take charge of factories, installations, special programmes. This was where he showed his personal favouritism. But he would have been a poor Minister if he did not choose his own team for implementing his policies. Judging from the progress of the various projects, he picked the right men.

Another favourite topic with Menon's critics was defence in-formation. Attacks under this head began almost as soon as he gave his first speech in Parliament as Defence Minister. The point made was that the Minister was withholding information from the House under the pretext of secrecy. It was said that the Minister was keeping the nation in the dark deliberately because he did not want his dubious activities to be known. The accent was once again on the 'totalitarian' methods of the Minister. He was arbitrary in his promotion policy; he was being arbitrary again in refusing to answer questions in Parliament.

The way in which Menon replied to these charges was revealing. When some M.P.s pointed out to him that in Britain the Defence Ministry gave Parliament figures on the precise numerical strength of the services, Menon characteristically delved into history. He said, 'It [the number of troops in Britain] is published as a historical relic as there are so many relics in the British

Parliament. For example, the Speaker is dragged to the chair ...
He is tied to the chair in order that he may not run away. Are we
going to do it here for that reason?' Menon also described the
difference in approach between a militarily strong country and a
militarily weak one, the significance of belonging to an alliance
like NATO and belonging to no alliance, etc.

There was one occasion, however, when Krishna Menon contributed to the delaying of information. This happened during the
Goa campaign. New Delhi's civilian representative in Goa was
primarily responsible for what happened, but as the Minister who
was directly in charge of the Goa action, Menon must share the
blame.

A battalion of Press correspondents had pitched camp on the
borders of Goa in December 1961 when Indian military action
appeared imminent. Until the action commenced their only
source of information was a Government publicity officer who
seemed to know less about the situation than some of the correspondents. When the Army began moving into Goa the pressmen thought they could move in too. But they were barred from
doing so; the same Government officer continued his unhelpful
briefings.

Perhaps the defence authorities did not want too wide a
coverage of the operation. Perhaps they expected difficulties and
wanted the Press to come in only after everything was over. But
as it happened, the Government's restrictions affected only Indian
newsmen; foreign reporters found their way into Goa mostly from
the other side and sometimes even from the Indian side. The
result was that those reporters who could have given a sympathetic description of the operation were kept out, while men
from the large hostile camp were privileged to report from the
spot.[1] It distorted the picture for one thing and, for another, it
left a bitter taste in the mouth of the Indian Press. Newspapers in
India which had supported the Government at every stage of the
Goa crisis were left with nothing more than inane Government

---

[1] A British journalist told the author, 'The Indian pre-action hand-outs were mostly
trivial. The propaganda was not just untrue but obviously untrue. Nothing did more
to prejudice Western correspondents against the action. If only the Government had
stuck to the one big and true fact – colonialism! I, for example, was wholly in favour
of the action, wholly against the propaganda. If you want an example, one foreign
reporter, me, got through the frontier with a pass issued by the Information Officer
on Monday, the first day; returned to Indian territory, sent a highly pro-Indian
dispatch. The next day, with the same pass, I was not allowed in. Result: No dispatch.'

hand-outs and the imagination of their men who were covering the operation without seeing it. It was an unnecessary precaution on the part of the Government and its only effect in India was an adverse one.

In spite of criticism, the services Menon has rendered to India as Defence Minister are great. He introduced a new concept of defence preparation. He showed that even an under-developed nation could have a modern defence organization. He reorganized the services and fitted them into the Indian socio-economic realities. He gave a sense of purpose and patriotism to the officers and men. He revolutionized defence production. He saved the country huge amounts of foreign exchange.

But his very success made his enemies more determined. Their attention now turned to the General Election. There began a phenomenal mobilization of forces aimed at liquidating Menon at the polls.

27

The War of 1962

THE election that took place in North Bombay in February 1962 was not an election; it was war.

The personal animosity felt against Krishna Menon was sufficient to make it so. Since he was identified with the Left wing of the Congress, his fight became symbolic of the ideological tug-of-war going on in the country. Since he was recognized as Nehru's alter ego, it also became symbolic of the urge to defeat the Nehru Government and to end the long period in power enjoyed by the Congress Party. Since he was the most widely known exponent of India's foreign policy, it developed an international character too and became a symbol of the big-Power interest in the course of Indian politics.

The issues in the 1962 elections were clear-cut – socialism and non-alignment. These constituted the heart of Nehru's politico-economic philosophy and therefore of the Nehru Government's policies. Powerful sections of opinion in India had risen in opposition to these policies. Socialist planning was anathema to the business class. The 'permit-licence-quota Raj'[1] had provoked them to don battle dress and organize themselves. The numerically strong Hindu parties were upset by New Delhi's refusal to go to war with Pakistan as much as the political Right was irritated by the Government's soft line towards belligerent China. No longer was Nehru above criticism. In the late 'fifties opposition to Nehru's policies became an organized and determined political force.

But of course it was not easy to challenge Jawaharlal Nehru himself in his constituency. Nehru's personal hold on the masses was still too strong. The opposition therefore turned to the obvious alternative.

---

[1] This phrase was coined by C. Rajagopalachari, founder of the Swatantra Party, to refer to Government restrictions on private enterprise.

Krishna Menon became an emblem. Everyone who disapproved of any aspect of Nehru's policies became interested in defeating him. There was no doubt in any quarter, not even among official Congress Party circles, that his defeat would be Nehru's defeat.

The opposition included, although under cover, a small but influential section of the Congress. It was this group that fired the first shot in what was soon to become a raging controversy.

On top of the organizational pyramid of the Congress is the All-India Congress Committee. Under it come the various regional committees, the Bombay Pradesh Congress Committee looking after the affairs of Greater Bombay. Below the B.P.C.C. is the Bombay Suburban District Congress Committee, which takes care of the vast suburbs of Bombay City. It is the Suburban District Committee that is directly responsible for all party decisions in North Bombay. (The Suburban District Committee has since been liquidated.)

On July 1st, 1961, the Suburban District Committee held a meeting of Congress workers in the suburbs. The man who took the initiative in convening this meeting was Shantilal Shah, a veteran Congress leader of North Bombay and a minister in the State Cabinet. He also conducted the proceedings despite the presence at the meeting of the President of the Suburban District Committee.

There was only one topic on the agenda: Who should be the Congress nominee for the North Bombay parliamentary seat. Shah proposed, without mentioning any names, that a local man should be endorsed by the Party. It was clear to everyone what this meant. Krishna Menon, the sitting member from North Bombay, was not a local man.

There were heated exchanges at the meeting. Not all were against Menon, and they questioned the motives that lay behind the 'local man' theory. The idea did have a momentary appeal to Congressmen, but many came out against the attempt to introduce regionalism into Congress politics.

Those who were anxious to nip Menon's candidature in the bud were undaunted. They started the second round with a demand for *mandal* election[1] to determine the wishes of Congress

---

[1] A *mandal* is a local unit of the Congress. Several mandals constitute a district. The Suburban District Congress Committee was composed of thirty-six mandal committees for purposes of parliamentary elections.

workers in the area. The Bombay Pradesh Congress Committee agreed and mandal votes were taken.

Three names were given to mandal Congressmen to choose from. Besides Menon, there were Babubhai Chinai, a millionaire industrialist, and Indravadan Oza, a suburban Congress leader who had teamed up with Shantilal Shah to propagate the 'local man' argument. Oza was an unknown man outside Bombay, but in the suburbs he was powerful. The mandal committees had been manned for years by Oza's men. Menon's supporters expected the voting to be overwhelmingly in Oza's favour. When the votes were counted Menon had 258, Oza 274 and Chinai 55. However, the figures were challenged by Menon's supporters who argued that Oza's votes contained those of one mandal committee which was not qualified to vote.

When the Bombay Pradesh Congress Committee met to make its final choice a leading Congress kingmaker of Bombay and a colleague of Menon's in the central Cabinet said that local opinion was against the sitting member. The Chief Minister of the State then pointed out that it was an artificially created controversy, that it was Menon who had carried the Congress Assembly candidates with him to victory in 1957 when regional passions were running high against the party. The Committee yielded to the Chief Minister. On August 19th Krishna Menon was unanimously selected as the Congress parliamentary candidate for North Bombay.

As soon as the objections raised by certain Congress circles against Menon's candidature for North Bombay became known, invitations were extended to him by Madras, Mysore, Kerala, Orissa, Punjab and Andhra states. But owing to the way the controversy developed in Bombay, it became an issue of prestige for Menon to stay there. If he had left Bombay then, it would immediately have been interpreted as a moral defeat.

Efforts were simultaneously being made by the opposition to find a candidate who would give a good fight to Menon at the polls. Finally Jiwatram Bhagwandas Kripalani[1] was persuaded to stand. A brilliant parliamentarian, Kripalani had set himself up as the most trenchant of Menon's critics in Parliament. He had

---

[1] Kripalani was a professor of politics in the Banares Hindu University and Acharya (Principal) of the Gujarat Vidyapit from 1922–7. The appellation 'Acharya' denotes a teacher.

spoken against Menon in nearly all the defence debates since he had taken office. Kripalani was a leader of the Congress during the freedom movement and had sacrificed and suffered much. For a good many years he was the General Secretary of the Congress and later became its President. He was an intimate associate of Gandhi and was known as one of the real Gandhians in the Congress movement. His intellect was sharp and his record inspiring.

As General Secretary of the Congress he had maintained correspondence with Krishna Menon in the 'thirties.[1] They were comrades in arms then, respecting each other. But after 1947 Kripalani had drifted away from the Congress. At the time of the transfer of power, he felt, Nehru had pushed himself to the forefront and left Kripalani, who was the President of the Congress, without his share of prominence. Kripalani became a very bitter man and the bitterness was directed especially at Nehru and the man who had apparently become Nehru's closest friend and adviser.

Following his break with the Congress, he had set up his own Krishak Mazdoor Praja Party (peasants', workers' and people's party) in 1951. This had later been merged with the Socialist Party to create the Praja-Socialist Party which he had left in 1954. He was an 'independent' and seventy-four years old when the challenge of Krishna Menon caught up with him in 1962.

Kripalani did not rush into North Bombay. He spent some time unobtrusively in the city, scouting around and carefully studying the situation. He met local leaders, including Congressmen, and assessed his chances. When finally convinced that he could rely upon substantial support, he made up his mind to stand.

There was massive support for Kripalani's candidature. The Swatantra Party, with its considerable resources, was fully committed to him. The Praja-Socialist Party mustered whatever strength it had to help him. The Jan Sangh, with a cadre of

[1] Nehru had to 'educate' Menon on how to write to Kripalani. In a letter from Lausanne in February 1936, Nehru informed Menon that the Congress would be sending the India League information bulletins but that Menon should also write directly to the General Secretary, Kripalani. Menon wrote back asking how he should address Kripalani in letters. Nehru replied, 'Kripalani can be addressed in any way you like. "Acharya" is too complicated for your office so you had better drop it. Usually in Congress India everybody is addressed as Syt. (short for Shriyut). In U.P. we address men and women both as Shri. You can make your choice. Probably Mr is best at your end.'

highly efficient field workers, identified itself completely with the Swatantra and the Praja-Socialist Party.

Most important of all, a section of the Congress Party went over to Kripalani. In the earlier stages they worked for him from inside the Congress. Once the campaign officially started, they began resigning from the Congress to the accompaniment of wide Press publicity. The resignations were cleverly spread out so that, as report after report appeared with big headlines in the Press, a popular impression gathered that there was a mass exodus of Congressmen from the Congress. The publicity did much damage to Krishna Menon's position.

The organization of this publicity was an expert job. Kripalani's supporters worked systematically on every political and social group in Bombay and other parts of the country. The groups came out one after another with statements endorsing Kripalani's candidature or decrying Menon's political affiliations. Each statement received a wide Press.

The entire organization of the Kripalani campaign was strikingly efficient. As the campaign progressed it became obvious that the planning was done by experts with a sure grasp of mass psychology. The literature produced by the propaganda units was immediately rushed to every doorstep in the constituency. Voters were individually canvassed, and on more occasions than one. Kripalani himself was present in the constituency from October, carrying on a vigorous personal campaign. He undertook regular walking tours, going from house to house, talking to little knots of people informally in drawing-rooms, porches and kitchens. At every stage and every level of his campaign, scientific organizational efficiency was evident.

By contrast Krishna Menon's campaign was slipshod and lacking in direction. There was little planning and less co-ordination. Groups were working for him, but the groups harboured a great deal of jealousy and animosity among them. The Congress as a party was hardly in the picture, except that official party posters carried his name. His campaign lacked a plan and it did not gather momentum until two weeks before polling day. The candidate himself was seldom in the constituency. He would come and go in a hurry, squeezing in a few public meetings when he was on the spot. Even a week before the election he was away in the Punjab and in Bangalore, campaigning for other Congress candidates. The almost total lack of Press publicity on his side added to his discomfiture. The publicity, voluminous as it was, was entirely unfavourable.

Kripalani set the tone, even before he formally entered the contest, by saying that people should be warned about the activities of 'enemies within the country and without who co-operated with each other'. Speaking at Lucknow on October 30th, he said he was fighting against Krishna Menon and not against the Congress. On January 4th, however, he told a public meeting in Bombay that the fight was not a personal one between himself and Menon but essentially a conflict between two ideologies – one emphasizing the integrity of the country and the other encouraging the forces of subversion.

The burden of the Kripalani campaign was that Menon was a communist and therefore an untrustworthy leader. It was said that he was surreptitiously helping the Chinese communists; he was talking tough about Pakistan only as a diversionary tactic; he had tarred the defence forces with a political brush. The choice, Kripalani said, was between Gandhism and Marxism.

That was an effective use of phraseology. He himself was an acknowledged apostle of Gandhism and now pictures began appearing in posters and in newspapers showing Kripalani in conference with Gandhi, Nehru and Sardar Patel. 'Where was Menon then?' asked the captions. C. Rajagopalachari said at a mass meeting in Bombay on February 9th, 'I do not want Gandhiji to be replaced by Marx in this country.'

Rajagopalachari, who was a stout supporter of Menon in 1957, was a bitter opponent in 1962. On February 8th he addressed a meeting in the suburbs and asked those who wanted Kripalani to raise their hands. Almost everyone in the audience raised hands. Rajagopalachari then said that, after such demonstrations of support, if the actual results of the election did not reflect the people's wishes, it would only show that 'there is something wrong with the election machinery itself'.

The most surprising statement he made during the campaign was Hindu in character. He told an audience that on election day the people should get up early in the morning and take their holy bath as on the day of the Hindu festival of Diwali, then go to the polling booths and cast their votes for Kripalani. If they did so, Rajagopalachari said, all their sins of the year would be washed away. Such was the temper of the campaign and such the alignment forces that no newspaper drew attention to the obvious appeal to communal instincts, a punishable offence under Indian electoral rules.

While the Kripalani campaign was systematic, powerful and based on a hit-often-and-hit-hard principle, the campaign on behalf of Menon was primarily defensive in character. It was inaugurated by Jawaharlal Nehru on January 15th – three whole months after Kripalani had started his drive – at a meeting attended by some 300,000 people. It was not an auspicious start, for Nehru was in an angry mood – and anger was not the most effective weapon against the concerted attack of the opposition.

Nehru spoke at length of the purpose behind the policies of the Congress Government. He described how Krishna Menon had modernized the fighting forces and given the nation a sense of self-respect. He then referred to the criticism of defecting Congressmen that Menon's actions were opposed to Nehru's policies. He could understand people opposing his policies, he said angrily, 'but it is insulting to me and my intelligence for anyone to say that my policies are correct but I should drop Mr Menon from the Cabinet. I have been in the Congress for some fifty years and I have known Mr Menon for some twenty-five years, and if some youngsters now come and tell me that they like Jawaharlal's policies but do not want Mr Menon, I would like to tell them to go to hell.'

Nehru had enough justification to feel angry at the 'youngsters' who were trying to have the best of both worlds. But as a campaign tactic, his angry tone and the 'go to hell' phrase did more harm than good.

In subsequent speeches, however, Nehru became an effective vote-getter for Menon. He dealt with anti-Menon propaganda item by item. In Poona on February 11th he said that Menon had no responsibility for India's stand towards China. If anyone had any responsibility for it, he said, it was the External Affairs Ministry alone. He said sarcastically that Congressmen opposing Menon were doing 'great honour to Jawaharlal, whose policies they profess to accept, by undermining the very roots of these policies by helping Acharya Kripalani, the arch-opponent of both the domestic and foreign policies of the Government and its Prime Minister'. It only meant, he said, 'that these Congressmen do not like Mr Menon because of his socialist ideas. We in the Congress who are socialist ourselves should like men like Mr Menon.'

On February 19th Nehru spoke in Gwalior about the manner in which 'backward minded people' had ganged up in Bombay to oppose 'our Government, our basic policies of non-alignment and socialism under the false, deceptive and mean façade of calling Mr Krishna Menon a crypto-communist'. Menon was no communist, Nehru said, but 'just a socialist as I am'.

He harped on the same theme in New Delhi the next day when he accused opposition parties of adopting 'McCarthy tactics' in North Bombay. These tactics harmed America a great deal, he said, and if they came to India they would ruin the country.

Then he came to the crux of the issue. 'Acharya Kripalani and his supporters hesitate to criticize me or say things against me,' he said. 'They don't do it perhaps because, by chance, people of India have love for me. So, whatever they want to say against me they say against Mr Menon. Let them openly say what they want to say against me. I have the strength to defend myself.'

This was perhaps the most effective passage in all of Nehru's public speeches during the election months. It did two things. First, it identified Menon completely with the Nehru ideology and personality, and that in Nehru's own words. Second, it showed up the opposition as a set of base tacticians resorting to cowardly techniques. This gave Krishna Menon the halo of a martyr. When Nehru uttered those words, his mammoth New Delhi audience burst into full-throated cries of 'Pandit Nehru Zindabad!'

Nehru had thrown himself whole-heartedly into the battle. Even though he visited Bombay only once in connection with the campaign, the North Bombay contest was the theme of his speeches wherever he went. He became a spirited campaigner for Menon because he saw that it was his own policies that were under fire in Menon's constituency. It was as much his own prestige as Menon's that was at stake.

One factor that contributed to his anger, as it did to Menon's, was the tempo and character of the Press campaign. He found the conspiracy between vested interests and big newspapers obnoxious. In his Gwalior speech he said, 'I am amazed how these people, including some big newspapers, have stooped to the lowest depth of falsehood, deception, low and mean tactics to frighten the people. All this propaganda is utterly wrong and baseless. It is only to incite the people.'

There was justification enough for Nehru's strong language. On February 18th Kripalani's supporters took out a three-truck, 3,000-man procession in the morning, and a 4,000-man procession in the evening, Kripalani participating in both. Menon's supporters organized a 108-truck, 20,000-man procession in the evening, though the candidate was absent. The next morning newspapers in Bombay carried large pictures and long reports of the Kripalani rallies. But the only reference to the Menon procession was a paragraph in the *Indian Express* which said, 'One man was injured when some unidentified persons threw stones at a procession of Mr Menon's supporters at Ghatkoper on Sunday afternoon.'

Menon's campaign began in earnest only two weeks before polling day. He was on his feet addressing meetings from eight in the morning till midnight. His campaigners now began to sense a perceptible change in popular emotions. Even a non-aligned observer could see that Menon's was no longer the hopeless fight it had seemed to be in the earlier stages of the campaign.

At last it was Sunday and election day. An ominous quiet descended upon the suburbs. The atmosphere was so calm, the proceedings so orderly that it was difficult to imagine that this was a day of destiny. As many as 483,190 men and women exercised their right to vote that day. The total number of those eligible to vote was 762,775 and in several areas those who actually voted represented as much as ninety and ninety-five per cent.

By dusk, when the ballot-boxes were sealed and removed under armed escort to the counting stations, everyone seemed to know the historic mandate they contained. Even the newspapers sensed the trend. On the morning after, the *Indian Express* gave the impression that it had all along been a great admirer and well-wisher of Krishna Menon; it carried on top of page 1 a two-column picture of Menon under the heading 'The Apparent Victor'. The *Times of India* also gave Menon 'a slight edge over Acharya Kripalani'.

Menon's campaign managers were now in no doubt about victory. Their concern was what margin he would gain. They tabulated reports from each polling booth and concluded that the margin would be not less, and not very much more, than his 1957 margin. That year he had run up a lead of 47,741 votes.

By Monday the first results began trickling in. And then eyes started popping out in amazement. Ballot-box after ballot-box revealed a gap between Menon and Kripalani far beyond the expectations of either. Menon started with a lead of 25,000 over Kripalani at the end of the first day's counting and went on increasing the margin as each box was opened. Areas which were thought to be heavily in favour of Kripalani went over to Menon in a landslide. Everywhere the preference was unmistakable, the difference overwhelming. By Tuesday night Menon's lead was 70,000. On the night of Wednesday it was 117,177 and victory – for only 75,000 votes remained to be counted.

In the office of one newspaper, the baron who had personally directed the paper's campaign against Menon sat before a teleprinter with a telephone line always open. He jotted down the figures as they came in. When the gap widened beyond hope on Wednesday, he threw down the telephone, called for his secretary and said resignedly, 'Now, don't let me hear a word more about the election. Get me the jute quotations from Calcutta.'

That was the end. The results were officially announced on March 3rd. The figures were 296,804 for Menon and 151,437 for Kripalani. The six other runners in the field all lost their deposits. Menon's lead over Kripalani was a shattering 145,367. It was almost a hundred thousand more than his lead in 1957.

Soon after the results were declared, Menon called on Kripalani at his city residence. On Sunday he spoke at a wildly cheering victory rally. Then he flew to New Delhi, a mass leader of India in his own right.

Many factors contributed to Menon's phenomenal victory. Apart from the fact that he belonged to the Congress, the two positive factors in his favour were the tone of his personal campaign and the popular appeal of Nehru socialism. Some negative factors helped him too, like the grotesque partisanship of the Press, indications of foreign interference on behalf of Kripalani and the very nature of the forces that lined up behind Kripalani.

Menon maintained a very high campaign standard all the way through. Consistently and deliberately he gave the impression that he was not interested in a personal victory as much as in the victory of his party. Although he would address twenty and thirty public meetings a day, not once did he ask his audience to vote for him. Not once did he mention his opponent by name. His speeches followed a strict rule of explaining to the people why the Congress Government was doing what it was doing. He described the nature of the Government's policies both at home and abroad and ended up by asking his listeners to decide for themselves whether these policies were not the best for the country.

The appeal of socialism was no less significant. The poverty and backwardness of India created in the minds of the ordinary citizens a great longing for the promises of socialism – for equality of status, for a fair distribution of wealth, for the rehabilitation of the under-dog. This longing cannot be easily diluted by crying 'wolf' over communism. Nehru and Menon are identified in the popular mind with socialism in its most egalitarian sense. Nehru personally did a great deal during the campaign to implant this in people's minds. A considerable proportion of the Menon votes must have been cast by those who simply wanted a happier life and a brighter future.

To make matters worse for Kripalani, it became common talk in Bombay as the campaign got into its swing that foreign countries were helping him. Prime Minister Nehru himself made the charge openly at one of his public meetings. The *Times of India*, inadvertently of course, had prepared the ground as early as October 31st, 1961, when it ran a story on 'Planned Anti-Menon Tirade In U.S. Press'. The Washington correspondent of the paper, a known critic of Menon, had described in the course of his story the virulence of the Press criticisms against Menon and India and said,

Thus far I had believed that the Press was, perhaps, expressing its own free opinions. My inquiries have now firmly established that the criticism is part of a concerted and planned campaign. Its authors can be traced to certain senior State Department officials. One of them told me yesterday, 'The Press is only catching up with our view of India.'

The victory as well as the victorious cause pleased Menon. As he looked back, he felt happy about his decision to stick to Bombay. 'I am not accustomed to run away from things,' he said. 'I held on to North Bombay and North Bombay held on to me. My duty to my own sense of self-respect wouldn't have permitted anything else. I will not take dictation from the opposition, or from other countries.' The election, he felt, was too exaggerated, 'and not because of the essential ingredients in itself'. He was smarting with memories of the hate campaign carried on by the Press when he said, 'The result of the election has shown the incapacity of newspapers to corrupt the mind of man.' But he was still the democrat and parliamentarian. 'I will never lift a finger,' he said, 'and as a member of the Government I will always resist any imposition of restrictions on the Press – even on the most scurrilous sheets. Restrictions usually restrict the wrong fellow.'

Menon could afford to be magnanimous towards the Press in the hour of his victory; for the victory was the more shattering for the humiliation it heaped upon the Press.

28

The End of the Road?

Be careful in dealing with a man who cares nothing for
sensual pleasures, nothing for comfort or praise or promotion,
but is simply determined to do what he believes to be right.
He is a dangerous and uncomfortable enemy, because his
body, which you can always conquer, gives you so little
purchase over his soul.

GILBERT MURRAY
on Mahatma Gandhi

On February 26th, 1962, Krishna Menon became a mass hero
in India. The restless youth of the early 'twenties, the socialist
agitator of London, the man who upset the balance of the United
Nations was now a prophet honoured in his own country.

Indications of his popularity became evident wherever he went.
His public meetings began attracting unprecedented numbers.
At the end of a meeting crowds mobbed him and followed his car,
shouting slogans in his support. It was as though an emotional
bond united him with the masses. They obviously trusted him –
and this moved Menon because powerful propaganda had made
such trust difficult.

The impact of the victory was felt abroad too. Political commentators for the first time saw him as a possible successor to
Nehru. The tendency, induced by untiring propaganda, to look
upon him as a political freak was no longer there. In its place was
an eagerness to understand the man, for it was now incontrovert-
ible that Menon was held in high esteem by his own countrymen.

The basic difference between Menon and the leaders of the
West was that the latter were essentially for the status quo in
world affairs, while to Menon, as to the whole of Afro-Asia,
status quo meant stagnation and death. Menon represented a
generation of revolutionaries.

I

It was only a coincidence that the communist bloc led by the Soviet Union also stood for revolution and change. This led to a few points of contact between India and the Soviet Union. The West attributed it all to Menon, seeing in him a sinister force. Menon's belief in non-alignment was no more sinister than George Washington's anxiety to keep out of Europe's entanglements while his fledgling nation stabilized itself.

Republican America failed to realize that Menon, like Nehru, was essentially a leader of India. The interest the two men showed in international leadership was only incidental to their main occupation, which was the Indian revolution. This conditioned their behaviour in a particular way. Missing this point, the United States started on a note of antipathy from the very outset, holding Menon up as a symbol of narrow regionalism, of ideological deceptiveness and of the lowest form of personal ambition. This created in Menon a suspicion that grew with the years. He became convinced that the Western combination, under American leadership, was out to suppress India. The conviction in turn led to an anger which affected all his actions in the international field. Menon is a man who desperately wants to be liked. But he wants to be liked on his own terms.

The Western Press seldom gives its reader an opportunity to judge Menon by his own words. In India, though the more powerful newspapers have been only too willing to emulate the example of the foreign Press, they have not succeeded in screening Menon off from the masses. Indians have had repeated opportunities to hear him and read him. Over the years this has led to a deep popular understanding of what he stands for and an appreciation of his aims.

The more the people of India came to know about his socialism, the more they seemed to like it. What gave his philosophy uncommon mass appeal was his ability to fit short-term solutions into a long-term perspective. He was concerned all the while with fundamentals. This frightened those whose interests were directly affected, for they knew that his axe was aimed not at a stray branch but at their very roots. For just the same reason the have-nots, by far the majority, stood by him with hope and confidence.

The more practical among Menon's supporters knew that his lofty scrupulousness was unrealistic in the Indian context. They

saw that the opposition too, profoundly disturbed by the unprecedented power the man had achieved as a result of the
election, was planning ahead. The defiance with which the
Right-wing leadership of the Bombay Congress proceeded to split
up the North Bombay constituency organization was a clear
enough straw in the wind.

Soon the opposition found an unexpected opportunity to
destroy Menon. China had been probing India's northern
frontiers ever since 1954–5. In September 1962 major incursions
occurred. On October 20th what was unmistakably an invasion
was under way.

The invasion met with a series of successes in the first week.
Outpost after Indian outpost fell to the Chinese. Everywhere
Indian soldiers were outnumbered and out-weaponed. On
October 25th the key town of Tawang in the North-East Frontier
Agency was captured by the invaders. The next day the President
declared a state of emergency.

These reverses numbed a nation unused to war. What was
meant by 'tactical retreat'? What lay behind the phrase 'advantage
of surprise'? What was 'regrouping' and 'withdrawing to a better
defensive position'? Government spokesmen went on explaining
the reverses as a normal thing in military history.

Then the 'Crush Menon' lobby sprang into action. The
Government, they said, was trying to cover up its mistakes, for
the Indian Army was clearly not prepared and the invasion itself
had not been anticipated by the Government. And who was
responsible for this twin blunder of political miscalculation and
military dilatoriness? The Minister for Defence, of course.

Pressure mounted against the Prime Minister. There was not
simply the war against China; there was as real a war against
Krishna Menon. For the first time the Right-wing leaders of the
Congress found it possible to mobilize forces inside the Congress
Parliamentary Party. Some senior members of the Cabinet, who
had tried hard to demolish Menon in North Bombay, now worked
incessantly to bring the issue to a head. Thanks to their organizing
abilities and the encouragement they received from what one
newspaper called 'the highest and the wisest in the land', a sizeable
section of the Parliamentary Party Executive asked the Prime
Minister to remove Menon from the Government.

At first the Prime Minister resisted the pressure. On October

31st, however, he took over the portfolio of Defence and appointed Menon as Minister of Defence Production. But the clamour did not die down. A Delhi newspaper declared that, having tasted blood, the people should go for the final kill. A majority of the Congress Parliamentary Party had been worked up to such an emotional pitch that they threatened to walk out of the crucial eve-of-Parliament meeting on November 7th if the Prime Minister refused to remove Menon. The President of the Union also played an active role and advised the Prime Minister to relieve Menon. Nehru, still numbed by the magnitude of the Chinese invasion, was in no condition to hold his own. On November 7th he announced that he had decided to accept Menon's resignation from the Cabinet. It was the first time the nation knew that Menon had been pressing his resignation for several months.

Two days later the Prime Minister said in Parliament that at 'a suitable time' an inquiry would be held to find out what errors were committed with regard to defence preparations and who were responsible for them. Enough, however, is already known to put the case in some sort of perspective.

Menon cannot escape his share of the responsibility for what happened to him. Having sown the wind, he had to reap the whirlwind. But his individual responsibility lay only in the fact that his personality provoked controversy in and around the armed forces which were, until he arrived on the scene, above controversy and gossip. For the rest, he was a victim of other people's deeds and misdeeds and a willing cross-bearer on behalf of his Cabinet colleagues. This became increasingly clearer in the months immediately following his resignation.

To understand the military debacle that befell India in the Himalayas, one must examine, firstly, India's traditional military policies; secondly, the way the Nehru Cabinet functions and the inter-relationship between the different ministries; and thirdly, the role of the opposition in Parliament and in the Press. Only against such a background can one fairly place Krishna Menon's own handling of defence with a view to seeing whether or not it contributed to the debacle.

The Gandhian philosophy of non-violence had taken such deep roots in Indian thought that in the early years of independence the Defence portfolio was sometimes regarded as rather un-Indian. Quite apart from this, even among professional military men, the

Himalayas had traditionally been neglected. In a letter to *The Times* of London, Field-Marshal Sir Claude Auchinleck said on November 6th, 1962,

> Under the British 'Raj' military vision was firmly fixed on the North-West Frontier and all plans were framed to meet a Russian invasion through Afghanistan. This fixed idea persisted into the early days of the Second World War in that defences were erected to stop a German invasion through the Caucasus via Afghanistan. The possibility of a major invasion of India across the main Himalayan chain was entirely neglected. When Japan invaded Burma and threatened eastern India our neglect and weaknesses were exposed.

The British tradition was continued in the first years of Indian independence, and only after Menon became the Defence Minister did the need to build up defences across the Himalayas receive appreciation in New Delhi. The fortification of the defence-line along the high mountains was necessarily a lengthy and costly affair. The Government as a whole was hesitant, even after it should have become clear that trouble from China could be expected. Krishna Menon was one of those who wanted concentrated attention to be given to the northern frontier, but his recommendations were not accepted. One reason might have been that hesitancy was supported even by Indian military experts. General Thimayya, writing in the *Seminar* magazine of July 1962, said,

> Whereas in the case of Pakistan I have considered the possibility of a total war, I am afraid I cannot do so in regard to China. I cannot even as a soldier envisage India taking on China in an open conflict on its own. China's present strength in man-power, equipment and aircraft exceeds our resources a hundredfold with the full support of the U.S.S.R. and we could never hope to match China in the foreseeable future. It must be left to the politicians and diplomats to ensure our security.

This was the thinking that governed New Delhi's approach to the question, even after 1957 when it was known that the Chinese had completed the Aksai Chin road in Ladakh. Krishna Menon then impressed upon the Cabinet the need to build up border defences more speedily. The Cabinet, however, felt that India should contain the threat diplomatically.

The result of this attitude was that the Defence Ministry under Krishna Menon ran against obstructions all along its path. At the execution stage all its plans got bogged down. The first full-scale assessment of the need for preparedness on the northern borders was made in October 1959. But the Finance Ministry insisted on phasing out the programmes put up by the Defence Ministry. The overall financial effect assessed by the Defence Ministry was 868 million rupees with a foreign exchange component of 137 million rupees. (A million rupees is equal to £71,500 approximately.) Finance refused to increase the foreign exchange allocation for defence, and said that demands should be covered only to the extent that foreign exchange was available from the periodical allocations made to the Defence Ministry. As a result of this decision, Defence could cover demands only to the value of 410 million rupees by March 1962; only 4.5 million rupees' worth of foreign exchange had been made available as against the 137 million required!

We can get an idea of the relationship between foreign exchange and military preparedness if we know that semi-automatic rifles and ammunition for equipping only one division of the Indian Army would mean a foreign exchange expenditure of 22 million rupees. As much as 1,600 million rupees' worth of foreign exchange would be required to equip ten heavy mortar regiments with 120-mm. mortars. Perhaps India would not have been unprepared if this kind of money had been available for defence; the Minister for Defence could have been held personally responsible for unpreparedness if such money had been made available to his Ministry and the armed forces had still been left without essential weapons. But such was not the case. The effectiveness of weapons is by and large relative to the weapons of the potential adversary. Despite the presence of an adversary of China's totalitarian advantages, the Government of India saw no need to put money aside for weapons – until it was too late.

Finance was only one of the obstacles that faced the Defence Ministry. Another check on speed and efficiency was provided by some of New Delhi's general policy directives. For instance, the Director General of Supplies and Disposals, the agency that had to provide clothing for the Army, could seldom execute indents in time because it was tied down to the Government's policy of supporting small-scale industries. It was obligatory for the D.G.S.D. to arrange supplies through small units, and this necessarily meant delay.

There was also the traditional character of the Indian Army top-brass to cope with. The Air Force and the Navy, being comparatively young, were easily adaptable to modern methods of defence organization. But the Army was prone to suffer from a hangover of the Imperial-Staff-College-dominated past. This, incidentally, was one of the reasons why Krishna Menon, planning specifically for Indian defence in Indian conditions and against Indian economic realities, sometimes fell out with some generals. The result of the top-brass being too attached to the old traditions was that they were slow to react to modern ideas. For example, the Defence Research Wing which Krishna Menon had brought into being perfected prototypes of automatic rifles as early as 1959. The project got stuck in Army Headquarters and the prototype was tested and passed only in March 1962. One of the charges hurled at Krishna Menon in the wake of the Himalayan fighting was that he had failed to provide the Army with automatic weapons!

While financial and organizational bottle-necks played havoc with Krishna Menon's modernization programme on the one hand, on the other opposition groups kept up an incessant barrage of criticism. The principal inspiration for them was the success with which Menon had withstood the pressures of private enterprise cartels and developed an immense state-owned industrial base for the manufacture of military hardware. But once criticism became the vogue, the very idea of spending any money on defence began to be ridiculed in Parliament and the Press. During the 1957 debate on the Defence budget, J. B. Kripalani made a scathing attack on defence policies in general and said, 'The mounting expenses on the Army should be cut down. The followers of Mahatma Gandhi and adherents of universal peace should not increase military expenses. Otherwise their profession would be hypocritical.' After the Chinese attack, Kripalani was among the loudest critics of 'unpreparedness'. But by then his earlier advocacy of unpreparedness as a policy had been forgotten.

Krishna Menon's achievement was that he made any headway at all with the money available and the opposition he had to face.

Seen against the background of the difficulties, his achievement was remarkable indeed. Indigenous production which expanded under his guidance included that of electronics, aircraft at Bangalore and Kanpur, trucks and heavy vehicles at Jubalpur, tanks at Avadi, explosives at Bhandara, guided missiles at Bangalore, marine engines at Bombay and Calcutta, automatic weapons, alloy steels and dehydrated food at Mussoorie. In fact, if he had had a few more months at his disposal, the Indian Army would have had quite different types of equipment with which to face the Chinese. He had pushed through plans to manufacture semi-automatic rifles, 7.62-mm. ammunition, 120-mm. Brandt mortars and Brandt mortar ammunition. These were scheduled to be ready for use by the end of 1962 and early 1963. China had timed her attack perfectly.

Even after the Chinese attack was mounted, Krishna Menon had a precise strategic plan with which he was confident of containing the threat. This was a plan of 'defence in depth'. He wanted to let the Chinese come through the Himalayan ranges in order to avoid pushing up Indian defences to the geographically unfavourable Thagla-Dhola heights. Indian forces were to make a planned withdrawal to the Se La Pass line, trap the Chinese there and mount an all-out counter-offensive. But opposition M.P.s and newspapers made it impossible for the Government to pursue this strategy. They magnified the early 'reverses' out of all proportion and let out howls of protests every time an inch of Indian territory was lost. Popular morale was so grievously threatened that the Nehru Government had to find a scapegoat. But in finding one, it destroyed all hopes of the Indian Army's eventually scoring a convincing victory in its own way.

Nehru was apparently aware of the unfairness of it all. In his speeches following Menon's resignation he repeatedly gave out information which, had it been digested, would have helped to establish the correct perspective on the situation. He said that the Cabinet had decided upon the strategy of planned withdrawal and that therefore many people 'had done an injustice, not to any minister or other, but to our armed forces as a whole in making various charges'. He said that the Defence Ministry had been insisting, from 1958–9, on the purchase of up-to-date weapons from various sources including the Western countries, 'but various difficulties arose and points of view differed'.

The End of the Road?

It has been asked why, if his plans were being frustrated by other ministries, Krishna Menon did not resign from the Government and make a public statement on the true state of affairs. He did in fact try to resign. But apart from privately requesting the Prime Minister to relieve him of office, he would not take any step that would embarrass his friend and comrade of many years. A demonstrative protest resignation in 1959 or 1960 might have made a hero of him personally. But his loyalty to Nehru would not have permitted it.

He finally left the Government because he believed that wartime was no time for recriminations and that recriminations would end if he sacrificed himself. On October 21st, the day after the Chinese invasion began in earnest, Menon repeated the resignation offer he had been privately making to the Prime Minister for some time past. As before, the Prime Minister would not entertain the idea, but Menon's conviction about the necessity for him to withdraw from the limelight only grew as the days passed. He had some differences of opinion with the Prime Minister on the timing of the counter-offensive, but the main consideration that weighed with him was that a concentrated war effort was necessary and all controversy should be ended in the interest of national unity. The Prime Minister was unmoved, but accepted Menon's compromise suggestion that he be made Minister for Production and Nehru himself take over the Defence portfolio. But the new arrangement failed to quell the controversy, with the result that Menon pressed his resignation anew and with more insistence. On November 7th he put his offer in writing.

> In the crisis that faces our country, the nation as well as our party should be enabled to face it in unity and zeal ... I am painfully aware of the fact that not only the opponents of our policy and party but even perhaps an appreciable number of our party members, some leaders among them, have proclaimed or implied their lack of faith in me and in the defence organization under my stewardship. These views may not, and in fact do not, represent the bulk of our party or the people. Nevertheless, in my humble submission, the reservations, amid the crisis, that are theirs are a weak link in our national and party unity ... It is not purposeful to argue

that such attitudes or facts are unreasonable or indeed un-
founded, or wrongly motivated. It is again of little value to
argue that these hostilities are misdirected. It is wrong for me
at the present time to seek to provide answers or to reveal the
hollowness of charges and allegations. The fact is that, whatever the factors, domestic or foreign, and whoever are
involved, the present situation must come to an end for the
simple reason that we cannot afford to let our energies be
dissipated ... I am content to rest in the belief that facts are
not altered by subsequent non-factual representation of
them ... The immediate concern and task of every Indian
today is the defence and then the counter-offensives against
the invaders for the redemption of the honour and integrity
of the country ... All this will be adversely affected by the
present tensions and arguments and unwholesome propaganda within our party and the nation, irrespective of
individuals ... If events should prove when the present excite-
ments die out that this confidence [which you have shown in
me] was misplaced or betrayed, I would willingly accept all
the consequences that must follow.

Later the same day, in order to emphasize that he was serious
about resignation, he wrote a second letter to the Prime Minister:
'I submit that it may be in the interests of the party that I should
be relieved of office ... If my resignation serves in a small measure
to forge the strength and unity of the country, the party and the
Government, I am amply rewarded.'

It was a strange spectacle – Krishna Menon standing among his
detractors and asking for his removal from office. Stranger still, he
held his silence when critics, unaware of Menon's repeated
resignation offers, loudly asked him to resign if only to 'save his
self-respect'. He made no effort to clear his name or to show how
others were also responsible for what happened in the mountains.
In the face of humiliating criticism he kept quiet so that the
Prime Minister might have time enough to decide and announce
the developments in his own way.

It is pertinent here to examine an attempt Menon made,
unknown to the world, in 1960 to settle the India-China border
dispute. He had read the Chinese mind, correctly as it turned out,
and realized that China's main interest lay in the Aksai Chin

salient of Ladakh, which India never physically possessed anyway. He also knew that if India adopted an inflexible attitude in Ladakh, China might mount military pressure in the North-East Frontier Agency which was valuable to India, and 'nibble away areas in the dark'. In the event his only miscalculation was about the size and scope of the Chinese 'nibbling'.

Menon conveyed his analysis of the situation to the Cabinet and suggested a political deal with China which would be in line with international practice, and which – and this was more important – would help India gain time to complete her developmental plans. The suggestion was to lease to China the Aksai Chin salient. In turn China would lease to India the narrow strip of Chinese territory projecting into India between Sikkim and Bhutan. This was a strategically important territory. Menon prepared his case thoroughly and collected a long list of instances of similar international lease arrangements in history.

Chou En-lai came to New Delhi in April 1960 to discuss the border dispute and Nehru agreed to place before him the Menon formula. In order to avoid the public controversy that was bound to follow if he put forth the idea as his own, Menon kept out of the talks with the Chinese Premier; another Cabinet minister was nominated the principal Indian negotiator.

Chou En-lai seemed willing to accept the plan and to give India some Chinese territory in return for the Aksai Chin area. But before the plan could be seriously discussed with the Chinese Premier, it was torpedoed by the combined efforts of two of the most senior members of the Cabinet. One of them, the late Gobind Vallabh Pant, sat in his bathroom and carried on a dialogue with Nehru who stood outside the door. The gist of the conversation was that Pant would revolt and resign if Nehru agreed to the lease idea. The other Cabinet minister met Chou En-lai and started riling him with talk of China's stupidity and India's moral grandeur. So offended was the Chinese leader that he walked out of the room and started talking in terms of 'taking revenge' on India.

Menon's lease proposal would have given India plenty of time to build up her military potential, industrial strength and general economic vitality. And then, when the agreement came up for reconsideration, India would have been able to speak from a position of strength.

Has Krishna Menon reached the end of his political road? Reading newspapers one would think he had. In the West, for the most part, the news of his leaving the Government was given, not as it happened, but as the newspapers would have liked it to happen. Some leading newspapers, for instance, said in so many words that the Prime Minister had 'dismissed' Krishna Menon.

In India at no time did anyone seriously think that Menon's days were over. Indeed, his sworn enemies were chagrined to find that, out of office, Menon was still an influence on popular thinking in the country. Despite the 'dismissal' his relations with Prime Minister Nehru continue to be close and cordial; Menon was the only non-family member present at Nehru's birthday breakfast on November 14th, less than a week after he had laid down office. In his acceptance letter the Prime Minister had told Menon, 'This is of course not a parting, as both you and I are dedicated to serve our country in whatever position either of us may be placed. In the grave crisis that we are facing today I am sure your help in many ways will be a great assistance. I hope that it will be possible in the future to utilize your high abilities in the cause of the nation.'

As for Menon, he does not sulk. Loss of office has not dampened his spirits or destroyed his will. On the contrary, he is more relaxed and happier than before. He continues to enjoy overwork. He has become India's most sought-after barrister, and once when he appeared in a case in Hyderabad the crowd was so great that admission to the court had to be restricted by passes. Among those who flood him with briefs are many of the country's wealthiest industrial tycoons, who seem to have forgotten all about the man's socialism and how they planned his destruction when he was in office. Menon has also turned an expert gardener and won prizes at a New Delhi flower show.

Only one thing can destroy Menon politically – a conviction that the common people do not want him. The circumstances under which he left the Government did not give him that feeling even remotely. On the contrary, his buoyancy is sustained by the knowledge that, despite the shock of military reverses and despite persistent propaganda, the common people continue to have faith in him.

This knowledge grew out of events. On November 6th, after he had been 'demoted', he agreed to speak at a public rally in

The End of the Road?

New Delhi. Rightist parties had whipped up considerable passion against the 'treacherous' Defence Minister, and he was advised by friends to avoid going to a public meeting, but no persuasion could change Menon's mind.

When he was spotted climbing on to the dais, the assembled crowd of 20,000 people burst into shouts of 'Krishna Menon Zindabad'. The crowd was so enthusiastic and so generous with personal slogans in his support that he found it possible to write the next day in his resignation letter to the Prime Minister, 'I am personally grateful in my heart to feel that in every place I have gone, even till last night, they [the people] have gathered to accord me their faith and support, in considerable numbers, with enthusiasm reminiscent of the election campaigns earlier this year. In some places they have broken previous records in both these respects.'

Further and more touching evidence of popular support came the day after Menon's resignation was officially announced. With a smile of contentment on his face he walked into Parliament. A demonstration pledging support to the Government gathered outside Parliament House. Menon, alone among national leaders, went out to meet the demonstrators. As he emerged into sight the crowd, which was several thousands strong, broke into a frenzy of cheers. They again cried 'Jawaharlal Nehru Zindabad' and 'Krishna Menon Zindabad'. An old Sikh bent down and touched Menon's feet in admiration.

The feeling that the public has not rejected him is a feeling that will keep Menon alive and active. In his November 6th speech in New Delhi he said '... no one can prevent me from making my contribution in the fight whether I am in the Cabinet or whether I run a canteen.'

Nobody pretended that Krishna Menon's departure from the Government was something that concerned only himself. There was universal recognition of the fact that it would have a tremendous impact on India's domestic and foreign policies. There is no doubt that Menon's fall was the beginning of a vastly significant Rightist upsurge in the country; the real blow dealt by China was at India's democratic socialism. What he was forced to do in the first week of November was therefore something of an ideological suicide for Nehru. His life-long efforts to set India on a particular course are seriously jeopardized – unless the Prime

Minister fights back while it is still possible for him to do so. The natural desire to ensure the success of his policies and his work of half a century, if not any special solicitude for Menon, may prompt Nehru to reinstate Menon when an opportunity arises. However, in his old age and against men admittedly more crafty, Nehru may not be able to swing the national leadership back to a progressive frame of mind once he has, under the stresses of an emergency, helped to install conservatives in the saddle.

The real significance of Krishna Menon was that he provided a decent and popular alternative to conservatism on the one hand and communism on the other. To the middle and lower classes, disgusted with vested interests and distrusting communists, he was an attractive rallying point. To them he held out the promises of socialism without the violence and the dogma of communism. With his promise of a purposeful social revolution he blocked the chances of an indigenous communist revolution. The final removal of Menon from the scene may once again leave India with but two alternatives – conservatism and communism. Was this one of the objectives the Chinese had in mind?

By mid-1963, some eight months after Menon's exit from the Government, there does seem to be a growing feeling among top political circles that he was a victim of circumstances. Developments since November 1962 have only confirmed the view that Menon's basic doctrines and policies were after all correct. The most important of these was that the Soviet Union would be persuaded by self-interest if nothing else to strengthen the base of Indian defences against China on a long-term footing, while the West would be an uncertain partner in military collaboration because of its bonds with Pakistan. Every new phase of the friction between Russia and China is a vindication of Krishna Menon's political calculations – calculations that were made well before the Sino-Soviet rift became a talking-point round the world. The value of his other major doctrines – self-sufficiency in defence production, emphasis on manufacture as distinct from purchase of equipment, more financial allocation for defence, strict maintenance of civil over military authority – has also begun to be better appreciated.

A man whose impact on his nation has been so strong cannot be easily erased from the scene. Despite loss of office Krishna Menon remains politically potent. He draws his strength from the masses,

The End of the Road?

and can in turn give strength to the masses. Maintaining constant contact with them, he is in a position to continue influencing the direction of popular thinking in favour of his social ideals and to inspire and sustain basic political processes.

The lesson of his newest experiences cannot be lost upon Krishna Menon. It was his refusal to cultivate the articulate sections of public opinion that left him apparently friendless in a crisis. If not for his personal popularity, at least for the success of his programmes, he should have tried to win friends consciously and as a matter of policy. His political upbringing was in a country where, if one had merit, one's personal mannerisms were overlooked. It was different in India, and Menon did not adapt himself.

The accumulation of a ruinous reputation was his misfortune. He became, partly due to personal failings but largely due to the unreadiness of society's upper crust to accept his advanced ideas of social justice, a personification of all that was undesirable in a politician. Like Disraeli, he was thought artificial and cynical by those who knew him slightly, but natural and soft-hearted by true friends. And true friends were so hard to come by. So, as it was said of Lloyd George, hatred of Krishna Menon became a frame of mind, a kind of eleventh commandment.

While losing his own reputation, though, he built up his country's. His overbearing character drove home to the world the reality and political implications of Indian independence. Free India could well have lost her identity, as Pakistan did, but instead she became a face in the crowd. She developed a political power far in excess of what her material strength warranted. Krishna Menon was the symbol of this power. Inasmuch as he destroyed himself in order to build up his country, he offered a profile in courage. Menon was an historical necessity for India in the 'fifties.

Perhaps the exit of Krishna Menon from the Indian Cabinet symbolized the end of an era, just as his emergence into the limelight symbolized the beginning of another. But only the blind will say that, minus office, he is a write-off. Menon may be down, but Menonism will not be out. He may have been disliked, but the causes he fought for were popular. He has not won in a cause that will some day lose, but lost in a cause that will some day win. His contribution to the development of the Indian personality has been notable, and it will continue to be so.

Who's Who

BOSE, SUBHAS, was a dynamic Congress leader who grew to be a legend. He defied Gandhi and was elected President of the Congress. During the Second World War he escaped from imprisonment, travelled incognito to Germany, formed an alliance with the Axis powers, and was killed in an air crash in Japan while fighting to liberate India.

LOHIA, RAM MANOHAR, started out as a brilliant young Congressman, paying special attention to foreign affairs. With the coming of socialism, Lohia, who is prone to look upon his own socialism as the purest version, found himself standing alone. He leads the Socialist Party of India, which has a long list of lost causes to champion.

MALAVIYA, PANDIT MADAN MOHAN, one of the patriarchs of the Congress, was a stolid conservative, often described as 'a devoted friend of the Empire'. His most famous legacy is the Benarese Hindu University, which he founded. He was one of Indian nationalism's leading figures in the first two decades of the century.

MASANI, M. R., was once an ardent Congressman, then an ardent socialist and now an ardent anti-socialist. For a brief period he was Indian ambassador to Brazil. Following the rather abrupt conclusion of that office, he developed into a trenchant critic of Nehru's policies. He is now General Secretary of the Swatantra Party.

MEHTA, ASOKA, is a gifted economist and social theoretician who somehow fell by the wayside; as Chairman of the languishing Praja-Socialist Party, he was a leader in search of a following. Finding none, he has now become a government official. He was a pillar of the Congress Socialist Party in the 'thirties.

NARAYAN, JAYAPRAKASH, once an idol of Indian youth, is no longer an active politician. He was an inspiring socialist leader and universally recognized as Nehru's natural heir until he retired from politics, at least officially. He is now a non-party man, but a constant critic of the Nehru Government.

PATEL, SARDAR, the 'Iron Man' of the Congress, was essentially an organization man. Ultra-conservative and efficient, he was Deputy Prime Minister until he died in 1950, aged seventy-five.

RAMASWAMY AIYAR, the Hon. Sir C. P., is an outstanding member of the Madras Bar. Originally an adversary of Mrs Besant, he then became her close friend and associate. He was also prominent in the Congress. He gravitated to administrative and ministerial positions in British India and finally became Dewan of Travancore State. At the age of eighty-four he is still active.

RAO, B. SHIVA, a labour and constitutional expert, has been prominent in Indian public life since the late 'twenties. He represented India at various international forums, including the Round Table Conference in London in 1930–31. He was also an associate of Mrs Annie Besant and one of the leading lights of the theosophical movement in India.

SAPRU, TEJ BAHADUR, was a contemporary and friend of Motilal Nehru, Jawaharlal's father. He was a noted liberal of his time and often played the role of benevolent intermediary between Gandhi and the British Raj.

SINHA, SACHIDANANDA, was the uncrowned king of Bihar Province at the turn of the century and became a highly respected moderate leader of his time. He held various offices of distinction and represented India at several conferences in London.

SITARAMAYYA, PATTABHI, was a Congress leader of the Gandhian era. He became known as the historian of the Congress by virtue of a two-part, loosely-written work entitled *The History of the Indian National Congress*, published in 1935.

Bibliography

THERE is at the present time practically no literature on Mr Krishna Menon, even books like Mr Nehru's *A Bunch of Old Letters* having no reference at all to him. What is available is in the form of newspaper and magazine articles, and these, as is to be expected in the case of Mr Menon, are not always reliable as sources of information. However, the story of Mr Menon's life is essentially the political history of a period, and books pertaining to this period provide an excellent commentary on the events and movements that shaped his ideas and career. The following books in particular were of great help to the author:

Malabar Manual, by William Logan. Madras, 1906.
Janmi System in Kerala, by Elankulam Kunjan Pillai. (In Malayalam.) Kerala, 1959.
The History of the Indian National Congress, by Pattabhi Sitaramayya. 2 vols. Bombay, 1935.
An Autobiography, by Jawaharlal Nehru. London, 1936.
Discovery of India, by Jawaharlal Nehru. Calcutta, 1946.
Glimpses of World History, by Jawaharlal Nehru. London, 1935.
The Congress Socialist for 1935 and 1936, ed. by Asoka Mehta.
Nehru – A Political Biography, by Michael Brecher. Oxford, 1961.
Nehru: The Years of Power, by Vincent Sheean. London, 1960.
India: The Most Dangerous Decades, by Selig Harrison. Oxford, 1960.
Mission with Mountbatten, by Alan Campbell-Johnson. London, 1951.
The Transfer of Power, by V. P. Menon. Calcutta, 1957.
As It Happened, by C. R. Attlee, London, 1954.
India Wins Freedom, by Abul Kalam Azad. Calcutta, 1959.
A Continent Decides, by Lord Birdwood. London, 1953.

Bibliography

The Commonwealth, by Patrick Gordon Walker. London, 1962.

Communism in India, by Gene D. Overstreet and Marshall Windmiller. California University, 1959.

The New Dimensions of Peace, by Chester Bowles. New York, 1955.

Diplomacy of India, by Ross N. Berkes and Mohinder S. Bedi. Stanford, 1958.

'The continuing position of India', by Arthur Lall, in *The Evergreen Review*, vol. ii, No. 7.

The Condition of India (India League publication). London, 1932.

The Last Phase, by Pyarelal. Ahmedabad, 1956.

Diaries and account books maintained by Govinda Kurup (Krishna Menon's father's uncle) and Krishna Kurup (Krishna Menon's father) were made available to the author by the present *karanavar* of the family, Komathu Govinda Kurup.

Several school and college notebooks, scout notes, political papers, memoranda and personal correspondence of Krishna Menon were also seen by the author at India League, London, by courtesy of its present secretary.

A great deal of printed material was issued in Bombay at the time of the 1962 General Election. Of these, *Krishna Menon – Danger to India* (A. D. Gorwala, Bombay, 1962) presents a collection of 'scandals' in sensational style. More impressive were the articles written by Marie Seaton (the biographer of Eisenstein), who had collected a vast amount of original material on Mr Menon, particularly on his life in London and his relations with the Labour Party.

Index

INDEX

Index

Index

Index